CITIZENSHIP AS FOUNDATION OF RIGHTS

Citizenship as Foundation of Rights explores the nature and meaning of citizenship and the rights flowing from American citizenship in the context of current debates around politics including immigration. The book explains the sources of citizenship rights in the Constitution and focuses on three key citizenship rights - the right to vote, the right to employment, and the right to travel in the US. It explains why those rights are fundamental and how national identification systems and ID requirements to vote, work, and travel undermine the fundamental citizen rights. It also analyzes how protecting citizens' rights preserves them for future generations of citizens and aspiring citizens here. No other book offers such a clarification of fundamental citizen rights and explains how ID schemes contradict and undermine the constitutional rights of American citizenship.

RICHARD SOBEL is a political scientist, and author and editor of eight books and numerous scholarly, law, and policy articles. He graduated from Princeton University, New Jersey, and the University of Massachusetts, Amherst, and has taught at Princeton University, Smith College, Massachusetts, the University of Connecticut, Harvard University, Massachusetts, and Northwestern University, Illinois. At Harvard, he has also been a research associate of the Charles Hamilton Houston Institute and African-American Studies, fellow of the Hutchins Center, Shorenstein Center, and Berkman Center, and member of the Program in Psychiatry and Law. He is Visiting Scholar at the Buffett Institute, Northwestern University, and Director of Cyber Privacy Project. He has contributed to Supreme Court amicus briefs on voting rights and identification.

Citizenship as Foundation of Rights

MEANING FOR AMERICA

Richard Sobel

CAMBRIDGE
UNIVERSITY PRESS

CAMBRIDGE
UNIVERSITY PRESS

University Printing House, Cambridge CB2 8BS, United Kingdom

Cambridge University Press is part of the University of Cambridge.

It furthers the University's mission by disseminating knowledge in the pursuit of education, learning and research at the highest international levels of excellence.

www.cambridge.org
Information on this title: www.cambridge.org/9781107128293

First published 2016

Printed in the United States of America by Sheridan Books, Inc.

A catalog record for this publication is available from the British Library

Library of Congress Cataloging-in-Publication Data
Sobel, Richard, author.
Citizenship as foundation of rights : meaning for America / Richard Sobel.
Cambridge [UK] : Cambridge University Press, 2016.
LCCN 2016028962 | ISBN 9781107128293 (hardback)
LCSH: Citizenship – United States. | Civil rights – United States. | Constitutional law – United States. | BISAC: LAW / General.
LCC KF4700 .S65 2016 | DDC 342.7308/3–dc23
LC record available at https://lccn.loc.gov/2016028962

ISBN 978-1-107-12829-3 Hardback
ISBN 978-1-107-56803-7 Paperback

For my grandparents and great grandparents
who came to America

CONTENTS

FOREWORD

by Sidney Verba

This is a significant book, with a very apt title, for an understanding of the United States as a political and social system. The basic feature of a democracy is that the government is responsive to the needs and preferences of the citizenry. But what does it mean to be a citizen? Who has access to that situation? What rights are associated with it? And how have they evolved over time?

Few concepts – perhaps none – are more central to the functioning of the American political system than citizenship. Democracy depends on the relationship between the public and the government. In an authoritarian regime, governing rulers make policy without regard for the preferences of the citizens. In a democracy, the citizenry plays a major role. The dictionary tells us that "citizenship" is the status of being a citizen. If you have citizenship in a country, you have the right to live there, work, vote, and travel. Without consideration of the preferences of citizens, a polity is not democratic.

To understand citizenship, one needs to know its history. Its meaning was defined at the time of the formation of the Republic by the founders, and modified and redefined since then after the Civil War amendments with changes to the status of African Americans, women, and the poor and the rich. Citizenship is a legal, cultural, and social characteristic.

This book provides a close and careful analysis of Supreme Court and lower court cases of the legal issues and empowerment of citizenship as well as the civic obligations of citizens. It explores foundations of citizenship from the earliest days of the Republic to the current debates about voter identification requirements and immigration. Debates over citizenship occur with the partisan and racial implications over regulation of access to the polling booth and policy – as well as other citizen rights.

This is what makes *Citizenship as Foundation of Rights: Meaning for America* a major contribution to our understanding of America and the role of citizenship in it. It is a broad and deeply informed discussion of the subject of citizenship and hence to our understanding of democracy. Sobel is a major author of books on important public and political issues. Add this to your reading list about the meaning of citizenship for America and Americans today.

PREFACE AND ACKNOWLEDGMENTS

Because citizenship issues are "in the air," the fundamental nature of citizen rights needs to be founded "in bedrock" and articulated concretely. Though citizen rights go unrecognized in many debates around citizen responsibilities, immigration, and immigrant rights, the scholarship in this book highlights them in support of a critical perspective on citizenship, immigration, and national security issues, and the under-recognized perils of national identification systems. It serves as a cautionary tale about undervaluing citizenship rights and overlooking identification systems threats.

Writing books is sometimes a solitary project even when assisted by many others, and this book may have been the most challenging of eight. Fortunately, finishing it in a timely manner was a compelling goal and rewarding in itself because a full-length study of the nature of citizens' rights and the threat of identification regimes had yet to be written.

I would like to thank Henry Bienen for inviting a prior article that formed part of the basis for the book. I also thank David Harris and Johanna Wald for commissioning the voter ID report that preceded the chapter on voting rights. I appreciate the assistance of Gerald Jenkins, Mark Lerner, Rebecca Weaver, and Shamama Moosvi, among others, for reading draft chapters on rights. As Sidney Verba believed in this project and my prospects to tell a new story, he thoughtfully provided an insightful Foreword to the study. John Fennel, Edward Hasbrouck, Barry Horwitz, Timothy Madden, Michael Ostrolenk, Jenna Malamud Smith, Robert Ellis Smith, Daniel Solove, and Shaun Spencer contributed to predecessor conceptions.

I would also like to thank a fine group of interns and research assistants for this book and earlier articles over more than a decade. They include Lesley Arca, Matt Beamer, Ryan Backman, Robert Boswell, Matt Cannon, Jenni Chang, Mackenzie Eisen, Anjan Choudhury, Jason Crowley, Anna Crane, Dawid Danek, Kelsey Dennis, Kevin Doran, Lucy Filipac, Kathryn Gainey, Patrick Grimaldi, Annalie Jiang, Brian Kebbekus, Natalie Kim, Michael Kranovsky, Tim Lamoureaux, Shamama Moosvi, Catherine Nance, Wendy Netter, Darcy Paul, Emily Pollack, Ann Nunnerly, Nick Riley, Brad Smith, Ross Smith, Allison Trzop, Sarah Wald, Rebecca Wagner, and Michael Zhang. I especially appreciate the contributions of former interns and students Lesley Arca, John Fennel, Alexandria Guttierez, and Ramon Torres, who became colleagues, consultants, coauthors or editors. I appreciate the insights of coauthors and other analysts on issues particularly around travel and privacy. Margaret Ormes, Mellissa Gallaher, David Harris, Johanna Wald, Ed Baskauskas, Randall Kennedy, Charles Ogletree, Skip Gates, Abby Wolf, and Abigail Rose Sobel provided comments and support.

Reference librarians at the Northwestern and Harvard Law Schools and Evanston and Wilmette Public Libraries often found obscure citations and data and provided interlibrary loans, thanks especially to Heidi Kuehl, Gallagher, Roxie Mack at Northwestern Law School and Evanston Public Library librarians, including Ben Rensen and Heather Norborg.

Anonymous reviewers were helpful in asking for a clearer statement of the propositions of this book. John Berger served as a facilitating editor at Cambridge University Press. There, too, Sarah Starkey, Lakshmi Gobidass, Brianda Reyes, Morten Jensen, Manimegali Devi Mathuligam, Michael Duncan and Bret Workman shepherded the manuscript through galleys at the American Political Science Association meetings publication by the fall election campaign to contribute to the needed fuller debates over citizenship, immigration, national security, and national identification schemes as public issues. Colleagues at the Houston Institute, Hutchins Center and African-American Studies at Harvard, the Buffett Institute, Transportation Center, and Northwestern Institute on Complex Organizations at Northwestern provided affiliations and places to work. As noted in earlier acknowledgments, those friends, family, and colleagues who helped with time and space away from other projects, as well as those who were not helpful were also part of the process.

David Steele, Lisa Zimmerman, Charles Paddock, Ray Ollewerther, and Diana Marek provided invitations to speak on the topics of this book. Editors at Boston University's *Public Interest Law Journal* and *Journal of Science and Technology Law*, Harvard's *Journal of Law and Technology*, John Marshal Law School's *Journal of Information Technology and Privacy Law*, and *The Journal of Transportation Law, Logistics and Policy* provided opportunities to explore preceding ideas about rights and identification regimes. Earlier versions of parts of this analysis were presented at the Transportation Center at Northwestern, the College of Complexes in Chicago, a faculty–alumni forum at Princeton, a John Marshal Law School's conference, and the Program in Psychiatry and the Law seminar at Harvard Medical School. I welcome other opportunities to discuss these issues among colleagues and the wider public.

Mr. Schneider in his Shoe Shop and Hubert Wilson in his Princeton lectures provided inspiration for this book. Bob Gilmore's comments after the Immigration Reform and Control Act became law – that citizens have a bundle of rights – contributed to beginning this inquiry. A course on the Politics of Economics and Social Control at Princeton and Smith that included a burgeoning section on citizenship, immigration, and identification was the basis for moving from one week in a class to several journal articles and now a full-length book.

Citizenship as Foundation of Rights is dedicated to my grandparents and great grandparents for coming to America (or aspiring to) and becoming citizens here. Without their and my parents' – Betty Debs Sobel and Walter H. Sobel, FAIA – support and inspiration, this book would not have had the opportunity to air these contemporary controversies or see the light of day.

Richard Sobel
July 4, 2016

1 INTRODUCTION
Empowering Citizenship

The foundational nature of United States citizenship and the rights it empowers constitute essential bedrocks of American democracy. *Citizenship as Foundation of Rights* explores the unique constitutional and political bases and ramifications of American citizenship. It advances this understanding by explaining the character, fundamentals, meanings, powers, and consequences of American citizenship in its most basic rights.

Specifically, the book expounds on the meanings and policy ramifications of American citizenship for political, work, and travel rights. Here citizen rights and their exercise derive directly from the nature of citizenship: rights are exercisable by the empowerment of citizenship. The book explains political citizenship rights as inviolable and empowering, and thereby extends and deepens the discussion of the right to vote. Further, it explicates the right to employment in its constitutional and political aspects and thus extends fundamental citizen rights to working. It also develops the right to travel in its historical and constitutional dimensions, and locates citizen mobility rights in the natures of both political and economic union.

The current debates around citizenship, immigration, and national security generally neglect the nature of citizenship as a source of empowerment for citizens and others aspiring to join them. Similarly, most of these debates neglect the corrosive effects of anti-terrorism or immigration policies undermining citizenship and its rights by imposing identification regimes on the exercise of rights to work or travel. The book explains why requirements and restrictions, for instance, on citizens' political, work, and travel rights by identification requirements degrade the foundations and meaning of citizenship and democracy. It reveals why the "thick" empowerment of strong citizenship rights benefits all persons, including noncitizens, whose personhood, natural rights, and human rights provide significant but restricted protections. It explains why debates today need to include the benefits of exercising citizenship rights and highlight the detrimental effects of identification requirements and systems for those basic rights.

"Political and legal thought today are suffused with talk of citizenship." In Bosniak's terms (2006, 1), "citizen talk pervades our popular political discourse." The word "citizenship" is in the air today in profound and popular ways. From "path to citizenship" (Zamora, 2014) to "citizen scientists" (Ormes et al., 2014) to "citizen musicians" (Ma, 2013), the phrases are current and conversational. But the meaning of American citizenship at its most empowering levels needs a more thorough explanation and explication to inform both scholarly and policy debates. Alternative approaches to citizenship that emphasize benefits, responsibilities, human rights, cosmopolitanism, or global reach complement the conception here that concentrates on rights and empowerment of US citizenship.

In short, *Citizenship as Foundation of Rights* holds that American citizenship is constituted in fundamentally empowering political and proto-political rights. Those rights are exercisable *per force* of citizenship, and government must abet, and may not abridge, their exercise.

COMPONENTS OF CITIZENSHIP

The dimensions of "the most basic institution of our public life ... American citizenship" (Shklar, 1991, 23) are currently incompletely specified. From the "formal bundle of rights at the heart of the institution of citizenship" (Sassen, 2003, 16) flow the basic "political rights such as voting, jury service, militia service, and office holding" (Amar, 2006, 391). While the political rights are the most tightly held "bundle of rights" that "standing as republican citizens" embodies (Shklar, 1991, 17), citizenship empowers other rights. As elements of a unique democratic political system, the fundamental natures both of the US polity and of its basic rights require that natural-born, and naturalized, American citizenship and its concomitant rights be unassailable. Citizens exercise "full citizenship" (R. Smith, 1997, 506) in pursuing "the priority of the liberties of citizenship" (Rawls in R. Smith, 1997, 640), in experiencing a unique "package of rights" (R. Smith, 1997, 544) that are "peculiar to citizenship" (R. Smith, 1997, 593), and in following "the fundamental rights belonging to citizens of all free governments" (Field, 140, in R. Smith, 1997, 592).

Because citizenship originally derived from residency in states, which are the organic constituents of the more perfect union, state citizenship once encompassed national citizenship. Since the original US Constitution "left the status of citizenship undefined," "[l]acking any explicit definition of American citizenship, the Founders' Constitution was widely read in the antebellum era as making national citizenship derivative of state citizenship" (Amar, 2006, 381). During that era, citizenship was mainly limited to the basis that states residency bestowed it, except for particular persons who could not become citizens by birth or naturalization.

Chief Justice Roger Taney's opinion in *Dred Scott v. Sandford* (60 U.S. 393) in 1857 restricted the nature of membership in the polity to white citizens alone. While citizens play the central role in the political community, one may be part of the American community without being a citizen. Sovereignty as the locus of both political authority and the right to representation resides in the people here, not, as in Britain, in the parliament. Taney neglected the state's power to grant citizenship. He ignored the five Northern states in New England the *Scott* dissents pointed out as granting both citizen and voting rights to blacks. As Rogers Smith noted, "The Constitution proclaims itself the creation of 'We the People of the United States,' words that suggest a national political community and one not necessarily confined to its citizens" (R. Smith, 1997, 119).

After the Civil War, the Fourteenth Amendment overturned *Dred Scott* and fundamentally recognized citizenship in ways the original Constitution had not: "All persons born or naturalized in the United States, and subject to the jurisdiction thereof, are citizens of the United States and of the State wherein they reside."

"Citizenship is commonly portrayed," in Bosniak's framework, "as the most desired of conditions, as the highest fulfilment of democratic and egalitarian aspiration." Furthermore, "[t]he idea of citizenship is commonly invoked to convey a state of democratic belonging or inclusion" (Bosniak, 2006, 1).

Citizenship is "a binding relationship between the individual and the political community under which the polity is obligated to guard and respect certain fundamental rights" (Bobbitt, 1982, 89 in Bosniak, 2006). Citizens have their rights so firmly anchored that the government may not take them away. These protections are intrinsically intertwined with the Thirteenth Amendment's abolition of both slavery and involuntary servitude and the Fourteenth Amendment's protections of the rights of citizenship, particularly by birth. Citizenship is a bulwark against governmental actors' reimposing subservience. "It is only citizenship perceived as a natural right that bears a promise of equal political standing in a democracy" (Shklar, 1991, 57). There is no notion more central in politics than citizenship (Shklar, 1991 in Bosniak, 2006, 17).

Citizenship rests on an organic connection to the body politic. It is fundamentally about belonging to a community, comprising part of a "membership sphere" (Bosniak, 2006, 49). It derives from membership in the social community underlying membership in the political community (Marshall, 1965, 79). It is part of a "Marshallian rights-based conception of citizenship" (Bosniak, 2006, 20) in "Marshall's well-known formulation, not only with the rights of political participation, but also with civil rights (rights to legal personality)" (Bosniak, 2006, 20). "[L]egally and politically significant," it encompasses "an ensemble of rights enjoyed" by "formal members of the nation" (Bosniak, 2006, 82–83).

"Citizenship is a status bestowed on those who are full members of a community" (Marshall, 1965, 92). It is "always understood to denote ... membership in a political community or common society" (Bosniak, 2006, 103). It is "a binding relationship between the individual and the political community" (Bosniak, 2006, 183). "Citizenship designates formal, juridical membership in an organized political community ... in citizenship's classically political dimension" (Bosniak, 2006, 19). Similarly, "[c]itizenship is a precondition of influencing these [political] processes and institutions" because "citizens without citizenship are not really free" (Thompson, 1970, 3). Hence, citizenship must remain virtually immutable.

Citizenship is "a binding relationship between the individual and the political community under which the polity is obligated to guard and respect certain fundamental rights of individuals" (Note, 1989, 1931). It provides certain "nontextual guarantees" to members of the political community (Bosniac, 2006, 185).

As James Madison noted, "in Europe, charters of liberty have been granted by power [while] in America . . . charters of power [are] granted by liberty" (*The National Gazette*, January 19, 1792). Here "the sovereign is the people and the people are sovereign" (Sassen, 2003, 17). Indeed, Lincoln's Attorney General, and former rival, Edward Bates, reminded him that "[t]he Constitution itself does not make the citizens; it is, in fact, made of them [and] recognizes such of them as are natural – home born" (Bates, 1862). The generative nature of American citizenship in the people's creation of both sovereignty and the state further bulwarks it for the generation and protection of rights that remain fundamental to the body politic against transient majorities.

Fundamental political rights – full privileges and immunities – are anchored more securely for citizens than other persons (Amar, 2005, 384). The most completely grounded citizenship rights belong to native-born citizens whose births to American parents occur in the United States, because native citizenship embodies *jus soli* (birthplace) with *jus sanguinis* (descent). "Citizenship is automatically extended to those born in the national territory" (Bosniak, 2006, 135).

All birthright citizenship rules make citizenship "an inherited entitlement" that "secures the ability of its holders to enjoy a share in specific rights [and] protections" (Bosniak, 2006, 136). Also, constitutionally founded, if less secure, is birthright citizenship by *jus soli* for those born here of alien parents. Citizenship acquired by birth "ma[kes such] infants 'natural-born citizens'" (Schuck and Smith, 1985, 50). The children of US citizens born abroad are also native citizens (by *jus sanguinis*), if properly recorded (Naturalization Statute of 1790). Validly naturalized citizens have the same rights, except for presidential eligibility. Less rights protected are permanent residents, and other persons, including aliens.

The distinctiveness and "distinctive worth" (R. Smith, 1997, 489) of citizenship is maintained because birthright citizenship exists separately from governmental action, while fundamental rights to be free

and sovereign flow from citizenships. Hence, natural and valid naturalized citizenship is not removable by government. One cannot lose
natural-born citizenship by any governmental act, even for treason
(R. Smith, 1997, 156). Citizens may only shed their standing by voluntary renunciation through expatriation. Only naturalized citizenship
obtained illegally (8 U.S.C. Section 1451) can be lost by denaturalization, the government removal of citizenship (R. Smith, 1997, 578).
"Native born Americans ... could never truly be non-Americans"
(R. Smith, 1997, 578).

"Text, history, judicial precedent, and Executive Branch interpre-
tation confirm" that citizenship is granted exactly as the Fourteenth
Amendment says, to "all persons born or naturalized in the United
States" (Ho, 2006, 76). Citizenship is ascribed to those born here.
Birthright citizenship trumps the state because government may not
take native citizenship away. The potential threat of governmental
removal of birthright citizenship would weaken the foundation.
Hence, citizenship by birth must be immutable.

Denying birthright or naturalized citizenship would "mean that
a society could freely denationalize citizens against their will ... even
leaving them stateless" (Schuck and Smiths, 1985, 37). British and
American common laws grant citizenship by birth as a fundamental
right retained by the people against the enumerated government
powers (Schuck and Smith, 1985, 42, 58). By necessity, birthright
citizenship must remain an asymmetric relationship of individual
sovereignty in which right inheres in the citizen and the burdens fall
on the government. While citizens may sever their political band, "the
government could never do so" (Schuck and Smith, 1985, 87).
Citizenship is "of constitutional dimension, one not subject to the
whims and prejudices of transient majorities" (132–133).

"Citizenship [is] beyond the power of any governmental unit to
destroy" (*US v. Wong Kim Ark*, 1898). As Dellinger summarizes
(1995, 5), "the text and legislative history of the citizenship clause [of
the Fourteenth Amendment] as well as consistent judicial interpretation make clear that the amendment's purpose was to remove the right
of citizenship by birth from transitory political pressures."

Birthright citizen protections are intrinsically intertwined with the
Thirteenth Amendment's abolition of both slavery and involuntary

servitude by selection of place of birth (*jus soli*) for citizenship (naturalization appeared in the founding Constitution). "This is hardly sur-
prising," Shklar notes, "since the fear of slavery had always been at the
very core of this particular conception of citizenship" (1991, 57).

EXPLAINING EMPOWERING CITIZENSHIP

The foundations, sovereignty, presumptions, and empowerments of
citizenship, particularly by birthright, rest on the basis that citizens, by
the nature of citizenship, have political and proto-political rights.
Citizenship ultimately encompasses the rights and requisites to determine the nature of society and government. Citizens may exercise
rights *per force* by the empowerment in citizenship.

As Chief Justice Rehnquist noted in dissent in *Sugarman v. Dougall*
in 1973, the Constitution includes almost a dozen rights only citizens
may exercise (cf. Smith, 115, 149). These rights typically exceed the
essential protections for persons and human rights (R. Smith, 1997,
534). Citizenship laws, designating the criteria for membership in the
political community and the "key prerogatives that constitute members," are among the "most fundamental of political creations." "They
distribute power, assign status and define political purpose" (R. Smith,
1997, 30–31; Sparrow, 2006, 227).

Fundamental citizen rights are exercisable as parts and presumptions of citizenship. Among rights in the US Constitution reserved to
citizens alone (federal offices, jury duty, diversity suits), citizens' political rights provide the clearest demonstration of reserved prerogatives.

Requirements to produce government identification before exercising basic rights undermine the foundations of citizenship and those
freedoms. Rights that exist *per force* of citizenship may not be impeded
by the prior requirement to prove citizenship or identity through
official documents. The right to vote and the right to employment are
political in the sense of exercising authoritative actions essential to the
nature of the polity (Sobel, 1989, 1994). The privileges and immunities
clause is a "shield for citizens ... substantive rights that inhere in
American citizenship" (R. Smith, 1997, 538). If a citizen has to wait
to exercise a right until proofed by the requirement to show

government identification, then that person is constructively not a citizen and does not have the right.

Identification regimes, instead, threaten the sovereignty of citizenship and self-government. The debasing of fundamental rights occurs as a concomitant of requiring identification to exercise rights. The harm of an identification requirement measured only by the magnitude of burden trivializes the reality that restrictions on a right such as voting abridge a most fundamental right of citizenship. The policy consequences of making citizen voting rights contingent, for instance, on identification documents constitute constructive disenfranchisement and denationalization by the state selecting which citizens can participate in elections. Identification regimes accomplish what government laws may not otherwise do: stripping citizens of their citizenship rights prior to producing identification, the constructive equivalent of denaturalization or exile.

Moreover, requirements to obtain and provide identification prior to exercising basic rights transform and invert government by consent of the people into a regime of citizens' praying for privileges to be granted by permission of the government. This inversion of the proper relation of citizens to state undermines the nature of democratic and republican politics and government (Sobel and Fennel, 2007). Explicating the debilitating nature of a national identification regime for citizenship (Sobel, 2002a, 2002b) provides the basis for policies and mobilizations to enhance citizens' rights protections to reverse this inversion. The process thereby removes sovereignty from the people. Three of the clearest examples of threats to citizen rights occur in identification requirements for politics, work, and travel. The fundamental nature of citizenship rights raises the issue of how voter, worker, and travel identification requirements undermine citizen rights and are profoundly anti-constitutional.

THE RIGHT TO VOTE

Voting right inheres in the nature of a constitutional republican democracy. Civil rights-era court decisions such as *Reynolds v. Sims* (1964), *Wesberry v. Sanders* (1964), and *Harper v. Virginia Board of Education*

(1966) empowered disenfranchised voters by explicating voting as a fundamental constitutional right of citizenship, not to be abridged. The right is more recently contradicted by the *Burdick v. Takushi* (1992) administrative regime embedded in *Crawford v. Marion County* in 2008. The latter decision burdens the exercise of the franchise, for instance, by requiring official photo identification in order to vote. Instead, explicating the fundamental nature of the franchise in citizenship provides intellectual foundations for strengthening voting rights.

THE RIGHT TO EMPLOYMENT

Similarly, the right to take employment has long been fundamental for citizens. From the early republic to the civil rights era, US Supreme Court decisions from *Corfield v. Coryell* (1823) to *Butcher Union Co.* (1884) and *Truax* (1915) to *Roth* (1972) recognized that taking employment is a foundational citizenship right. The right to earn a living parallels suffrage (Shklar, 1991), and "the choice of profession" is "fundamental" (Urofksy, 561–562, 619). On this basis, citizens are guaranteed the right to take employment (though not promised a job). In short, a citizen may work without government permission.

THE RIGHT TO TRAVEL

Equally essential, the right to travel is a privilege and immunity of citizens in a broad federal union as guaranteed explicitly in Article IV of the Articles of Confederation and therefore implicitly in Article IV of the US Constitution and its Fourteenth Amendment. From *Corfield* (1823) to *Dulles* (1958) and *Guest* (1967) to *Saenz* (1999), courts have recognized that the right to travel makes America a more perfect union and sustains Americans as free in their pursuit of happiness. Identification restrictions tether travel rights. Requirements to carry and show identification like driver's licenses or passports for domestic travel impede the fundamental right of free movement across the republic.

VOTING RIGHTS RESTRICTIONS

The emergence of voter identification laws began after the spate of contested elections over the past two decades. While states began to consider voter identification laws in the late 1990s, the first laws in Missouri, Indiana, and Georgia in the early 2000s imposed stricter requirements on voters, with disparate impact on minorities. Though the Missouri Supreme Court outlawed voter ID under the state constitution, a split US Supreme Court permitted the Indiana voter ID law to remain in effect in 2008. More laws and further challenges based on the constitutional burdens the law imposes have ensued. At stake is not only voter identification burdens, especially on minorities and poor, but also restrictions on other voting procedures such as early voting and same-day registration that permit a wider range of voters to get to the polls.

EMPLOYMENT RIGHTS RESTRICTIONS

Recurring proposals since the 1980s to require national "worker" identification reinforce the barrier to what should be a directly exercisable employment right, with implications for the right to travel. Requiring first a simple ID and then a national one, ultimately to include fingerprints, digital photograph, or other biometrics in a government database and on identification cards in order for citizens to be "official" or "documented," compounds the separation of citizen rights from their political and economic exercise.

The problem for citizen employment began with a 1986 Immigration Reform and Control Act (IRCA) requiring citizens to produce government identification to get official permission to take employment. This prior restraint on exercising a basic occupational right of citizens constructively severed citizens from taking employment. The electronic verification system (E-Verify) is the more recent high-tech version of enforcing separation between citizenship and work rights that requires not only identification but location in a national databank.

Immigration laws and other social policies often abridge the rights of citizens and immigrants, legal or otherwise. The pejorative terms "illegal" or "undocumented immigrants" imply that people can be "illegal" and persons, including citizens, need to be documented. Similarly, they imply that citizens and residents are merely "legal" and "documented" entities. But these unfortunate formulations obscure and undermine the political bulwark that citizens are not mere "legals" but specifically constitutionally protected persons. Furthermore, citizens do not need to be "documented," because citizenship rights by their nature and under the Constitution are exercisable *per force* of citizenship and its presumptions. Citizens are citizens with rights prior to and without government documentation or identification. The burden of proof is on the government to demonstrate that a person is not a citizen. No identification demand is justified for citizens and others for doing nothing wrong.

TRAVEL RIGHTS RESTRICTIONS

Similarly, the requirement to provide identification in order to fly, begun after the TWA 800 crash in 1995 from mechanical malfunction, and later augmented by profiling and risk assessment, inhibits the right to travel. Requirements to provide identification in order to board an airline since 1996, and more recent rules since 2008 to cooperate on identification and since 2010 under "Secure Flight" to reveal birth date and declare gender in order to get an airline reservation, also interfere with the exercise of citizens' travel rights. Similar identification requirements to purchase Amtrak train tickets or to board interstate buses to travel nationally are equally detrimental and burdensome. The ability to travel domestically without a passport is the hallmark of a free society. The proliferation of identification requirements to move around the country adds to the degradation of citizenship and its inherent rights. They set the foundation for an internal passport system, anathema to a free and open society.

ENDURING SIGNIFICANCE OF PROTECTING FUNDAMENTAL CITIZENSHIP RIGHTS

These seemingly "philosophical" arguments about the nature of citizenship and its concomitant rights, as well as "theoretical" explanations of why identification requirements are detrimental to citizenship and the polity, are instead powerful foundations for preserving and protecting the rights of citizens and others. Close examination and explication of citizen rights are missing from current security and immigration debates. Their absence has real political consequences because the failure to recognize in policy analyses and political debates the fundamental rights of citizenship – the empowerment to exercise rights *per force* and to be immune from identification demands absent probable cause – abets the increasingly frequent misconception that rights do not exist unless invoked and that the imposition of identification requirements and regimes is acceptable.

When identification demands become ubiquitous, they consequently demean citizenship, personhood, and citizens and thereby desensitize people to the harm of being constantly "proofed." Rights thereby illegitimately become alienated and unexercisable prior to "verification." This sundering of citizenship from its constitutional perquisites undermines the rights of citizens and noncitizens alike. In fact, rights may not be degraded in order to "save" or "extend" them. Like winning the battle in the Civil War to preserve the union and end slavery, maintaining citizenship now preserves it for our posterity (McPherson, 2015, 170).

Protecting citizenship rights also protects the rights of others, including noncitizens. Solidifying citizens' rights also enhances the human rights protections for aliens. Maintaining citizen rights assures the goal of many noncitizens – to become full citizens – and that it not be devalued in the process of allegedly defending it. Preserving and protecting the nature and continuity of citizen rights makes citizenship ultimately more inclusive than exclusive. Conversely, undercutting citizens' rights in order to punish the "undocumented" or "illegals" degrades citizens and citizenship. While there can be penalties for noncitizens attempting to exercise citizens' rights, the rightful exercise of those rights by citizens must be protected by current and future practitioners. A key responsibility of citizenship is to maintain and protect the integrity of citizen rights by exercising them and sustaining them for the next generations. Protecting citizen rights can also strengthen personhood rights, natural rights, and human rights protections.

OVERVIEW OF THE BOOK

Citizenship as Foundation of Rights provides a direct statement of the empowering nature of citizenship, its meaning, and its concomitants. The two introductory chapters explicate the nature of citizenship and the rights flowing from it. In highlighting the thrust of the book, Chapter 1 on "Empowering Citizenship" identifies the nature of American citizenship against the limitations of alternative conceptions, and it introduces the nature of political, occupational, and travel rights. Chapter 2 on "The Nature of American Citizenship as the Foundation of Rights" explicates American citizenship's essence and critiques existing formulations. It also explains what other rights citizens have besides voting, working, and traveling.

The next three chapters explain the nature of fundamental citizenship rights to vote, take employment, and travel. Explicating the foundational nature of electoral rights, Chapter 3 on "The Right to Vote" develops more fully the nexus between citizenship and voting franchise. Chapter 4 on "The Right to Employment" explains how taking employment as a right is also fundamentally enmeshed as a constitutional privilege and immunity of citizenship. Similarly, Chapter 5 on "The Right to Travel" explains the nature of travel rights in citizenship and their constitutional foundations and warns of ID perils.

Chapter 6 on "Threats to Citizenship Rights in Identification Regimes" explains how identification requirements undermine the nature of citizenship. The chapter synthesizes and extends the analysis of problems identification requirements create for exercising fundamental rights. Chapter 7 on "Other Countries' Systems Constitute Warnings" distinguishes foundations of American constitutional rights from other even other democratic regimes.

The conclusions in Chapter 8 on "Sustaining Empowering Citizenship" point to new insights into citizenship and to the empowerment from sustaining the strength and integrity of citizen rights for those approaching and aspiring to citizenship. The section "Protecting Citizenship Rights Protects Human Rights" explains how reinforcing the fundamental nature of US citizenship can empower citizens and those aspiring to join them. While Human

Rights may protect others' interests, American citizenship is an expansive force that ramifies into rights for those who exercise it as well as for those who aspire to its protections.

CONCLUSION: CITIZENSHIP AS EMPOWERING RIGHTS

In short, *Citizenship as Foundation of Rights* provides provocative insights into the empowering nature of American citizenship and its constitutional foundations for political, employment, and travel rights. It explains the philosophical, policy, and practical consequences of strengthening citizenship rights in politics, work, and travel against identification systems that undermine them daily. The wider public recognition in public explanations and that the burdens of discussions identification barriers must not be allowed to compromise citizens' constitutional rights strengthens those basic rights. Detrimental ID experiences elsewhere provide cautionary tales of what could be happening here.

Scholarly and public awareness and debate of these issues solidifies recognition of the essential nature of citizenship and citizen rights in politics, work, and travel. *Citizenship as Foundation of Rights* is an extensive exposition of how the unassailable nature of citizenship supports the foundation of rights for and prevents ID injuries to the healthy body politic. Bringing these perspectives prominently to public forums enhances understanding of their significance and promotes their continuity and the reversal of the erosion by a national identification regime of citizenship's foundational qualities. The provocative explication of the nature and rights of citizenship will fire the imagination and energize debate across the nation.

2 THE NATURE OF AMERICAN CITIZENSHIP AS THE FOUNDATION OF RIGHTS

The current expositions of citizenship present incompletely specified dimensions of "the most basic institution of our public life ... American citizenship" (Shklar, 1991, 23). From the "formal bundle of rights at the heart of the institution of citizenship" (Sassen, 2003, 16) flow the basic "political rights such as voting, jury service, militia service, and office holding" (Amar, 2006, 391). While the political rights are the most tightly held "bundle of rights" that "standing as republican citizens" embodies (Shklar, 1991, 17), citizenship rights empower other rights. As elements of a unique democratic political system, the fundamental natures both of the United States polity and maintaining its basic rights require that American citizenship and its accompanying rights be unassailable. While there are alternate conceptions of US citizenship that do not involve concomitant fundamental rights, using the rights-enhancing view of citizenship creates stronger bases for citizenship rights.

CITIZENSHIP IN AMERICAN HISTORY

Although the term "citizen" appears in both the Articles of Confederation and the US Constitution, it was not given "an authoritative and precise definition until after the civil war" (Fehrenbacher, 2001, 64). In the early national period, "citizen meant any domiciled inhabitant except an alien or a slave" (64). The Articles treat "citizen" as interchangeable with "inhabitants": The "free inhabitants" of each state are entitled to the privileges and immunities of "free citizens" of the several states (65). Sometimes citizen included "active partners" in sovereignty, with full civil and political rights and privileges, including suffrage and public office eligibility (65). In short, citizenship was "free status and domicile in a state" (Fehrenbacher, 2001, 445).

The Thirteenth and Fourteenth Amendments, respectively, abolished slavery and involuntary servitude and by recognizing that citizenship empowers "All persons born or naturalized in the United States . . . are citizens of the United States and of the state in which they reside," set the parameters for citizen rights. "The Fourteenth Amendment can be read to approach citizenship at once as a kind of formal status and as the enjoyment of basic rights" (Bosniak, 2006, 14). Indeed, Lincoln's attorney general reminded him that "The Constitution itself does not make the citizens; it is, in fact, made of them [and] recognizes such of them as are natural – home born" (Bates, 1862).[1]

Bates's conception precedes slavery's abolition after the Civil War in late 1865 and the enshrining of birthright citizenship in 1868. These amendments undermined the "fear of slavery," Shklar located, "at the very core" of creating the birthright conception of citizenship. In clarifying the source of American citizenship inalterably in birth, the Fourteenth Amendment overturned Dred Scott's imposition of rightlessness among blacks after that infamous decision.

Early in the Republic, the relationship between state and national citizenship was also undefined. Essentially, before the Civil War, state citizenship bestowed national citizenship. After the war and the Fourteenth Amendment, national citizenship bestowed state citizenship.[2]

ALTERNATIVE AND OVERLAPPING CONCEPTIONS OF CITIZENSHIP

While there are numerous definitions of citizenship, most do not address these issues of political powers and rights of American citizenship. Bickel declared a generation ago "that the concept of citizenship is of little significance in American constitutional law" (1973, 369 in Bosniak, 2006, 77). Walzer associates citizenship with territoriality.

"Walzer clearly links . . . membership to a territory and to the state and calls this relationship citizenship" (Townsley, 2004, 4). He considers political rights as part of the "consequentiality of citizenship" within a stable, prosperous state (Glover, 2011, 1; Walzer, 1983, 29). "If the manyness of America is cultural, its oneness is political" (Walzer, 2004, 638).

Jacqueline Stevens relies on territoriality to define citizenship, and eschews birthright citizenship in preference to "use residence to define citizenship" similar to the nineteenth-century practice of a state versus national basis for citizenship (J. Stevens, 2012). "The problem," she maintains, "is the age-old, irrational linkage between citizenship and birthplace." For Stevens, "the use of residence to define citizenship" makes people "citizens of the states where they happen to reside – period." Contrary to the Fourteenth Amendment, Stevens claims "Citizens are created by politicians, the citizen-makers." Of course, if a government can create citizens or remove "citizenship" based on residence, they can make a citizen into a noncitizen when "governments renders their own legal citizens stateless" (cf. R. Smith, 1997, 538, n. 44).

Honig contrasts citizenship to foreignness. In the movement from "foreign" to "American," the consent to become citizens distinguishes naturalized citizenship from citizenship by birth. At most, natural-born citizens provide tacit consent to the regime (2001, 75). Appiah's focus on the international aspect of cosmopolitan citizenship of the world creates "world citizenship." "[A] cosmopolitan's role is to appeal to 'our own' government to ensure that these nation-states respect, provide for, and protect their citizens" (2006, 3).

Agonistic conceptions of citizenship highlight the benefits to Americans of the contrasting foreign model that may be incorporated into a mainstream model. As "political theory that does not place any institutions, procedures, principles or values beyond political contestation," agonistic views of citizenship are inherently within "the agonistic theory of politics as contestation" (Fossen, 2008, 1).

For Van der Brink, "citizens in privileged positions must develop dispositions for civic responsiveness, a willingness to recognize that their own beliefs and ideals may be contested and that the civic order may not be sufficiently responsive to the legitimate needs of people in less fortunate, or dominant social position" (2005, 121–122). These involve "mutual recognition in social contexts marked by disagreement" (122).

From the "civic republican tradition, Mouffee retains the emphasis on political association and argues that it is fundamental to recognize that individuals acquire their rights and sense of identity through their inscription in the political community." Citizenship identity is a constructed or constituted identification (Tambakaki, 2006, 7). Agonistic citizenship is "a constructed form of identity, open to many different interpretations" (8).

Closer to the empowered conception in this book are Arendt's highlights of the political and participatory aspects of citizenship. Here, citizenship constitutes rights empowering agency. She emphasizes "the exercise of effective political agency" (d'Entreves, 2006, 23) in which "citizenship is viewed as the process of active deliberation" (23–24). Concerning political agency, Arendt draws a connection between "political action, as the active engagement of citizens in the public realm, and the exercise of effective political agency" (24). She values "direct involvement of the citizens" over representation. By "direct political participation" or "engaging in common action and collective deliberation," she holds "that citizenship can be reaffirmed and political agency effectively exercised" (24).

Similarly, Bosniak holds that "constitutional citizenship should be read to encompass and ground our most basic individual rights" (Bosniak, 2002, 1). As opposed to the "thick" conception in "the idea of citizenship as a foundation for constitutional rights," the idea of rights grounded in the status of personhood is excessively "thin" (2). "Constitutional citizenship [serves] as the central foundation for rights" (3). "The idea [is] citizenship as rights itself" (4). The "meaning of citizenship" treats citizenship as "an ensemble of rights" (5). The citizenship rights approach treats citizenship as the "exclusive preserve of citizens" (7, 9) based on the privileges and immunities clause of the US Constitution, "ensuring citizens' rights only for people who possess citizenship status" (9). Bosniak also asks "to what extent is the constitution concerned with the rights of citizenship, and what, precisely, would those [rights] be?" (14). Yet her analysis encompasses the conception that "the restoration of citizenship does not necessarily entail the elimination of rights grounded in personhood" (2).

Bosniak's distinction between "'thin' and 'thick' versions of citizenship" (2006, 87) differentiates "citizenship status" versus "citizenship rights." Thin citizenship is citizenship-as-status – "mere status." Status citizenship lacks "the enjoyment of rights citizenship and the practice of republican citizenship" (Bosniak, 2006, 118). The thicker and "more robust substantive conception" is "citizenship as the meaningful enjoyment of rights," the "mode of democratic engagement and self-governance" (87). In Karst's formulation, it is "the dignity of full membership of society" (1991, in Bosniak, 2006, 87).

Yet Powell (2004) also notes that "personhood became a presumption bestowed to all citizens at birth." He adds, "the rise [of] the nation-states" in the "creat[ion of] a new political space for personhood (and membership) rooted in citizenship" had the effect "to limit personhood to citizens" (987).

Benhabib (2005) develops the liberal idea "of citizenship as the practice and enjoyment of rights and benefits" where "[c]itizen[s are] the subject of rights and entitlements" (673). "The privilege of political membership" constitutes "the sense of access to the rights of public autonomy and the entitlement of social rights and privileges" (675). For Benhabib, the key issue now is "access to citizen rights, or the attainment of political membership by non-members" (674). Here citizenship is the "right to have rights" (Benhabib, 2001). "The political element was constituted by the rights to participate in the exercises of political power" (Townsley, 2004, 5, quoting Marshall, 1965).

Yet Benhabib, among others, "argue[s] that we are witnessing a 'disaggregation' of citizenship rights' in which the civil, political, and social rights associated with membership are increasingly 'unbundled' from one another" (Benhabib, 2002, 2003, 2005, cited in Glover, 2011, 7). "The losers in the process are the citizens from whom state protection is withdrawn, or, more likely, who never had strong state protection in the first place" (Benhabib, 2005, 676) by "the uncoupling of jurisdiction and territory. '[P]roto-citizenship' rights can now be exercised at both the local and supranational levels by an array of actors" (Glover, 2011, 1). This parallels Honig's concern for the "devaluation of citizenship" (Schuck and Smith, 1985, 161) by giving social benefits to legal or illegal residents in court decisions like *Graham v. Richardson* (1971) and *Plyler v. Doe* (1982). While not begrudging noncitizens social rights, the empowered conception of citizenship holds that citizens' political rights may not be shared or stripped from them.

Schall distinguishes between liberal and republican views of citizenship rights and prerogatives (2006, 69, 85). Quoting Jones and Gavanta (2002), he notes that liberal theories "promote the idea that citizenship is a status, which ent[itles] individuals to a specific set of universal rights granted by the state" (69). He also holds that "Republicanism regards citizenship not as a series of rights, as liberalism does, but as the fulfillment of certain duties" (85).[3]

The "public law" (or communitarian) view of mutual consent for citizenship (Schuck and Smith, 1985, 68) as a supposed way to grant citizenship is actually a way to remove it. This is so because the government, under political pressure, could withhold consent for citizenship from those disfavored minorities born in this country. "By stressing the right of the existing community of citizens to 'consent' to newcomers, Schuck and Smith perversely turn Lockean consent from a device designed to limit state power into a device for its enhancement" (Honig, 2001, 160, n.60). Rather than the government deriving its just powers from the consent of the governed, people would need government permission to join the polity (see Sobel and Fennel, 2007). Consent or identification requirements intervening before the exercise of citizen rights devalue citizenship itself.

Sparrow (2006, 227) describes four levels of citizenship. For persons born in US territories, there is single, "second-class" citizenship. For those born in the District of Columbia, there is one-and-a-half (national and electoral college). For those born in any of the fifty states, it is double (state and national). And for those born as Native Americans, there is treble citizenship (state, federal, and tribal nation).

Crafting together these kaleidoscopic dimensions of citizenship produces a more coherent conception of empowered citizenship. But no single exposition has yet explicated the totality of citizen rights and powers as undergirding constitutional rights writ large. *Citizenship as Foundation of Rights* pursues that path.

CITIZENSHIP COMPONENTS

By nullifying *Dred Scott*, the Thirteen and Fourteenth Amendments solidified citizenship rights. Those rights are anchored to bulwark against reimposing subservience. "Citizenship is a precondition of influencing" political processes and institutions because "citizens without citizenship are not really free" (Thompson, 1970, 3). Fundamental political rights – full privileges and immunities – are anchored differently for citizens than other persons (Amar, 2006, 384). It is essential that citizens do not lose natural-born citizenship by any governmental act, not even for treason (R. Smith, 1997, 156). Involuntary denaturalization is limited to invalid naturalization, and expatriation may only occur voluntarily.

The potential threat of governmental removal of birthright citizenship would weaken its foundation: "Birth, alone ... gives a man permanent rights as a citizen" (R. Smith, 1997, 545, n. 62). Denying birthright citizenship would "mean that a society could freely denationalize citizens against their will ... even leaving them stateless" (Schuck and Smith, 1985, 37). The asymmetry of relationship in favor of the citizen enhances the bases for democracy. Its inversion undermines democracy.

It is essential to the United States as a free society that certain rights are obtained from citizenship because citizenship is "preservative" of other rights (*Yick Wo v. Hopkins*, 1888; *Harper v. Board of Elections*, 1966). Citizens have fundamental political and economic rights among their privileges and immunities of citizenship (Amar, 1999, 169–171; *Saenz v. Roe*, 1999).

"PEOPLE" IN THE CONSTITUTION INCLUDES CITIZENS AND OTHERS

Despite Chief Justice Roger Taney's holding in the infamous *Dred Scott* decision, the people and citizens are not the same group of persons. "[T]he words '[p]eople of the United States' and 'citizens,'" Taney tendentiously held, "are synonymous and mean the same thing. They both describe the political body who, according to our republican institutions, form the sovereignty" (60 U.S. 393). As congressional apportionment in the Constitution is by the number of residents, not citizens, "people" and "citizens" are not necessarily synonymous.

Yet, "[t]he Constitution does distinguish," as Cole noted, "in some respects between the rights of citizens and noncitizens." For instance, "the right not to be discriminatorily denied the vote and the right to run for federal elective office are expressly restricted to citizens" (Cole, 2003, 370). "The fact that the Framers chose to limit to citizens only the rights to vote and to run for federal office is one indication that they did not intend other constitutional rights to be so limited" (370).

Still, unless the Constitution explicitly states that a right is for "citizens" only, "people" refers to both citizens and noncitizens alike. Accordingly, the Supreme Court has squarely stated that neither the First Amendment nor the Fifth Amendment "acknowledges any distinction between citizens and resident aliens" (Cole, 2003, 370). If citizens are also part of the people and persons, does this mean citizens and noncitizens have equal rights? Concurring in *Zobel v. Williams* in 1982, Justice O'Connor noted that "the word 'citizen' suggests that the [privileges and immunities] clause also excludes aliens."[4] Yet *Hicklin v. Orbeck* (1978) holds, "While the [Privileges and Immunities] Clause refers to 'citizens' this Court finds that the term 'citizens' and 'residents' are 'essentially interchangeable' for purposes of most cases under the Privileges and Immunities clause."[5] In *Foley v. Connelie* in 1978, the Court held that exclusion of aliens "from participation in its democratic political institutions" is part of the "sovereign's obligation 'to preserve the basic conception of political community' ... It represents the choice, and right, of the people to be governed by their citizen peers" (Bosniak, 2006, 164, n.121).

In *INS v. Lopez-Mendoza* (1984), Justice Rehnquist distinguished provisions of the Fifth and Sixth Amendments that speak "in the relatively universal term of 'person'" from the Fourth Amendment terms which is guaranteed to "the people."[6] Hence, some persons are "not necessarily among the people of the United States" (Bosniak, 2006, 166).

"The view that foreign nationals do not deserve the same constitutional protections as U.S. citizens was given some support in April 2003 when a divided Supreme Court in *Demore v. Kim* upheld a 1996 statute imposing mandatory detention on foreign nationals charged with being deportable for having committed certain crimes" (Cole, 2003, 368). In *Demore v. Kim* (2003), "the majority ... expressly invok[ed] a double standard, claiming that in regulating immigration, 'Congress regularly makes rules that would be unacceptable if applied to citizens'" (Cole, 2003, 368).

Foreign nationals are entitled to reduced rights and freedoms. "On the one hand, the Court has insisted for more than a century that foreign nationals living among us are 'persons' within the meaning of the Constitution, and are protected by those rights that the Constitution does not expressly reserve to citizens" (Cole, 2003, 368).

> On the other hand, the Court has permitted foreign nationals to be excluded and expelled because of their race. It has allowed them to be deported for political associations that were entirely lawful at the time they were engaged in. It has upheld laws barring foreign nationals from owning land ... It has permitted the indefinite detention of "arriving aliens" stopped at the border ... And it has allowed states to bar otherwise qualified foreign nationals from employment as public school teachers and police officers. (368–369)

"The general rule," Cole noted, "is that where foreign nationals and citizens are similarly situated, they must be treated equally. Indeed, the Court treats alienage as a 'suspect' classification, and state laws discriminating on the basis of alienage, nationality, or national origin are generally as presumptively invalid as laws discriminating along racial lines" (380). In short, while there are rights that only citizens may exercise, most rights apply to the people and persons with equal force.

In *Sugarman v. Dougall* (1973), the Supreme Court "suggested in dictum" that "matters resting firmly within a state's constitutional prerogative" to "define a political community" need only a rational basis to be constitutional (Bosniak, 2006, 61). Justifiable discrimination may exist in restricting to citizens "participation in [our] democratic political institutions" (Bosniak, 2006, 61).

Smith opines that "[t]he very robustness of American traditions of natural rights, common-law rights and rights of state citizenship independent of U.S. citizenship evacuated most of the 14th Amendments clause's potential content" (R. Smith, 1997, 406). While individuals have other rights as persons, under human rights law, and in common law (135, 406), they have different levels and strengths than citizenship rights. While the body of the Constitution typically protects citizens, the Bill of Rights largely protects persons. In short, many rights are stronger for citizens than others, including US persons (nationals), permanent residents, and other persons such as aliens.

As James Madison argued, "those subject to the obligations of our legal system ought to be entitled to its protections." His words ring as true today in the debates about immigration as during the Revolutionary era (Cole, 2003, 371):

> [I]t does not follow, because aliens are not parties to the Constitution, as citizens are parties to it, that whilst they actually conform to it, they have no right to its protection. Aliens are not more parties to the laws, than they are parties to the Constitution; yet it will not be disputed, that as they owe, on one hand, a temporary obedience, they are entitled, in return, to their protection and advantage. (371)

WHAT MAKES A RIGHT FUNDAMENTAL AND A FUNDAMENTAL RIGHT OF CITIZENSHIP?

Two kinds of rights are deemed "fundamental": The first are those explicitly guaranteed by the Constitution, and the second are "those felt to be so important that they are considered implicitly granted by the Constitution, such as the right to vote."[7] Black (1991) defines "fundamental rights" as "those rights which have their source and are explicitly or implicitly guaranteed in the federal Constitution and state constitutions" (465). "Challenged legislation that significantly burdens a 'fundamental right' ... includ[ing] First Amendment rights, privacy and the right to travel interstate, will be reviewed under a stricter standard of review" (465).

Fundamental rights comprise a group that has been recognized by the Supreme Court as requiring a high degree of protection from government encroachment. These rights are specifically identified in the Constitution, and especially in the Bill of Rights, or have been found under due process. Laws limiting these rights must generally pass strict scrutiny to be upheld as constitutional.

In *Palko v. Connecticut* in 1937,[8] the Court identified those "immunities that are valid against the federal government by force of the specific pledges of particular amendments that have been found to be "implicit in the concept of ordered liberty" (325).[9] In 1938, the Supreme Court clarified what rights are so "implicit" in the concept of ordered liberty in *United States v. Carolene Products Co.*, when the Court identified the following rights as falling under substantive due process: "the rights contained in the first eight amendments to the Constitution; the rights that affect people's ability to participate in the political process, including the rights to free speech, freedom of association, and voting; and the rights of "discrete and insular minorities."[10]

When a substantive due process case comes before the Supreme Court, it asks if the right argued is a "fundamental right." The rights in *Carolene Products* are used as a guideline, but the Court may also ask whether the right is "implicit in the concept of ordered liberty" or "deeply rooted in the Nation's history or traditions."[11] If it is, the Court applies "strict scrutiny" when analyzing the law. A law can only stand under "strict scrutiny" if it is narrowly tailored to serve a compelling state interest. This test is so strict that some legal scholars have called it "strict in name, but fatal in fact," and few laws survive strict scrutiny.[12]

"Substantive due process" provides heightened protection against government interference with certain fundamental rights and liberty interests. As noted in *Washington v. Glucksberg* (1997), the protected rights and interests include those that "are, objectively, deeply rooted in this National history and tradition, and implicitly in the concept of ordered liberty, such that neither liberty nor justice would exist if they were sacrificed" (720–721). In contrast to the procedural component of due process clause, substantive due process "protects individual liberty against certain government actions regardless of the fairness of the procedures used to implement them."[13]

Being fundamental does not make a right a fundamental right of citizenship since many apply to the "people," or "persons," citizens or not.[14] Basic rights that only citizens may exercise and that the government may not abridge are found in a document like the Constitution and require strict scrutiny by the courts (though requiring strict scrutiny does not mean the right is fundamental for citizens). These include political citizenship and other quasi-political rights. Only some rights are fundamental rights of citizenship.[15] Political rights provide the clearest examples.

POLITICAL CITIZENSHIP

"The Constitution itself recognizes a basic difference between citizens and aliens," as the future chief justice William Rehnquist wrote in 1973.[16] "That distinction is constitutionally important in no less than 11 instances in a political document noted for its brevity."[17]

There are political activities, few in number but essential in importance, that one must be a citizen to participate in.[18] According to the US Constitution, one must be a citizen in order to vote or serve as an elector, to run for national and most other governmental offices, and to sue a citizen of another state (diversity jurisdiction) (Amar, 2006, 385, 391). In Amar's formulation, political as opposed to civil rights include voting, running for office, jury services, and service in the militia (385, 391).

In short, the Constitution gives certain rights only to citizens. Perhaps most tellingly, in Article II, only "natural born" citizens may become president: "No Person except a natural born Citizen, or a Citizen of the United States, at the time of the Adoption of this Constitution, shall be eligible to the Office of President" (Article II, Section 1, Clause 4) [No. 1].

For other federal offices, in Madison's words, "any citizen may be elected" (Amar, 2006, 69). Many elected offices in the United States require US citizenship. Article I requires that Members of the House of Representatives and Senate be citizens: "No Person shall be a Representative who shall not have ... been seven Years a Citizen of the United States. Similarly, Senators have to be at least "nine Years a Citizen" (Article I, Section 1, Clause 2 and Article I, Section 3, Clause 3) [Nos. 2, 3].

Article I, Section 2, also requires citizenship to vote in national elections. "The House of Representatives shall be ... chosen ... and the Electors ... shall have the Qualifications [of citizenship and age] requisite for Electors of the most numerous Branch of the State Legislature" (Article I, Section 2, Clause 2). State constitutions and laws require citizenship to vote [No. 4]. Although Section 2 says that the electors are the "people" of the states, in context, this refers to citizens.

Article III, Section 2, discusses the citizens' rights to judicial process:

> The judicial Power shall extend to all Cases, in Law and Equity, arising under this Constitution, the Laws of the United States, and Treaties made ... to all Cases affecting ... to Controversies ... a State and Citizens of another State; – between Citizens of different States; – between Citizens of the same State claiming Lands under Grants of different States, and between a State, or the Citizens thereof, and foreign States, Citizens or Subjects. [Nos. 5–8]

Article IV mandates that the full privileges and immunities fall only to the citizens of the several states. "The Citizens of each State shall be entitled to all Privileges and Immunities of Citizens in the several States" (Article IV, Section 21, Clause 1). Similarly, the Fourteenth Amendment holds, "No State shall make or enforce any law which shall abridge the privileges or immunities of citizens of the United States" (Fourteenth Amendment, Section 1) [Nos. 9–10].

In addition, under the Eleventh Amendment, modifying a provision of Article III about "controversies ... between citizens of different states," one must be a citizen to sue someone in another state: "[N]o suit may be brought against persons in another state except by citizens of one state against the other" (Article III, Section 2.9; Eleventh Amendment). This issue of "diversity jurisdiction" arose in the *Dred Scott* case about whether Scott could sue his alleged owner living in New York state for freedom under the *Somerset* principle of "once free always free" (Amar, 2006, 258) [Nos. 11–12].

All the extensions of suffrage involve citizenship.[19] The Fifteenth Amendment holds that "[t]he right of citizens of the United States to vote shall not be denied or abridged by the United States or by any State on account of race, color, or previous condition of servitude" [No. 13]. The Nineteenth Amendment holds that "[t]he right of citizens of the

United States to vote shall not be denied or abridged by the United States or by any State on account of sex" [No. 14]. The Twenty-sixth Amendment gave the vote to citizens eighteen years old. "The right of citizens of the United States, who are eighteen years of age or older, to vote shall not be denied or abridged by the United States or by any State on account of age" [No. 15].

The Twenty-fourth Amendment outlawed poll taxes and other taxes against citizens voting: "The right of citizens of the United States to vote in any primary or other election for President or Vice President, for electors for President or Vice President, or for Senator or Representative in Congress, shall not be denied or abridged by the United States or any State by reason of failure to pay poll tax or other tax" [No. 16].

The demise of the poll tax in 1966, however, has not blunted the reincarnation of "other taxes," which at one point required voters as citizens to be property owners or taxpayers (R. Smith, 1997, 171, 541, n. 11). These included paying property taxes as precursors of identification requirements for voting that burden fundamental rights. They are particularly pernicious when the costs fall disproportionately on classes of poorer and minority citizens. In short, only citizens have certain political and related rights, which are often under attack, by identification requirements as a form of or alternative to a tax.

OTHER CITIZENSHIP RIGHTS

There are other citizenship rights, largely constitutional, that are also fundamental. Although not always as basic as the rights to vote, work, or travel, their exercise distinguish citizens from other persons. Some statutory rights of citizenship are not fundamental because they do not have stronger constitutional foundations.[20]

Right to Enjoy Equally the Privileges and Immunities of Citizenship

Article IV protects "the privileges and immunities of citizens" against federal actions, while the Fourteenth Amendment holds that "No State shall make or enforce any law which shall abridge the privileges or immunities of citizens of the United States."[21] There are numerous privileges and immunities citizens enjoy, though rights need not be a privilege or immunity of citizenship for only citizens to enjoy them. There may be other sources in the Constitution or equivalent court decisions undergirding the citizen's (and others') right (Bosniak, 2006, 79). "The revival of the privileges or immunities clause ... provid[es] a sounder basis than the Due Process clause for the protection of the substantive rights, protect[ing] ... United States citizens" (79).

While there is no definitive list of what comprises the privileges and immunities of citizens, the classic definition appears in *Corfield v. Coryell* (1823), where Justice Bushrod Washington identified the privileges and immunities of citizens in the several states as "those privileges and immunities which are, in their nature, fundamental, which belong, of right, to the citizens of all free governments." These included "protection by the government; the enjoyment of life and liberty, with the right to acquire and possess property of every kind, and ... the right of a citizen of one State to pass through, or to reside in, any other State for purposes of trade, agriculture, professional pursuits."[22] *Palko* identified the "immunities that are valid against the federal government by force of the specific pledges of particular amendments that have been found to be 'implicit in the concept of ordered liberty.'"[23]

Unenumerated Rights and Reserved Powers

Similarly, there is no list of unenumerated rights (or undelegated powers) protected by the Ninth and Tenth Amendments.[24] The Ninth Amendment states: "The enumeration in the Constitution of certain rights shall not be construed to deny or disparage others retained by the people." The Tenth Amendment adds, "The powers not delegated to the United States by the Constitution, nor prohibited by it to the states, are reserved to the states respectively, or to the people." A partial list includes the rights to travel, privacy, autonomy and dignity, freedom of association, fair trial, and presumption of innocence ("Unenumerated Rights," 2015). While the first is a right to citizenship, the others are rights of persons.

The Rights to Citizenship Rights and Their Exercise

United States citizens have the right to exercise citizenship and its rights. They may not to be stripped of their citizenship, even for treason. This applies universally to birthright citizens and those validly naturalized (Taranovsky, 2003). Thus, a citizen cannot be deprived of US citizenship and may only give it up with informed consent. The government has no power to withdraw or strip citizens of citizenship. If it did, the government could ignore its people through these actions and systematically violate their fundamental rights.

In a similar sense that United States citizenship may not be removed from US citizens, citizens may not be required to prove citizenship or provide identification to exercise rights of citizens, either constitutional or statutory. Proof of citizenship may not be required prior to exercise of rights lest the citizenship and rights be constructively removed from citizenship, and only returned with governmental permission or identification. Similarly, citizens may not be required to prove "lawful presence" in the United States because a foundational right of citizenship is to have and exercise rights here without proving citizenship. This principle of not being required to prove citizenship prior to exercise of citizen rights applies particularly to exercising fundamental constitutional rights such as the rights to vote, work, and travel.

The Right to Live and Live Freely

One of the privileges and immunities of citizenship is to live. In this sense, the right to live is stronger from citizens because they may not be killed by government and public officials without due process and arguably at all, especially on US territory. The president does not have the authority "to kill an American not engaged in combat on American soil." Citizens have more protections against capital punishment. They have a right to be "protected by the government when in federal custody" (R. Smith, 1997, 616, n. 205).[25]

Specifically, the president has no authority to carry out drone strikes on US citizens in the United States (Bendery, 2013). For instance, "The president has not and would not use drone strikes against American citizens on American soil," the president's spokesman said.

"The legal authorities that exist to use lethal force are bound by, constrained by, the law and the Constitution ... Whether it's a drone strike or a gun shot, the law and the Constitution apply in the same way" (Bendery, 2013).[26] This includes presidents and police.

Arguably, in the case of an American citizen, even accused of treason or as an enemy combatant, the government is obligated either to try him or to release him (Breyer, 2015, 72–73, 80).[27] The Court's ruling in *Hamdi* has "long since made clear that a state of war is not a blank check for the president when it comes to the rights of the Nation's citizens" (Breyer, 2015, 73; *Hamdi*, (542 US 536, 2004)).

The Right to Live in and Enter the United States

Citizens have the right to reenter the United States if they leave: "Citizens have the right to return to this country at any time of their liking."[28] While simple and straightforward, the rights to live in, leave, and reenter the United States are fundamental bases and liberty interests for rights such as travel.

According to Bosniak (2006, 111), "Possession of citizenship status in a particular state ... has consequences. Among other things, those who are status citizens may travel unconditionally into the country of citizenship."

The Right Not to Be Deported or Exiled

A citizen may not be deported and may only be extradited for a crime that is directly related to the country to which the person is being sent after a proper due process judicial proceeding. As Taranovsky notes, "a person cannot be stripped of citizenship without the person's informed consent." A citizen may be deported "only for a crime" that "must be directly related to the country to which the person is deported." And this only "after a proper judicial proceeding and then only to a country where the person will retain all fundamental rights." Otherwise, "If the government has a broad right to deport its citizens or to strip people of citizenship or not grant citizenship in the first place, the government can ignore the people through these actions and violate fundamental rights" (2003).[29]

As Justice Brandeis noted in *Ng Fung Ho v. White*, "To deport one who so claims to be a citizen obviously deprives him of liberty ... [and may] result also in loss of both property and life, or of all that makes life worth living. Against the danger of such deprivation without the sanction afforded by judicial proceedings, the Fifth Amendment affords protection in its guarantee of due process of law."[30]

The government has no power to deport its citizens. The citizen right not to be either exiled by being kept out of the country or deported is fundamental. The government may not prevent citizens from leaving or entering the country (kept in exile) without documents, or force citizens to leave (deportation). They may not be deported and are in fact not deportable (Schuck and Smith, 1985, 104).[31]

Citizens' right not to be exiled means citizens may not be forced or kept out of the country.[32] The right of US citizens to enter the United States "has long been recognized as one of the most fundamental aspects of the Constitutional right to travel" (Papers Please, 2014). Citizens are entitled to US passports and US protection abroad.[33] Traveling with a US passport is another fundamental right of citizens related to the right to travel. A US passport allows citizens to get assistance from the US government when overseas.

In addition to the right to travel within one's country founded in *Shapiro v Thompson*,[34] among fundamental rights of citizens is for those who are already abroad that they "may travel unconditionally into the country of citizenship" (Bosniak, 1998, 111; Sobel, 2008, n. 27). "A United States citizen has a right to reenter the United States." The Court concludes that a US citizen's right to reenter the United States entails more than simply the right to step over the border after having arrived there. See, e.g., *Newton v. INS*, 736 F.2d 336, 343 (6th Cir. 1984) (noting that citizens "have the right to *return* to this country at any time of their liking" (emphasis added)) (*Mohamed*, 2014, 536). The default, for a US citizen, cannot be that one does not have a right to travel to and from the United States. Otherwise, "This is a blatant violation of US citizens' Constitutional rights, and of US obligations as a party to the [International Covenant on Civil and Political Rights]" (Papers Please, 2013).

Normally,

> U.S. government permission is provided, invisibly to the traveler, in the form of a boarding pass printing result transmitted electronically to

the airline's reservation system in response to the transmission to the DHS of the would-be traveler's reservation details. But now that the default has been changed from "yes" to "no" (or, more precisely, from "fly" to "no fly"), and the U.S. government has deemed travel to be a privilege rather than a right, a government permission-to-travel letter might be needed just to override prior erroneous or superseded no-fly instructions, but to ensure that an individual would be allowed to board in the absence of the usual electronic boarding pass printing instructions from DHS (Papers Please, 2013b).[35]

The Right to Leave the Country

Just as citizens may not be exiled or deported, they may not be forced to stay in the United States or become internally exiled. Citizens may by right leave the country at any time without government permission. This derives from the nature of citizenship and the right to travel. In *Kent v. Dulles* (1958) the Court noted,

> [T]he right of exit [from the United States] is a personal right included within the word "liberty" as used in the Fifth Amendment. If that "liberty" is to be regulated, it must be pursuant to the lawmaking functions of the Congress. And if that power is delegated, the standards must be adequate to pass scrutiny by the accepted tests. Where activities or enjoyment, natural and often necessary to the well-being of an American citizen, such as travel, are involved, we will construe narrowly all delegated powers that curtail or dilute them. (128–129)

The Right to Consular and Embassy Protection Abroad

"The U.S. Department of State and our embassies and consulates abroad have no greater responsibility than the protection of U.S. citizens overseas."[36] The point of having a passport is that it requests and ultimately guarantees protection for US citizens abroad. The text of a passport notes that it requests the protection of the host government. This is embodied in the US passport's passage, "The Secretary of State of the United States of America hereby requests all whom it may concern to permit the citizen/national of the United States herein named to pass without delay or hindrance and in case of need to give all lawful aid and protection."

The Right to Serve in the Militia and Receive Militia Training

"A Well-regulated militia being necessary for a free society," citizens have the right in the Bill of Rights to join the militia. "Congress shall have the power ... To provide for organizing, arming, and disciplining, the Militia, and for governing such Part of them as may be employed in the service of the United States."[37] The US Code under "composition and classes" indicates the militia of the United States consists of all able-bodied males at least seventeen years of age ... [and] under forty-five years of age who are, or who have made a declaration of intention to become, citizens of the United States and of female citizens of the United States who are commissioned officers of the National Guard."[38]

The Right to Serve on a Jury

Only American citizens may serve on grand juries or petit juries.[39] The qualifications for jury service includes the provision that "any person [is] qualified to serve on grand and petit juries ... unless (1) not a citizen of the United States eighteen years old" (U.S. Code 28 § 1865). A jury of one's peers means a jury of citizens of the same community. Though sometimes avoided, jury service is actually one of the most valuable rights (and obligations) of citizenship for local participation in government.

The Right to Obtain Citizenship for Children Born Abroad

The right to citizenship by birth applies even if born abroad to parents who are US citizens (Katyall and Clement, 2015).[40] "Grant of citizenship must be almost automatic for people born ... in the country" (Taranovsky, 2003).[41] This right includes "Birth Abroad to Two U.S. Citizen Parents in Wedlock provid[ing] that one of the parents had a residence in the United States or one of its outlying possessions prior to the child's birth." Birthright citizenship also applies to "Birth Abroad to One Citizen and One Alien Parent in Wedlock, Birth Abroad Out-of-Wedlock to a US Citizen Father, Birth Abroad Out-of-Wedlock to a U.S. Citizen Mother"; and if the mother was a US citizen at the time of the person's birth and if the mother was physically present in the United States or one of its outlying possessions for a continuous period of one year prior to the person's birth. This extension of the Fourteenth Amendment definition of citizenship also permits citizen parents to bring children born abroad into the United States.[42]

Other Rights Citizens May Exercise

There are still other rights citizens may exercise make experience as enhanced prerogatives. For instance, citizens have the right to travel navigable waters in the United States. In general, the rights to privacy and due process are stronger for citizens.[43] Citizens have a right against privacy invasions in international surveillance and may not be put under surveillance inadvertently in international communications. Other claims for fundamental rights of citizenship may be compared with the rights of all persons.[44]

Conclusion: Empowering Citizenship

Citizenship ultimately encompasses the "thick" rights and requisites for persons to act individually under their civic power and to determine collectively the character of the nation and government. Citizens may exercise rights *per force* of citizenship. These rights typically exceed the protections for personhood and human rights. Among the dozen rights in the US Constitution reserved to citizens alone, citizens' political rights provide the clearest demonstration of reserved citizenship prerogatives.

Citizens do not need to prove their citizenship. They may exercise rights because they are citizens. They need not provide proof of citizenship first in order to exercise their constitutional rights. The reason parallels the presumption of innocence: The burden of proof is on the state to show one is not a citizen. One may exercise citizen rights because one is a citizen, simply by the status or by averring it.[45] If one had to prove citizenship first before exercising its rights, then s/he would not have citizen rights.

While Douglas (2008, 148, 175) identifies voting and travel as fundamental rights for these reasons, the right to employment is equally foundational as a source of autonomy and self-governance. As *Palko* noted in 1937, fundamental rights are "those found to be implicit in the concept of ordered liberty," as the privileges and immunities of citizenship surely are.

The debasing of fundamental rights occurs as a concomitant of requiring identification to exercise rights. The harms of an identification requirement are both qualitative and as measured by the magnitude of burden on a right like voting that abridges a most fundamental right of citizenship. The policy consequences of making citizen voting rights contingent, for instance, on identification documents constitute constructive disenfranchisement by legislatures selecting which citizens may and may not participate in elections.

Instead, identification regimes threaten the sovereignty of citizenship and its fundamental rights. "Rights that are inherent in protecting individual autonomy and self-governance are properly construed as fundamental. Thus, it makes sense to think of the fundamental right to vote as an individual right" (*Douglas*, 2008, 143, but see R. Smith, 1997, 588). Similarly, "the right to interstate travel ... receives consistent treatment as a fundamental right" (*Douglas*, 1964, 175, n. 205).

Requirements to produce government identification before exercising basic rights undermine the foundations of citizenship and those freedoms. Like the right to vote, the right to employment is political in the sense of exercising authoritative actions essential to the nature of the polity and society (Sobel, 1989, 1994). As Shklar (1991) noted, there are parallels between suffrage and earning. As work is a system of authority relations (Sobel, 1989), the formality of work authority parallels and leads to higher levels of voting. Similarly, travel to the seat of government is fundamental for seeking redress of grievances.

Government provisions that require citizens to prove their citizenship in order to exercise fundamental rights devalue citizenship and democracy while undermining the proper consenting relationship between citizen and the state (Sobel and Fennel, 2007). Identification requirements and systems invert the proper relationship between citizens and the state from one in which the people provide (or withhold) consent to the government to one in which the government provides or withholds "consent" for the people's identity.

In short, requirements prior to exercising basic rights, for citizens to get and provide identification, transform and invert government by consent into a regime of citizens praying for privileges to be granted by the government. This inversion of the proper relation of citizens to state undermines the nature of democratic and republican politics and government.

Expounding here and in public discussions the strong nature of citizenship rights against the debilitating strictures of a national identification regime provides the basis for policies and mobilizations to enhance citizens' rights protections to reverse this inversion. Threats to these rights undermine government by consent, the *pursuit* of happiness, and *securing* the blessing of liberties. Three of the clearest examples of strong rights that identification regimes abridge occur in politics, work, and travel.

3 THE RIGHT TO VOTE

The right to vote is a fundamental right of citizenship. The history of voting rights involves a long struggle to obtain and extend the franchise for all American citizens. Voting is fundamental in itself as an expression of popular sovereignty and as preservative of other rights. The right to vote as a fundamental constitutional right for citizens bulwarks and preserves other rights.

Voters may vote by right. Laws that interfere with the exercise of the right to vote and burden that right beyond constitutional standards undermine citizenship. The requirement, for instance, for government photo voter identification unconstitutionally abridge that right by restricting and burdening basic citizen rights to participate effectively in the political process.

The struggle for voting rights has been particularly evident in civil rights arenas. As with earlier Jim Crow restrictions in literacy tests and grandfather clauses, voter identification laws also have a disparate impact on minority voting under the Fourteenth and Fifteenth Amendments. Those laws deny minority groups the equal opportunity to participate in the political process.

The right to vote is a constitutional guarantee to American citizens. The right in national elections appears in Article I, Section 2, of the US Constitution and the Seventeenth Amendment. It is further found in the First, Fourteenth, and Fifteenth Amendments. It is extended by the Nineteenth, Twenty-fourth, and Twenty-sixth Amendments. These provisions and amendments create a right to vote. They do not just prohibit discrimination in its exercise. The right must not be abridged by bureaucratic burdens.

Explicating the fundamental nature of the franchise in citizenship provides intellectual foundations for strengthening voting rights. The right to vote derives from Article I, Section 2, of the US Constitution. "The House of Representatives shall be composed of Members chosen every second Year by the People of the several States, and the Electors in each State shall have the Qualifications requisite for Electors of the most numerous Branch of the State Legislature."

Though Article I, Section 3, originally provided for state legislatures to choose US Senators, the Seventeenth Amendment in 1913 changed it to popular elections: "The Senate of the United States shall be composed of two Senators from each State, elected by the people thereof, for six years ... The electors in each State shall have the qualifications requisite for electors of the most numerous branch of the State legislatures." As the Constitutional Accountability Center explains (2011), "Nearly a century ago today, the 17th Amendment ... expanded democracy and the right to vote by providing that the people of each state would elect their own U.S. Senators."[1]

VOTING AS A CONSTITUTIONAL RIGHT

Voting is most prominent among several political rights that only citizens may exercise.[2] "Only U.S. citizens can vote in Federal elections. Most States also restrict the right to vote to U.S. citizens."[3]

Moreover, the right to vote is also a privilege and immunity of citizenship guaranteed in Article IV and the Fourteenth Amendment (R. Smith, 1997, 256, 257, 177 v. 538). Under *Corfield v. Coryell* in 1823, "the elective franchise" was considered a "particular privilege" and immunity of citizenship. "The very foundation of a republican government" was "the right of suffrage" as an "immunity" inseparable from citizenship (R. Smith, 1997, 256). The right to vote, particularly in state elections, also derives from the First Amendment (assembly) and Fourteenth Amendment (liberty and equal protection) (*Veasey v. Perry* 2014).[4] It also has constitutional support in Article I and in the First Amendment right to association.

The foundations and reach of the right to vote go back in American history. Besides *Corfield v. Coryell* in 1823 holding "the elective franchise" as fundamental for citizens, court decisions from the 1870s mandate "vigorous enforcement of the laws" for whites in congressional elections (R. Smith, 1997, 408). *United States v. Goldman* in 1878 held that Article I, Section 4, "provided a right to vote in congressional elections to anyone eligible to vote in a state legislative election" (R. Smith, 1997, 408). In 1879, *Ex Parte Siebold* (1879) ruled that Congress had the power to protect the right as the Supreme Court agreed (R. Smith, 1997, 408).

In 1884, *Ex Parte Yarbrough*[5] ruled that "[t]he exercise of the right [to vote in general] ... is guaranteed by the constitution, and should be kept free and pure by congressional enactments whenever that is necessary." This right is basic to citizenship. "[W]hen congress undertakes to protect the citizen in the exercise of rights conferred by the constitution of the United States, [it is] essential to the healthy organization of the government itself."

In 1886, *Yick Wo v. Hopkins* articulated voting as a "fundamental" right. "The case of the political franchise of voting is one ... regarded as a fundamental political right, because preservative of all rights."[6] The theme of voting as preservative of other rights reinforces the significance of electoral rights in numerous future decisions. In 1915, *Guinn & Beal v. United States*[7] ruled that "grandfather clauses" in state constitutions were unconstitutional because they violate the Fifteenth Amendment's "restrict[ions on] the power of the United States or the States to abridge or deny the right of a citizen of the United States to vote on account of race, color or previous condition of servitude." While lacking explicit text granting a right to suffrage, the Fifteenth Amendment has "self-executing power" that makes any infringement upon its scope inherently unconstitutional.

In *United States v. Bathgate* (1918),[8] the Court articulated that "the right to vote" is "personal" and "definite." It recognized that U.S. citizens who reside in the states have the right to be a candidate for office and the right to vote (if duly qualified). The case recognizes not only the right for a qualified voter to vote but also the necessity to protect the entire voting process from malice or corruption.

In 1941, *U.S. v. Classic* declared the right to vote as constitutionally based and locates it in Article I. "[T]o the question whether that right is one secured by the Constitution, Section 2 of Article I commands that Congressmen shall be chosen by the people of the several states by electors, the qualifications of which it prescribes. The right of the people to choose . . . is a right established and guaranteed by the Constitution." Hence, voting "is one secured" by the Constitution "to those citizens and inhabitants of the state entitled to exercise the right" (314).[9]

Classic further articulated that "[i]ncluded within the right to choose, secured by the Constitution is the right of qualified voters within a state to cast their ballots and have them counted at Congressional elections. This Court has consistently held that this is a right secured by the Constitution" (313 US 315).

Moreover, the *Classic* Court held in 1941, as the Supreme Court said with respect to a congressional election, "The right to participate in the choice of representatives includes . . . the right to cast a ballot and to have it counted at the general election, whether for the successful candidate or not." *Classic* further held the right to vote is unrestricted. "And since the constitutional command is without restriction or limitation, the right, unlike those guaranteed by the Fourteenth and Fifteenth Amendments, is secured against the action of individuals, as well as of states" (299).

CIVIL RIGHTS ERA

During the Warren Court era, the US Supreme Court extended the meanings and reach of voting rights. Decisions in *Wesberry v. Sanders* (1964), *Reynolds v. Sims* (1964), and *Harper v. Virginia* (1966) empowered disenfranchised voters by explicating voting as a fundamental constitutional right of citizenship. That right, not to be abridged, inheres in the nature of a constitutional republican democracy.

Echoing *Yick Wo* in 1886 on voting as "preservative" of other rights, in 1964 *Wesberry v. Sanders* held that

> No right is more precious in a free country than that of having
> a voice in the election of those who make the laws under which, as

good citizens, we must live. Other rights, even the most basic, are illusory if the right to vote is undermined. Our Constitution leaves no room for classification of people in a way that unnecessarily abridges this right [to vote].

As Chief Justice Earl Warren noted in *Wesberry*, "The right to vote freely for the candidate of one's choice is of the essence of a democratic society, and any restrictions on that right strike at the heart of representative government and the ability to exercise their right to vote."

Similarly, in 1964, *Reynolds v. Sims* held, "Undoubtedly, the right of suffrage is a fundamental matter in a free and democratic society. Especially since the right to exercise the franchise in a free and unimpaired manner is preservative of other basic civil and political rights, any alleged infringement of the right of citizens to vote must be carefully and meticulously scrutinized (377 US 561)."

Echoing *Classic* from 1941, in *Harper v. Virginia* in 1966, the Court again articulated the Constitutional foundation of voting rights:

> While the right to vote in federal elections is conferred by Art. I, § 2, of the Constitution ... the right to vote in state elections is nowhere expressly mentioned. It is argued that the right to vote in state elections is implicit, particularly by reason of the First Amendment, and that it may not constitutionally be conditioned upon the payment of a tax or fee.[10]

Further, the *Harper* Court stated regarding burdens to voting, "For, to repeat, wealth or fee paying has, in our view, no relation to voting qualifications; the right to vote is too precious, too fundamental to be so burdened or conditioned" (670). In short, voting is fundamental as a right based in the constitution and is essential for political empowerment for citizens. Voting is foundational "since the right to exercise the franchise in a free and unimpaired manner is preservative of other basic civil and political rights."[11]

Furthermore, *Lubin v. Panish* in 1974 summarized that voting rights develop from the First Amendment freedom of association, in conjunction with the incorporation through the Fourteenth Amendment of the Bill of Rights on the states. "The right to vote derives from the right of association that is at the core of the First

Amendment, protected from state infringement by the Fourteenth Amendment."[12]

Wright v. Mahan in 1979 elaborates the source of the right to vote in the First Amendment rights to free expression and association. The right also derives from the equal protection guarantee in the Fourteenth Amendment.

> A careful reading of these and other cases convinces this Court that the right to vote and the right to reasonable access to a ballot derive not only from the equal protection clause of the Fourteenth Amendment, but also from the First Amendment. The guarantee of free political expression would have diminished practical value if it did not include the right to cast a ballot. Similarly, the right to associate freely in a political party, and to advance a political cause, would lack meaning if the right of reasonable access to a ballot were denied.[13]

Williams v. Sclafani in 1977 held, "It is well settled that voting is a fundamental right, *Reynolds v. Sims* (1964, 910). "Furthermore, in considering the important state interests ... involved here, this Court cannot overlook the compelling federal interest in protecting the fundamental right to vote." The courts found that the protections of the First Amendment encompassed the right to vote and to reasonable ballot access (917).

In 1992 in *Burdick v. Takushi*, the Court upheld the fundamental nature of voting rights. "It is beyond cavil that 'voting is of the most fundamental significance under our constitutional structure.'"[14] Yet *Burdick* permitted burdens on voting rights. *McCutcheon v. FEC* in 2014 underscored the basic nature of voting rights. "There is no right more basic in our democracy than the right to participate in electing our political leaders."[15]

In short, the courts have repeatedly upheld the fundamental political rights of citizens to vote. They do so particularly for the "preservative" character of voting for protecting other citizen rights.

MAJOR VOTING RIGHTS LEGISLATION

The Civil Rights Act of 1964 (HR 7152) entitled "an Act to enforce the constitutional right to vote ..." included pioneering voting rights provisions. For the first time, it barred unequal application of voter registration requirements by requiring voting rules and procedures be applied equally to all races. It set up the Civil Rights Commission to investigate allegations that certain citizens of the United States were being deprived of their right to vote, and to have that vote counted, by reason of their color, race, religion, or national origin.

The Voting Rights Act of 1965 became the premiere voting rights protection by reinforcing the fundamental right to vote in an "act to enforce the Fifteenth Amendment." By eliminating most voting qualifications beyond citizenship, Section 2 of the 1965 Act prohibits any jurisdiction from implementing a "voting qualification or prerequisite to voting, or standard, practice, or procedure ... in a manner which results in a denial or abridgement of the right ... to vote on account of race," color, or language minority status (Garrine, 2008). Section 2 holds that "[n]o voting qualifications or prerequisite to voting, or standard, practice, or procedure shall be imposed or applied by any State or political subdivision to deny or abridge the right of any citizen of the United States to vote on account of race or color."

Section 3 permitted "bailing in" (inclusion under the Act's coverage) more jurisdictions by demonstrating purposeful discrimination. In short, the section permitted the federal government to add jurisdictions with records of discriminatory patterns to those identified under existing laws.

Section 4 set the formula for coverage of those jurisdictions with a long history of voting discrimination using myriad "tests and devices" under the statutory mandate to get "preclearance" (prior permission) from the US Justice Department or a federal court. It was this section that was declared unconstitutional by the Supreme Court in *Shelby v. Holder* in 2013,[16] effectively gutting Section 5 (preclearance) of the act.

Section 5 required "preclearance" of any voting-related changes in nine mostly Southern states. It says that "[w]henever a State or political subdivision with respect to which the prohibitions set forth in section 4(a) are in effect shall enact or seek to administer any voting qualifications or requisite to voting, or standard, practice, or procedure with respect to voting ... such State or subdivision may institute an action in the United States District Court for the District of Columbia for a declaratory judgment that such qualification, prerequisite, standard, practice, or procedure does not have the purpose and will not have the effect of denying or abridging the right to vote on account of race or color, and no person shall be denied the right to vote for failure to comply with such qualification prerequisite, standard, practice, or procedure: Provided, that such qualification, prerequisite, standard, practice, or procedure ... has been submitted ... to the Attorney General and the Attorney General has not interposed an objection .... Any action under this section shall be heard and determined by a court of three judges ... and any appeal shall lie to the Supreme Court."

POLITICAL SUPPORT FOR VOTING RIGHTS

Political leaders have provided some of the most persuasive articulations of the importance of the right to vote. As Voting Rights Act sponsor, Senator Everett Dirksen (R-IL), noted in a radio interview in 1965 that "the right to vote is still an issue in this free country ... There has to be a real remedy [for] the denial of the right to vote by ruses and devises and test, and whatever the mind can contrive to either make it very difficult or to make it impossible to vote" (Zeliger, 2014).

One of the best descriptions of the fundamental right to vote as preservative of other rights came, echoing *Reynolds* and *Harper*, in the September 2005 confirmation hearings for John Roberts to become chief justice of the United States. In the hearing, Senator Edward Kennedy asked if then appellate Judge Roberts believed that "the right to vote is a fundamental constitutional right" (Hoxie, 2014). In response to questions about his views of the Voting Rights Act, Roberts replied, "[The right to vote] is preservative, I think, of all the other rights. Without access to the ballot box, people are not in a position to protect any other rights that are important to them. And so I think it's one of, as you said, the most precious rights we have as Americans" (Berman, 2015a, 250; Hoxie, 2014).

Judge Roberts was also asked if he had any questions about the constitutionality of the Voting Rights Act. "The existing Voting Rights Act the constitutionality has been upheld, and I don't have any issue with that," Roberts answered. Further he noted, "Any issues that come before me under the Voting Rights Act, I will confront those with an open mind and decide them after full and fair consideration of the arguments, in light of the precedents of the Court, and in light of a recognition of the critical role that the right to vote plays as preservative of all other rights" (Berman, 2015a, 251).

As the appellate dissent noted in *Crawford v. Marion County Election Board* (2007), "Even if only a single citizen is deprived completely of her right to vote ... this is still a 'severe' injury for that particular individual."[17] The Supreme Court dissent in *Crawford* noted that the right to vote is fundamental and that laws like the Indiana voter identification statute are facially unconstitutional, in the sense that they generally widely abridge a fundamental right. In short, withholding such a fundamental right significantly injures citizen rights. Voter identification requirements are facially unconstitutional as profound impediments to voting as a right. They are also unconstitutional "as applied" as they constitute impermissible burdens on the exercise of the right to specific groups of people, typically minorities.[18]

Furthermore, legislatures may not make rules that subvert the rights of popular choice of their legislators. Because the people choose the legislators and not the legislators their electors, citizens have the fundamental right to vote without government identification: *League of Women Voters v. Walker* (2012) makes explicit that requiring government photo voter identification damages and abridges the democracy-sustaining right of voting.

> These qualifications [to vote] are explicit, exclusive, and unqualified ... and the Constitution ... confers no authority upon the legislature to change, impair, add to or abridge them ... Until the people's vote approved the Constitution, the legislature had no authority to regulate anything, let alone elections. Thus, voting rights hold primacy over implicit legislative authority to regulate elections ... [A]rgument that the fundamental right to vote must yield to legislative fiat turns our constitutional scheme of democratic government squarely on its head ... If citizens are deprived of that right, which lies at the very basis of our Democracy, we will soon cease to be a Democracy.[19]

In short, citizens may exercise their rights as citizens to vote. Democratic government must protect the exercise of that right as

a primary responsibility for remaining democratic. Legislative interference with the citizen franchise by identification requirements undermines the legislature's role in the democratic process. In a democracy,
the people's consent legitimates the government's exercise of power;
the government's exercise of power should not be required to legitimate
the identities of the people (Sobel and Fennel, 2007).

As *Elrod v. Burns* held in 1976, "[N]o right is more jealously
guarded ... under our constitutions ... than is the right of
suffrage ... enjoyed by the people before the adoption of the constitution and is one of the inherent rights."[20] In sum, citizens have the right
to vote first and may not have prior restrictions burdening this
exercise.[21]

Because citizens are eligible to vote, each one has a vested right in
the electoral franchise that may not subsequently be denied simply for
lack of a government ID. Requiring individuals to obtain photo identification as a condition to exercise that vested right amounts to
a modern-day re-registration requirement (outlawed by the Voting
Rights Act)[22] and frequent voting roll purges that constitute a denial
of fundamental political rights and due process.

VOTING RIGHTS ABRIDGEMENTS BY VOTER ID LAWS

Both citizens and governments have equally strong interests in
protecting constitutional rights as the bedrock of "ordered liberty."
Citizens may carry out constitutional liberties unmolested. Justice
Brennan wrote that "offensive to the sensibilities of private citizens,
identification requirements ... even in their least intrusive form,
must discourage ... participation [in the political process]."[23]
Essentially, voter identification laws "drive out [of the political
process] people who are useful national resources, even if they
are not political allies" (R. Smith, 1997, 34). They contradict the
inherited Anglo-American practice of letting all "freemen vote"
(R. Smith, 1997, 127).

Even a short halting of the exercise of fundamental rights constitutes a constitutional harm. As noted in *Elrod*, "The deprivation of
a constitutional right for even a brief period of time amounts to

irreparable injury."[24] "The loss of First Amendment freedoms, for even a minimal period of time, unquestionably constitutes irreparable injury."

The violation of the right to vote need not be an absolute denial of a voter's entry into the polling booth. Abridgement may lie in the creation of burdens that discourage qualifying for or exercising of the right.[25]

As the Wisconsin decision noted, "[P]hoto ID requirements impermissibly eliminate the right of suffrage altogether for certain constitutionally qualified electors ... who ha[ve] incontrovertible ... proof at the polls that [they are] a qualified elector ... but lack statutorily acceptable photo ID ... Thus ... photo ID requirements are unconstitutional because they abridge the right to vote."[26]

Citizens have rights to exercise their citizen rights. As a demand for identification constitutes a search under the Fourth Amendment, only those people suspected of committing voter fraud can be required to furnish identification any more intrusive than simply stating one's name and address or signing a poll book. As *Kolender v. Lawson* established in 1983, citizens do not require identification for legal activities. In the electoral context, a citizen can state his name and business and be on his way to the polling booth.

Two years earlier in 1981, the Ninth Circuit had held in *Lawson v. Kolender* that the requirement to identify oneself "impermissibly intrudes upon the fourth amendment's proscription against unreasonable searches and seizures." The circuit court

> agree[d] with the courts and commentators who have concluded that statutes ... which require the production of identification, are in violation of the fourth amendment. The two reasons for this conclusion are that as a result of the demand for identification, the statutes bootstrap the authority to arrest on less than probable cause, and the serious intrusion on personal security outweighs the mere possibility that identification may provide a link leading to arrest.[27]

The Supreme Court's affirmation in *Kolender v. Lawson* in 1983 on vagueness validated the Ninth Circuit's judgment that the identification statute violated the Fourth Amendment. The appellate court identified identification demands as searches that violate the Fourth Amendment. "The appellate court determined that the statute was unconstitutional in that it violates the Fourth Amendment's proscription against unreasonable searches and seizures, it contains a vague enforcement standard that is susceptible to arbitrary enforcement, and it fails to give fair and adequate notice of the type of conduct prohibited."[28]

In affirming the appellate decision in *Kolender v. Lawson* in 1983, the Supreme Court invalidated a statute that allowed police to demand identification without suspicion of criminal conduct. Justice O'Connor called the requirement for "credible and reliable" identification "unconstitutionally vague on its face because it encourages arbitrary enforcement." In concurring, Justice Brennan explained that, absent probable cause, the circumstances under which the state may infringe upon a citizen's Fourth Amendment rights are "strictly defined by the legitimate requirements of law enforcement and by the limited extent of the resulting intrusion on individual liberty and privacy."[29] Voting as a type of expressive conduct is protected by First Amendment freedom of expression. As such, it includes the right also under the Fourth and Fifth Amendments not to be coerced to express oneself in identification.[30]

Moreover, Justice Brennan's concurrence clarified how the demand for identification is a search when he held that, even if the statute had not been vague, it would still have violated the Fourth Amendment.[31] "Even if the defect identified by the Court were cured, however, I would hold that this statute violates the Fourth Amendment" because "States may not authorize the arrest ... for failing to produce identification."[32] In short, the *Kolender* court struck down the requirement to provide identification when involved in legal behavior.

As *Hiibel v. Nevada* also holds, only upon reasonable suspicion of criminal conduct under the state stop-and-identify law may government require citizens to reveal their names. The Court in *Hiibel* recognized that the government may not require citizens to identify themselves, unless there is already a state stop-and-identify law, to any degree more intrusive than stating their names, absent probable cause to arrest (2004, 187–189). By analogy, any infringement upon another fundamental right – whether freedom from unreasonable searches or to vote – must limit the intrusion on protected rights to situations when there is evidence of criminal conduct. Moreover, any government intrusion upon individual liberty and privacy must be narrowly tailored to fulfill the governmental interests.

VOTER IDENTIFICATION LAWS REQUIRE A CONSTITUTIONAL STANDARD FOR DEMANDING IDENTIFICATION

In order to preserve citizens' constitutional right to vote, there must be a predictable, constitutionally sound standard that defines when, and to what degree, the government regulates voting. This includes a standard for when a citizen can be required to furnish identification before being allowed to exercise the right to vote (Smith and Sobel, 2009).

By their very nature, across-the-board demands for identification lack standards for application. Voter identification laws for all voters contradict a reasonable standard because their coverage is overbroad and they lack a basis for intrusion in requiring every citizen wanting to vote in person to furnish government photo identification. Requiring photo identification is not the least intrusive means to prevent in-person voter fraud. Without reasonable suspicion, the government may not infringe Fourth Amendment rights and require citizens to identify themselves any more intrusively than stating their names (*Hiibel v. Nevada*, 2004).[33] *Hiibel* extends the holding in *Kolender* (1983) that people carrying on law-abiding activities may not be required to provide identification.

The requirement that all in-person voters present photo identification in order to vote infringes upon the fundamental electoral right by failing to comply with any proportional, constitutionally justifiable standard. The extent the government may require citizens to identify themselves must be carefully tailored. For example, many states simply require voters to state their names and addresses and sign a poll book.

There are many steps on the spectrum of identification, from requiring a name, address, and signature, or presenting a piece of US mail, to requiring government-issued photo identification. The simpler steps are effective but not burdensome. Requiring a government-issued photo identification is at the far end of the spectrum of identification and among the most intrusive forms.

The government may not require more intrusive forms of identification unless it can articulate reasonable grounds for questioning a voter's identity. Even then, the government may not require official photo identification based upon less-than-probable cause that the voter is attempting to commit fraud.

Although *Classic* held in 1941 that electoral rights are "without restrictions and limitations," legislatures and courts propose different standards for evaluating the constitutionality of electoral laws (see, e.g., *Burdick*, 1992, 434). The standard of at least reasonable suspicion of illegal activity is required for an allegation of in-person voter fraud, the purported basis for requiring photo identification at the polls (*Crawford*, 2007a, 953–954) and thereby infringing on citizens' right to vote. As the appellate dissent recognized in *Crawford*, "voting is a complex act that both helps to decide elections and involves individual citizens in the group act of self-governance" (*Crawford*, 2007b, 438). Justice Kennedy aptly noted in dissent in *Burdick* (1992, 447), "For those who are affected by [write-in] bans, the infringement on their right to vote for the candidate of their choice is total."

VOTER IDENTIFICATION LAWS ARE OVERLY INCLUSIVE

Requiring every voter to supply government photo identification is an overbroad application of government requirements. Virtually all voters are not suspected of fraud or irregularities. Voter identification laws contradict this standard, because they arbitrarily require that every citizen wishing to vote in person furnish official photo identification without suspicion of voter fraud. This requirement of a license to vote imposed a constitutionally unsustainable burden.

Voter identification laws are overbroad in requiring photo identification from everyone wishing to vote in person. This may not be the requirement when there is no suspicion that the person wishing to vote is intending to commit voter fraud. By not requiring reasonable suspicion of fraud before imposing more intrusive identification, voter identification laws contradict the reasonable standard in *Kolender* and

Hiibel by arbitrarily allowing the government to impose restrictions on exercising the right to vote without cause.

Voter identification laws create a system whereby citizens are required to obtain a license to vote in order to exercise their right in the electoral franchise. Any system of electoral licensing contradicts the values embedded in the Constitution. As the government may not require intrusive identification without suspicion, states may not apply overbroad and disproportional identification laws in ways that essentially require licenses to vote.

In short, voting rights come first and do not require identification to exercise them. Only when a predictable, constitutionally sound standard is breached, in voter conduct, can the government require citizens to identify themselves, and can identification requirements be imposed on citizens to exercise the right to vote. Moreover, those laws must be narrowly tailored to accomplish their goals in the least intrusive ways.

PHOTO IDENTIFICATION LAWS ARE NOT THE LEAST INTRUSIVE WAY TO PREVENT VOTER FRAUD

Depriving even one voter of the opportunity to exercise this fundamental right to vote is too substantial a burden to withstand constitutional scrutiny. As the dissent in *Crawford* held, "Even if only a single citizen is deprived completely of her right to vote ... this is still a 'severe' injury for that particular individual" (*Crawford*, 2007b, 438). Any intrusion on constitutionally protected rights must be the most narrowly tailored way to serve government interests. However, by requiring that every voter provide photo identification, voter identification laws are not the least intrusive means to achieve the stated goal of preventing in-person voter fraud.

A more narrowly tailored approach better serves the government's interest in fair voting. Alternative approaches are less intrusive and more precisely tailored than requiring every voter to furnish government-issued photo identification. Election officials can identify voters without requiring government photo identification. Asking voters to sign poll books and comparing the signatures to those on file perform as non-intrusive and effective ways to identify voters in many states (Indiana Democratic Party, 2007, 4–5). When someone does not appear to be who they say they are, officials can ask potential voters their addresses or length of residency to develop a reasonable certainty. This might include additional questioning that can as effectively discourage and detect voter fraud.

Indeed, modest identification measures and criminal penalties for misrepresentation in voting have worked for many years before the passage of voter identification laws. As another dissenting appellate judge affirmed in *Crawford*, "the defenders of [the Indiana] law candidly acknowledged that no one ... had ever been charged with" voter fraud (2007a, 955). There has never been a reported instance of in-person voter fraud in Indiana (*Crawford*, 2007a, 955) and Wisconsin history. If no one has been charged, no one should be asked for identification.

If potential voters are unable to answer legitimate identifying questions like current address or their signature clearly does not match that on file, the election official may reasonably ask those people to prove who they claim to be. At that point, the official could investigate a voter's identity by requesting another form of identification, such as a document. Only upon probable cause to arrest for voter fraud, however, may the government require a voter to furnish photo identification (*Hiibel*, 2004, 188–189).

In sum, not requiring identification is most compatible with citizens' right to vote. Levels of identification, from stating one's name and address to providing a piece of mail, can be asked when there are standards met for further documentation. Only if there is reasonable suspicion about a voter's identity, may more extensive identification be asked. But photo- or government-issued identification may only be required if there is probable cause that a voter is attempting fraud. The government may not require intrusive forms of corroborative documentation without transgressing that constitutional threshold.[34]

REQUIRING PHOTO IDENTIFICATION ABRIDGES EQUAL OPPORTUNITY TO VOTE

Moreover, requiring all in-person voters to present photo identification violates equal protection because it has a disparate impact on the right to vote, particularly of minority groups. As the appellate dissent in *Crawford* noted, the voter identification law "is a not-too-thinly-veiled attempt to discourage election-day turnout by certain folks believed to skew Democratic" (*Crawford*, 2007a, 954). Moreover, these "folks" are "mostly ... people who are poor, elderly, minorities, disabled, or some combination thereof" (955). The law would result in the "denial or abridgement" of the right to vote of many of these citizens.

Practical burdens, such as lack of necessary documentation, infrequency of other occasions for identification, and difficulty traveling to obtain identification, are issues for minorities, particularly from voter identification laws. Because poor and minorities are less likely to have identification, or have the resources to obtain them, voter ID laws deny and abridge the equal opportunity of minority and other voters to participate in the political process.

VOTER IDENTIFICATION REQUIREMENTS DISPARATELY IMPACT POOR, MINORITY, AND ELDERLY GROUPS

Voter identification laws are additionally discriminatory in their impacts on poor, minority, and elderly voters: "[T]hese disenfranchised citizens would consist of those struggling souls who ... will lack the ... resources to comply with [Voter ID], but are otherwise constitutionally entitled to vote ... The right to vote belongs to all Wisconsin citizens who are qualified electors, not just the fortunate majority for whom [Voter ID] poses little obstacle at the polls."[35]

Poor voters often do not have access to, nor frequently use, government-issued photo identification because they lack cars and rarely travel by air. Many in this category are minorities, particularly African Americans and Hispanic Americans. *Minority voters* who tend to be poorer and less educated are less likely to have driver's licenses or the resources to obtain official photo identification. *Minority-language voters* whose identity documents are not in English may have difficulty in reading, understanding, and writing English, particularly complex regulations like voter identification laws (Sobel and Smith, 2009).

Elderly voters are also likely to encounter greater difficulty in traveling any distance to obtain identification. They may have been born before birth certificates were mandatory or in rural areas where birth registrations were delayed or erratic. *Women voters* whose family names have changed or become hyphenated risk having the name on their photo identification differ from, and hence do not "conform" to, the one on their birth certificates. *Disabled voters* may experience much greater difficulty in traveling to obtain identification or in communicating with government officials. They may not have frequent need for government photo IDs, for instance, to drive.

VOTER IDS DISCOURAGING PARTICIPATION TRIGGER CONSTITUTIONALLY LOST REPRESENTATION

Because voter identification laws discourage voter turnout, particularly among minority groups, their implementation abridges a fundamental constitutional right (Sobel and Smith, 2009).[36] The Fourteenth Amendment includes a little-known remedy for denying or abridging the right to vote that reduces a state's congressional representation in proportion to the extent of the abridgements. The constitutional remedy for voter discrimination appears in Section 2 of the amendment in a "never exercised tool for aiding black citizenship in the states" (R. Smith, 1997, 310). This rarely recognized Fourteenth Amendment passage in Section 2 says that "when the right to vote" in an election is "denied" or "in any way abridged," a state's "representation . . . shall be reduced" proportionally. The Fourteenth Amendment spelled out the constitutional remedy for the abridgement before the Fifteenth Amendment's promise that the "right of citizens of the United States to vote shall not be denied or abridged . . . on account of race, color, or previous condition of servitude."[37]

Abridgement of the right to vote does not require complete denial of voting rights but rather evidence of a burden discouraging exercise of the right. This occurs when a law makes it less likely that an individual or member of a group will try to or succeed in exercising the elective franchise. When the right to vote of citizens, including disparately impacted minority groups, is widely abridged, the remedy in the Fourteenth Amendment for voter ID law is the reduction in the size of the state's congressional delegation. This reduction, according to the Constitution, is in proportion to the percentage of its population whose right to vote is abridged or denied, in this case, by the voter identification law.

The abridgement of the right to vote consists in requiring identification without reasonable suspicion of committing a crime while voting. More pointedly, the abridgement consists in a state passing a voter ID law when a significant proportion of the citizenry does not have governmental identification.[38] The first group of affected citizens includes all in-person voters asked for a government identification without reasonable suspicion (see Smith and Sobel, 2009). The second includes anyone who does not have governmental identification with a photograph and current expiration date.

Additionally, evidence that minority groups, particularly blacks and Hispanics, are less likely to have required identification and are more likely to be burdened in its acquisition also constitutes evidence of abridgement to trigger the remedy (see Drew, 2007; Barreto et al., 2008). Not every member of the group needs to be prevented or discouraged to trigger the remedy when a substantial proportion in the class are more likely to be discouraged from voting by the photo identification requirement (Sobel, 2009).

Following the Fourteenth Amendment's prescription of proportional reduction of representation for voter abridgements, a state like Indiana, source of the *Crawford* challenge, would lose one-ninth to one-sixth of its representation, or one of its nine seats in the House (retaining two Senators). Hence, the state would also lose one of eleven electoral votes. Other discriminating states, with larger congressional delegations, would lose larger representation.

The consequences of the Fourteenth and Fifteenth Amendment proscriptions on voting discrimination are that governmental actions that "in any way" abridge the right to vote, as the voter identification law does, fail constitutional scrutiny and reduce representation. Yet, rather than risking losing representation, the appropriate remedy is for the state not to pass and to outlaw voter identification requirements.[39]

CONCLUSION: VOTING AS A CITIZENSHIP RIGHT
IS PROTECTED BY CONSTITUTIONAL STANDARDS

The right to vote is fundamental as a constitutional right for citizens because it preserves and bulwarks other rights. Voters as citizens may vote by right. The long history of the struggle for the franchise for working people, including minorities and women, underlies the importance of maintaining and exercising the right to vote and opposing tests and devices that abridge and undermine it.

Voter identification laws interfere with the exercise of the right to vote and burden that right beyond constitutional standards for identification demands. The requirements also have a disparate impact on the minority franchise under the Fourteenth and Fifteenth Amendments. They deny minority groups the equal opportunity to participate in the political process by imposing a "qualification or prerequisite to voting" that unfairly disadvantages groups.

Citizens' right to vote needs to prevail. Denying voters the opportunity to exercise the fundamental electoral rights is too severe a burden to withstand constitutional scrutiny. The constitutional remedy of depriving states of representation protects citizen rights in the amendments that anticipated laws like voter identification requirements as inherently antidemocratic and unconstitutional. Legislatures need to repeal them or courts strike them down as unconstitutional infringements of a most fundamental right.

The fundamental nature of citizen voting rights derives from the meaning and power of citizenship. Voting is the simple yet potent expression of the nature of sovereignty among the constituent elements of a democratic society. The right to vote must be unimpeded for democracy to operate effectively in a sustained manner. Other rights like employment and travel underlie the ability to exercise voting rights.

4 THE RIGHT TO EMPLOYMENT

The right to employment has long been fundamental for citizens. From the early republic to the civil rights era, United States Supreme Court decisions from *Corfield v. Coryell* (1823) to *Butcher Union Co.* (1884) and *Truax* (1915) to *Roth* (1972) recognized that taking employment is a foundational citizenship right and is preservative of other rights.

Though less recognized than voting rights, the constitutional right to take employment facilitates and undergirds other rights to pursue the American dream and happiness in social and political dimensions. The right may not be abridged by burdens to its exercise in, for example, worker identification requirements as aspects of systems of employment surveillance.

THE NATURE OF THE EMPLOYMENT RIGHT

"The right to earn," in Judith Shklar's formulation, "has a history parallel to that of the suffrage" (Shklar, 1991, 19). The right to take employment is an inalienable right of citizenship. In the quest for inclusion in citizenship, Shklar expanded on the "parallelism" between "what was unique about American citizenship: voting and earning" (Shklar, 1991, 67, 15). "This vision of economic independence, or self-directed 'earning' as the ethical basis of democratic citizenship took the place of an outmoded notion of public virtue and it has retained its powerful appeal. We are citizens only if we 'earn'" (67).[1]

Because "[n]ot to work is not to earn," as Shklar noted, "and without one's earnings one is 'nobody'" (92), "[o]nly those who act on their

own behalf ... can count as full citizens. If they lack the identifying
marks of citizenship, they must fall into a proscribed category" (99).
"The Jacksonian faith," she reminds us, "creates a presumption of
a right to work as an element of American citizenship" (99). In short,
Shklar maintains that the right to "earning is implicit in equal American
citizenship" (100).[2] Absent the right to earn, there is "the reduction of
standing and demotion to second-class citizenship" (100) or a form of
"subjectship" (Schuck and Smith, 1985, 13). The "right to earn," even
when not exercised, is a "right not to be deprived of one's standing as
a citizen" (Shklar, 1991, 101).[3] In sum, the right to take employment
flowing from citizenship may not be abridged.[4]

Social theorist T. H. Marshall treated the right to work as an
element of "civil citizenship" (Bosniak, 2006, 105). This conception
of employment represented an appeal to liberal republican consensu-
alism and "Lockean labor theory" (R. Smith, 1997, 247–248). In fact,
Lockean labor theory of civic values also makes the right to employment secure for citizens because "those who owned a country should
run it" (R. Smith, 1997, 248). For Delany, civic ownership came not
just from possession of property but from contributing civically beneficial labor. Those who "made the greatest investments" of their pro-
ductive industry in a country could be counted on to be most interested
in its well-being, and so they deserved "the most sacred rights of the
country." This argument links employment and citizenship across
races (R. Smith, 1997, 250, 351, 567, 592). In short, in creating and
"enjoying the fruit of their labor," citizens obtained citizenship rights
(R. Smith, 1997, 245).[5]

THE CITIZEN RIGHT TO EMPLOYMENT

The right to employment is a privilege and immunity of American
citizenship. In 1823, in *Corfield v. Coryell*, Justice Bushrod
Washington identified the privileges and immunities of citizens in the
several states as "those privileges and immunities which are, in their
nature, fundamental, which belong, of right, to the citizens of all free
governments."[6] These included "protection by the government; the
enjoyment of life and liberty, with the right to acquire and possess

property of every kind, and . . . the right of a citizen of one State to pass through, or to reside in, any other State for purposes of trade, agriculture, professional pursuits."

Similarly, in 1871, in *U.S. v. Maryland* (79 U.S. 430), the Court noted that privileges and immunities "plainly and unmistakenly secure and protect the right of a citizen of one state to pass into any other state of the Union for the purpose of engaging in lawful commerce, trade or business."

The dissent in *Slaughterhouse* in 1873 (83 U.S. 36) prefigured the finding of the fundamental nature of employment rights. Justice Bradley's *Slaughterhouse* opinion raised these themes: "the right of any citizen to follow whatever lawful employment he chooses to adopt . . . is one of his most valuable rights, and one which the legislature of a State cannot invade" (114).

In the landmark *Butcher's Union Co. v. Crescent City Co.* decision in 1884, the US Supreme Court proclaimed "occupation as a fundamental right of citizenship" (111 U.S. 746, 756 (1884)). The Court declared that one of the privileges and immunities of citizenship is "the right to follow any of the common occupations of life [a]s an inalienable right." Justice Stephen Field concurred that employment was a right of citizenship. "Among these inalienable rights, as proclaimed in that great document, is the right of men to pursue their happiness . . . the right to pursue any lawful business or vocation, in any manner not inconsistent with the equal rights of others, which may increase their prosperity . . ., so as to give to them their highest enjoyment."

Accordingly, 'The common business and callings of life, the ordinary trades and pursuits . . . must therefore be free in this country to all alike upon the same conditions. The right to pursue them, without let or hindrance . . . is a distinguishing privilege of citizens of the United States, and an essential element of that freedom which they claim as their birthright."[7]

Furthermore, in *Butchers Union Co.*, Justice Joseph Bradley also concurred that "The right to follow any of the common occupations of life is an inalienable right . . . under the phrase 'pursuit of happiness' in the declaration of independence . . . that they are endowed by their Creator with certain inalienable rights; . . . life, liberty, and the pursuit of happiness." This right is a large ingredient in the civil liberty of the citizen.

Most pointedly justice, Bradley "deem[ed] a fundamental one, that the ordinary pursuits of life, forming the large mass of industrial avocations, are and ought to be free and open to all" (111 U.S. 746, 763). Bradley further concurred that "I hold that the liberty of pursuit – the right to follow any of the ordinary callings of life – is one of the privileges of a citizen of the United States" (764).[8]

On that point, Bradley found *Corfield* "very instructive," because Article IV of the Constitution declares that "the citizens of each State shall be entitled to all the privileges and immunities of citizens in the several States." Among those privileges and immunities, both Justices Washington in *Corfield* and Bradley in *Butcher's Union* included the right to employment.

Later Supreme Court decisions have affirmed the centrality of employment as a citizen right. In 1887, *in re Sam Kee* (680) described "implicit liberty to select one's own occupation" as a fundamental right (R. Smith, 1997, 615). In 1897, *Allgeyer v. Louisiana* (589) affirmed the holding in *Butchers Union Co.* "that the liberty of pursuit – the right to follow any of the ordinary callings of life – is one of the privileges of a citizen of the United States" (764).

In 1915, in *Coppage v. Kansas*, the Court reiterated that "[i]ncluded in the right of personal liberty and the right of private property – partaking of the nature of each – is the right to make contracts for the acquisition of property. Chief among such contracts is that of personal employment, by which labor and other services are exchanged for money and other forms of property."

In *Truax v. Raich* (1915, 41), the Court maintained that "[i]t requires no argument to show that the right to work for a living in the common occupation of the community is of the very essence of the personal freedom and opportunity that it was the purpose of the [Fourteenth] amendment to secure."

In *Meyer v. Nebraska*, (1923, 399), the Court held that "The term [liberty under the Fourteenth Amendment] … denotes not merely freedom from bodily restraint but also the right of the individual to contract, to engage in any of the common occupations of life … The established doctrine is that this liberty may not be interfered with under the guise of protecting public interest by legislative action." Into the post-New Deal era in 1949, in *AFL v. American Sash and Door*, the Supreme Court held that "the right to work is one of the essential freedoms of man without which citizenship would be but an empty name" (538). Similar to Shklar's later articulation (1991), this decision closely links earning and franchise.

In the civil rights era, *Board of Regents of State Colleges vs. Roth* (408 U.S. 564) (1972) reprised *Truax* (1915) on the "right to work for a living in the common occupation of the community [a]s of the very essence of the personal freedom and opportunity ... the [Fourteenth] amendment ... secure[s]." It also repeated from *Meyer* (1923) that liberty denotes "the right of the individual to contract, to engage in any of the common occupations of life."

Brandeis held that the Fourteenth Amendment granted citizens employment rights (Urofsky, 2009). "Brandeis ... never believed that the Court should have used the Due Process Clause to strike down the other laws." "But if his more conservative brethren intended to use the clause to protect property rights, then they ought to be willing to use it to protect other rights as well." This includes such basic rights "as choice of profession" (and travel) (Urofsky, 2009, 561–562). Due process "had to be applied and to protect what he considered fundamental rights," such as "choice of profession, and the right to travel – none of which should be restricted except on a showing of clear-and- present danger" (Urofsky, 2009, 619). Indeed, in the "Brandeis-Frankfurther Conversations" (Urofsky, 1985, 320), Brandeis said due process "must be applied to substantive laws" for "things that are funda-mental," such as "the right to choice of profession."

Like voting and travel, the right to employment is equally fun-damental as a source of autonomy and self-governance. This is underscored by the social parallels between suffrage and earning. Because work is a system of authority relations, the formality of work authority parallels and leads to higher levels of voting (Sobel, 1989; 1994). In the sense that *Palko* notes of fundamental rights as "those [immunities] found to be implicit in the concept of ordered liberty" (302 U.S. 324–25, 1937), working is fundamental for citizens (and others).

CITIZENSHIP EMPLOYMENT RIGHTS ARE FUNDAMENTAL

Among their privileges and immunities American citizens have is the inalienable right to take employment.[9] Since the nineteenth century the US Supreme Court has affirmed "occupation as a fundamental right of citizenship," and "the right to follow any of the ordinary callings of life" as "a distinguishing privilege of citizens of the United States."[10] This right may be exercised without government permission. No verification system may destroy that right.

The unassailable qualities of citizenship, and its closely held political and employment rights, explain why requirements to prove citizenship in order to exercise fundamental rights also in taking employment are detrimental and corrosive of Constitutional rights. Citizens have work rights of citizenship without government permission. The right is with the citizen. The burden of proof is on the government or accuser to demonstrate probable cause that someone is not a citizen. Citizens do not need to be "documented," because citizenship rights by their nature under the constitution are exercisable *per force* of citizenship and the presumptions of rights that go with it. For citizens and others doing nothing wrong, no identification demand for working is justified.

The joint nature of citizenship and employment as its concomitant means citizens need not prove citizenship to take a job. Because citizens have the right not to prove citizenship, they can simply seek work or at most attest to their citizenship. At this point, the burden of any question about citizenship falls on the state to prove the person claiming citizenship is not one.

Having to prove citizenship to exercise the right to work undermines a constitutional right. Authorities may not demand identification from people for exercising constitutional rights and doing nothing illegal.[11] Court decisions make clear that there needs to be at least reasonable suspicion or probable cause of criminal activity to require identification, even stating one's name.

Immigration and national security laws requiring proof of citizenship and government photo identification in order to work are doubly degrading to fundamental rights because they first deny citizenship and then they withhold the right by bureaucratic obstacles. Being forced to prove citizenship before working undermines both the immunities of citizenship and the rights to employment. As citizenship is conferred by American personhood and birth or naturalization, citizenship also empowers employment as a right in itself that does not require proof for citizens.[12]

THE CITIZEN RIGHT TO EMPLOYMENT UNDERMINED

The problem for citizen employment began with the Immigration Reform and Control Act of 1986 (IRCA) requiring citizens to produce government identification to get official permission to take employment. Employees not only had to swear to being citizens (or having government permission to work) on a governmental I-9 form (kept locally) but also had to provide government identification (Sobel, 1986). Like halting at a stop light, citizens cease to have the right if required first to provide identification and can only then proceed once the interfering identification demand is met. This prior restraint on exercising a basic occupational right of citizens constructively severs citizens from taking employment. These disenfranchising barriers instantly turn citizens into persons without rights.[13] As in *Elrod v. Burns*, in 1976, "The deprivation of a constitutional right, even for a brief period of time, amounts to an irreparable injury" (427).

The requirement for citizens to prove citizenship in order to work constructively removes citizenship, and it degrades its concomitant rights by presuming one is an illegal immigrant unless otherwise proven. Because requirements to prove citizenship take away *sine die* fundamental rights inhering in citizenship, and only return them when bureaucratic identification standards are met, these laws unconstitutionally undermine the power of citizenship.

The presence and assertion of citizenship authorize the right to employment unless the state meets the burden to question it. Because the privileges and immunities of citizenship include the "right to follow any of the common occupations of life [a]s an inalienable right" (*Butchers Union Co.*), citizens have the right to work. The key right deriving as a concomitant of the joint nature of citizenship and employment is that citizens may take a job without proving citizenship. Citizens have the right to be presumed citizens and not have to prove citizenship, and may simply seek work and take a job offered. At most, they may be asked to attest to their citizenship. At that point, the burden of any question about citizenship falls on the state to prove the person claiming citizenship is not a citizen. While there may be penalties for false claims of citizenship in order to obtain work, and noncitizens may be required to prove authorization to work, assertions of citizenship invoke work rights unless proven otherwise.

ELECTRONIC "VERIFICATION" AS DENATURALIZATION

In 1997, the federal government began to require electronic verification for governmental employees and contractors when the Illegal Immigration Reform and Immigration Responsibility Act expanded electronic verification under E-Verify. The problem was expanded by proposals to apply Electronic Employment Verification Systems (EEVS) or E-Verify universally to all employees. Under E-Verify, employees must prove their identity and citizenship in order to take a job. Currently, it is required for federal government jobs, and many state positions, and those under federal contractors. The E-Verify system in place in some state and federal government programs requires official identification in order to work. This process *de facto* denationalizes citizens by unconstitutionally infringing their privileges and immunities as US citizens to work. The electronic verification system (E-Verify) constitutes the high-tech separation of citizenship from work rights (Sobel 2013a, b).

Buried in "Comprehensive" Immigration "Reform" legislation are provisions that impose on Americans expansive national identification systems, tied to electronic verification schemes. Under the guise of "reform," these requirements trample fundamental rights and free-doms (Sobel, 2013a). The digital identification scheme in Comprehensive Immigration Reform eliminates that fundamental citi-zen right to take employment and transforms it into a privilege. This constitutional guarantee to work can in effect be taken away by bureau-cratic rules or deleted by a database mistake.

Particularly pernicious to citizenship are proposed systems for worker identification systems matched with technologically complex ID cards in the Senate Comprehensive Immigration Reform Bill (S744). It includes a mandatory, universal system of employment verification and mandates a centralized databank containing digital and biometric identification information for all potential employees. The Department of Homeland Security (DHS) would create and maintain a databank of digital information on every American citizen in the labor force in a form that could be shared internationally.

Any citizen wanting to take a job would face the regulation that his or her digitized high-resolution photo on a US passport or driver's license also be collected and stored centrally in a DHS Citizenship and Immigration Services databank. Each citizen would have to bring a high-tech identification card in the form of a driver's license or passport that would be matched by a "photo tool" to the photograph in the DHS databank. If they did not match electronically (even visual matches would not count), the citizen could not work (Calabrese, 2011; Stanley, 2013). A key problem with some immigration and national security laws is that they undermine the rights of citizens (Sobel, 2008). Requiring that a national worker identification include digital photographs, fingerprint, or DNA samples in a government databank at Homeland Security and on identification cards in order to be "official" ("documented") compounds the separation of citizen rights from their political and economic exercise.

The DHS database raises national security implications that working is a threat to the society, when in fact it is a public and personal good. Comprehensive Immigration Reform and E-Verify essentially equate all Americans with "undocumented" or "illegal immigrants."[14] Instead of naturalization freeing legal immigrants from carrying mandatory "green cards," universal E-Verify would impose national identification on American citizens, old and new. E-Verify effectively creates a "no-work" list for the "undocumented" and unverified, including citizens. This creates the prospect of "undocumented" and "unauthorized" citizens.

American citizens would have to have their digital photographs in the Department of Homeland Security databank or they could not work. By capturing passport photos and state driver's licenses pictures from state Motor Vehicle Agencies and passport photographs from the US Department of State, the DHS database copy would have to match the digital, facial recognition photograph on the original driver's license or passport, using a complex and costly facial recognition "photo tool."[15] These images and fingerprints would all have to be digitized for "interoperable" transmission to both national and international governmental and intelligence agencies.[16]

The determination of whether someone has a right to take a job would be made by two computer files: one in the Department of Homeland Security database and the other on a government-issued identification card. As often is embossed on simpler ID cards, identity and identification become "property of the U.S. government." Any citizen or immigrant whose digital image in the DHS databank did not match the one embedded in their government-issued identification would be without a job (and benefits).[17]

The beneficial aims in the immigration debate cannot obscure that "E-Verify" constitutes what Hoover Institution senior fellow John Cochrane calls "the monster lurking in proposed immigration reform" (Cochrane, 2013). As one immigration policy expert said in the *Wall Street Journal*, a biometric E-Verify system is "not only a gross violation of individual privacy, it's an enormously high-cost policy that will have an incredibly low to negligible benefit" (Yadron, 2013).

Like Comprehensive Immigration Reform, the standalone "Legal Work Force Act" would make E-Verify mandatory for all jobs and employees. Not only would citizens have to provide identification to work but their identity would have to be confirmed in a government databank. The requirements would expand those in the Illegal Immigration Reform and Immigration Responsibility Act of 1996 that further extended electronic verification.

A citizen has citizenship determined by his or her American person-hood at birth or naturalization. Instead, requirements under CIR for placement in a national databank of mandatory biometrics, including digital photographs, "captured" from people's images substitutes digital representations for personhood. This contradicts and undermines Locke's formulation that "every man has a Property in his own Person." Government provisions of identification schemes undermines Lockean "consent of the governed" animating the Declaration and constitutional government. Requiring personal data be obtained under identification schemes, stored centrally, encoded in worker identification cards, and in national databases of identifying information and digital facial images separates persons from personhood and citizenship. Suggesting that citizens would be "eligible" to get a national worker identity card like a "REAL ID" rather than simply be able to take work offered undercuts the foundation that citizenship means employment is a right in itself that does not require proof for citizens.

CITIZENSHIP CONTRADICTS NATIONAL WORKER IDS' ABRIDGING EMPLOYMENT RIGHTS

A half century of repetitious proposals to require a national "worker" ID reinforces the burdens to directly exercise citizen employment rights. They create the separation of citizen rights from their political and economic exercise. Requirements for mandatory worker IDs and electronic verification remove the right of citizens to take employment and only "give" it back as a privilege if proper proof is presented and the government so permits.

In *The Right of Mobility* in 1979, Gerald Houseman raised the concern that identification such as a proposed upgraded Social Security card would become a national passport acting as a worker ID and restricting the right to take employment. In the late 1970s, Houseman foresaw the Congress establishing "a system of 'forgery-proof' Social Security cards, complete with photographs and plastic lamination ... Houseman identified this Social Security card acting as a national passport, or internal passport, by acting as a work ID." "Any potential employer must then refuse to hire anyone who fails to produce this card" (42). Mobility as a right that makes many other rights tenable and possible – the rights of association, privacy, equality of opportunity, and employment – would be restricted by the national worker identification cards constituting an "internal passport."

Houseman argued that a national identification system confronts the American with "a totalitarian potential of invasion of privacy, harassment, and denial of mobility" (43). A national identification can easily become an internal passport as an instrument of "mobility control" and feature of totalitarian governments, what Houseman called the "hallmark of repressive regimes such as [Apartheid] South Africa, the Soviet Union, or Nazi Germany."[18] E-Verify and comprehensive Immigration Reform identification requirements fulfill the prediction of such a system of employment and social control.

Under Comprehensive Immigration Reform, uses of worker IDs will proliferate, as has utilization of Social Security Numbers – once, as noted on the cards, intended "not for identification purposes." Similarly, the REAL ID nationalized driver's license under the REAL ID Act of 2005[19] would transform driver's licenses – once simply proving driving skill in national and international identification documents. Worker IDs could become "travel licenses" for "official purposes," as defined by the Secretary of Homeland Security, such as entering government buildings or flying on a commercial airliner (still possible without ID) (Posner, 2014, 21; Sobel, 2014), and buying or selling items (Lerner, 2013). These systems and restrictions undermine the rights to petition government and to travel. Even though the Comprehensive Immigration Reform bill says it does not authorize a national ID, its provisions do. The failure to recognize the photo matching scheme in the Comprehensive bill constitutes a "Trojan horse" of a national identification system imposed on all Americans and obscures the pernicious nature of these provisions for the rights of citizenship here (Sobel, 2016).

ALTERNATIVES TO WORKER IDENTIFICATION REGIMES

Reform can address immigration without deforming the rights of citizens and those who aspire to join them.[20] Reforming immigration policy and targeting workplace enforcement can reduce the imperative for employee verification. Most simply, enforcement of Wage and Hours laws discourages the incentive to impose low wage jobs on unauthorized employees. Simpler and constitutional forms of reform are low-tech and local. Citizenship attestation programs permit citizens offered a job to take it directly.[21]

Under the longstanding provisions of Citizen Attestation Programs, "an employee who attests to U.S. Citizenship or nationality . . . does not have to present any documentation." In fact, "Employers verify employment eligibility only for all newly hired alien employees." Employees and employers need only fill out a simple form, and they need not participate in a bureaucratic nexus of high-tech identification image matching and verification.

Moreover, there are simpler and less invasive alternatives to E-Verify, such as citizen attestation of rights. In fact, before proposing computer matching of identification for everyone in DHS databases, the Congress considered a simple approach where others can "answer questions about previous addresses or other details" (Yadron, 2013). These can be implemented straightforwardly and inexpensively on forms kept at the workplace.

Protecting the constitutional right to employment of a diverse group of citizens helps everyone who wants to contribute to prosperity and become an American citizen by maintaining citizenship as the foundation for rights. Citizenship needs to remain the standard for both current Americans and those seeking to settle here.

Universal electronic verification as a "comprehensive" part of immigration reform or legal workforce enforcement is unconstitutional. E-Verify and REAL ID as a worker ID and a substitute for immigration reform and anti-terrorism policy imposes detrimental barriers to the exercise of fundamental rights. Mandating universal E-Verify and REAL ID to "do something" about immigration merely burdens citizens without addressing the problems of the need for workable immigration policy. The discussion over workplace and immigration reform needs to focus on the pernicious nature of E-Verify and REAL ID for American citizenship. As Houseman foresaw, worker IDs have traveled the path toward a national ID system.

CONCLUSION: THE CITIZEN RIGHT TO EMPLOYMENT IS FUNDAMENTAL

The fundamental right to take employment has protected citizens since the early Republic – from *Corfield v. Coryell* (1823) to *Butcher Union Co.* (1884) and *Truax* (1915) to *Roth* (1972) – by recognizing that taking employment is foundational for citizens. The right to earn parallels the right to vote. The citizen right to take employment may not be abridged by identification requirements.

The joint nature of citizenship and employment as its concomitant means that citizens can simply seek work and take a job offered. They need not prove citizenship to take a job, or at most may be asked to attest to their citizenship. The burden of any question about citizenship remains on the government. Having to prove citizenship to exercise the right to work is a pernicious undermining of a constitutional right to employment in *Corfield* through *Kolender*. Debate on workplace roles in immigration reform need to recognize citizenship rights to employment and how national identification systems like E-Verify tied to REAL ID undermine those rights. Immigration reform is essential, but must not deform citizenship.

The right to employment, like the right to vote, is a constitutional immunity that may be exercised without government permission or identification requirements. For foundational constitutional reasons, the fundamental right to employment may not be abridged. Like voter IDs, worker IDs can become travel IDs. Without the right to work, the right to travel is also abridged. The constitutional right to employment is also preservative of other rights as it provides the resources and occasions for citizens to travel broadly across the American union.

5 THE RIGHT TO TRAVEL

The right to travel is a far-reaching and essential privilege and immunity of citizenship in a broad federal union. It is guaranteed explicitly in Article IV of the Articles of Confederation and thus implicitly in Article IV of the United States Constitution and the Fourteenth Amendment. Since *Corfield v. Coryell* in 1823, courts have recognized that the right to travel makes America a more perfect union, political and commercial. The major thrust of the Constitution for American civic identity is to make Americans citizens of "a large, commercial, national republic" (R. Smith, 1997, 120). The Constitution sustains Americans as free in the pursuit of happiness. Flying in the face of the fundamental right of free movement across the republic are requirements to show identification like the REAL ID driver's licenses or US passports for domestic and interstate travel.

The right to travel pervades United States history, with roots back into English law. The Magna Carta held that "[a]ll merchants shall have safe and secure exit from England, and entry to England, with the right to tarry there and to move about as well by land as by water, for buying and selling by the ancient and right customs."[1] In *Commentaries on English Law*, Blackstone recognized that "the personal liberty of individuals" protected under the Magna Carta "consists in the power of locomotion, of changing situations, or removing one's person to whatsoever place one's own inclination may direct, without imprisonment or restraint."[2]

In 1770, Thomas Jefferson maintained that freedom of movement is a personal liberty by birth. "Under the law of nature, all men are born free, everyone comes into the world with a right to his own person, which includes the liberty of moving and using it at his own will. This is what is called a personal liberty" (Jefferson, 1892). The Articles of Confederation of 1777 stated the travel right fundamentally for the founding era and beyond.[3] The appearance in Article IV of the Articles of Confederation of a right to travel informed its implicit incorporation in the privileges and immunities clause of Article IV of the US Constitution in 1789. The right inheres in both the union and citizenship.

Article IV of the Articles stated, "The better to secure and perpetuate mutual friendship and intercourse among the people of the different States in this Union, the free inhabitants of each of these States … shall be entitled to all privileges and immunities of free citizens in the several States; and the people of each State shall have free ingress and regress to and from any other State, and shall enjoy therein all the privileges of trade and commerce." The Fifth and Fourteenth Amendments also provide a due process liberty interest in the right to travel.

THE RIGHT TO TRAVEL AS FOUNDATION FOR CITIZENS AND UNION

American political history and US Supreme Court jurisprudence crafted the right to travel as a fundamental one accruing naturally to every US citizen and to the nation. The Court has consistently recognized the right to travel as one of citizenship, preceding and contributing to the establishment of a federal constitution and union. Although the text of the Constitution no longer mentions the right to travel, Article I and Article IV as well as the First, Fifth, Ninth, Tenth, and Fourteenth Amendments protect the right. Here facilitation of imports and exports (Article I, Section 9) and the commerce clause coincide with the privileges and immunities of citizens of all states (Article IV and the Fourteenth Amendment). Due process liberty interest and equal protection (Fifth and Fourteenth Amendments) intersect with rights reserved to the people and states (Ninth and Tenth Amendments).[4] All these constitutional and statutory sources of rights provide a justifiable reliance on these rights existing as the default.

In short, multiple constitutional provisions underlie the right to travel and related rights.

While paralleling travel as a right of union, from the perspective of individual rights, the ability to move freely in the United States is a personal liberty, inherent by birth and US citizenship. The travel right is essential to guaranteeing equality of opportunities and *the pursuit* of happiness for citizens of the federal union. Freedom of personal movement is a natural liberty that citizens exercise among fundamental rights and privileges.[5] Black defined "[r]ight to travel" as a "basic constitutional right" (1991, 92) and he included among "fundamental rights" "the right to travel interstate."

The right to interstate travel encompasses rights and privileges to personal, political, and commercial movement. This interconnection between the rights of individuals and the character of the nation guarantees unrestricted geographical mobility to citizens in the American political and economic union. The right to interstate travel is based on the Founders' desire to structure a federal union under the Constitution to create a strong political union and a common market composed of sovereign states. By "plac[ing] the citizens of each State upon the same footing with citizens of other States,"[6] the privileges and immunities clause in Article IV of the US Constitution guarantees the freedom to move from state to state and set up residence anywhere in the country. By securing that liberty, citizens of one state are entitled to the same privileges and immunities as the citizens of any other state. Article IV of the Constitution "carried over into the comity article of the Constitution in briefer form but with no change in substance or intent, unless it was to strengthen the force of the clause in fashioning a single Nation" (*U.S. v. Wheeler*, 1920).[7]

An essential element manifested in the notion that the states belong to a more perfect union is the right to travel between the states on a basis of equality as a fundamental right (Kreimer, 1992). "The right to travel within the United States is guaranteed to all persons by the federal system of government."[8] The *Paul* Court recognized that without this constitutive dimension "the Republic would have constituted little more than a league of States; it would not have constituted the Union which now exists."[9] Therefore, the right to travel is fundamental and structural to a larger union because without it the founding vision of a transcontinental nation and federal union could not be attained. As Justice Brennan concurred in *Zobel v. Williams* (1982),[10] the origin of the travel right's "unmistakable essence [is] that document that transformed a loose confederation of States into one Nation."

As a commercial union, the United States is a common market that enjoys the right of free interstate movement of people and goods in order to guarantee economic prosperity of the political union. "The Founders had a desire to create one nation with regard to economic movement and change . . . The Founders established national control of commerce[11] to encourage through the commerce clause individuals who seek to move from state to state for economic reasons" (Kahn, 1994).[12] In short, the commercial and political interests and nature of the union intersect and mutually reinforce each other under travel rights.[13]

The original expansive conception of the right to travel encompassed all available modes of transportation, including the then newly developed technology of rail travel in the 1820s. The right to interstate travel has connected the parts of the nation since its founding. Travel is fundamental and structural to maintaining a strong political and economic union of sovereign states. As Ronald Kahn articulated, "[t]he [Supreme] Court views the concepts of the federal union and personal liberty rights in the Constitution as closely related. Their union requires that all citizens be free to travel, uninhibited by regulations that unreasonably burden their movement" (Kahn, 1994).[14]

Because Congress does not possess "general police power," its authority is restricted to what the Constitution expressly grants (Tribe, 1988, 5–2). The Ninth and Tenth Amendments reserve all other unenumerated rights to the states and the people to ensure that citizens may not be deprived of those rights not delegated to the federal and state governments without due process under the Fifth and Fourteenth Amendments. The right to travel as inherent in intercourse among the states is also one of the implied and unenumerated rights reserved to the people.

THE COURT DEVELOPS RIGHTS TO TRAVEL

Early courts explicated this broad conception of travel rights. As well in 1823 in *Corfield*,[15] the Supreme Court recognized the travel right in explaining the relationship between the "free ingress and regress" clause in Article IV of the Articles and the privileges and immunities clause in the Constitution.[16] The Court affirmed that the privileges and immunities of citizenship encompass "the right of a citizen of one state to pass through, or to reside in any other state, for purposes of trade, agriculture, professional pursuit, or otherwise."[17] The imperative of free interstate travel was "better to secure and perpetuate mutual friendship" of the states.[18]

Moreover, just a year later, in 1824, the Supreme Court established in *Gibbons v. Ogden* that commerce, as intercourse between the states, proceeds as a right by the creation and adoption of the US Constitution.[19] "[T]he public [has] an interest in the use of the road, and the owners of the . . .franchise are liable to respond in damages, if they refuse to transport an individual or his property upon such road, without any reasonable excuse, upon being paid the usual rate of fare."[20] Hence, the public interest in the use of road coincides with the right to free movement.

The 1831 Court ruling in *Beckman v. Saratoga & Schenectady Railroad*[21] established that whenever there is a compelling public interest in a technology available to the public, for instance, a new mode of transportation like railways, then all citizens are equally entitled to enjoy its benefits and to access it and its instrumentalities. This ruling established transportation service providers as "common carriers" in scheduled passenger transport of various kinds in an era of mainly horse and stagecoach travel.[22]

The 1849 *Passenger Cases* declared the right to travel may be exercised without interference. The Court established that state taxation of imports and exports unconstitutionally imposed constraints on commerce and interstate travel.[23] It ruled against New York and Massachusetts' imposing taxes on nonresident passengers arriving from ports out of state.[24] To ensure uniform treatment of citizens across the states, and to bind together the Union, the Constitution empowered Congress alone with the power to regulate commerce between the United States and among the states.[25]

The right to travel is "so rooted in the traditions and conscience of our people as to be ranked as fundamental."[26] The 1867 case of *Crandall v. Nevada*, for example, recognized the necessity for interstate travel in order to exercise other personal rights and liberties. A Nevada monetary charge at the boarded state constituted "a tax on the passenger for the privilege of passing through the State by the ordinary modes of transportation."[27] Even one state's imposing a tax on those leaving the state could weaken the federation of states. "If one State can [levy such a tax], so can every other State. And thus one or more States covering the only practicable routes of travel from the east to the west, or from the north to the south, may totally prevent or seriously burden all transportation of passengers from one part of the country to the other."[28]

The Court determined that Nevada's imposing per passenger tax on railroad or stagecoach companies for passengers transported out of the state unconstitutionally limited citizens' right to interstate travel. The tax levied by Nevada on passengers for the privilege of passing through the state unconstitutionally burdened the travel right:[29] "We are all citizens of the United States, and as members of the same community must have the right to pass and repass through every part of it without interruption, as freely as in our own States."[30] The tax hindered citizens' exercising other fundamental rights, such as approaching the government for redress of grievances and accessing ports where commerce was conducted.[31]

In 1869, in *Paul v. Virginia*, the Court stated, "It was undoubtedly the object of the [privileges and immunities] clause in question to place the citizens of each State upon the same footing with citizens of other States, so far as the advantages resulting from citizenship in those States are concerned." The Court extended that the clause gives citizens "the right of free ingress into other States, and egress from them; it insures to them in other States the same freedom possessed by the citizens of those States in the acquisition and enjoyment of property and in the pursuit of happiness; and it secures to them in other States the equal protection of their laws."[32]

In 1871, *Ward v. Maryland,*[33] also upheld the right to travel, particularly for pursuing work. *Ward* held that the privileges and immunities clause of the Constitution protects the right of a citizen of one state to travel into another state in order to engage in commerce, trade, or business.

As in *Corfield, The Slaughter House Cases*[34] in 1873 affirmed the right to travel, determining that "the privileges and immunities intended [in Article IV of the US Constitution and Article IV of the Articles of Confederation] are the same in each."[35] By asserting such a close link, the Court confirmed the right to interstate travel is protected, as in the Articles of Confederation, by the Constitution's commerce clause in Article II and as a privilege and immunity of citizens under Article IV.[36]

In *Williams v. Fears*, the Supreme Court in 1900 declared, "Undoubtedly the right of locomotion, the right to remove from one place to another according to inclination, is an attribute of personal liberty, and the right, ordinarily of free transit from or through the territory of any State is a right secured by the 14th amendment and by other provisions of the Constitution."[37]

In *In re Quarles and Butler, and in re McEntire and Goble* in 1895, the Court held that the right to interstate travel was implicit in the "creation and establishment by the Constitution itself of a national government" (1895).

Similarly, *U.S. v. Wheeler* in 1920 outlined the elements of the right to travel. It reinforced the privilege and immunity of travel by holding that the "people of each State should have free ingress and regress to and from any other State."

In *Buck v. Kuykendall* in 1924,[38] Justice Brandeis noted that "the right to travel interstate by auto vehicle upon the public highways may be a privilege or immunity of citizens of the United States. A citizen may have, under the Fourteenth Amendment, the right to travel and transport his property upon them by auto vehicle" (267 U.S. 307 (1925)).

Complementing Fifth Amendment due process guarantees,[39] the Court established in *Edwards v. California*[40] in 1941 that the Fourteenth Amendment extends due process liberty protections to all citizens of the United States in their rights to assist others in traveling from one state into another. Here it struck down a California law prohibiting the bringing of indigents into California during the Depression. It thereby protects citizens from infringement on travel rights by states and the federal government.

As the Supreme Court affirmed in 1958 in *Kent v. Dulles*, citizens have a liberty interest in the right to travel: "[t]he right to travel is a part of the 'liberty' of which the citizen cannot be deprived without due process of law under the Fifth Amendment . . . In Anglo-Saxon law that right was emerging at least as early as the Magna Carta . . . Freedom of movement across frontiers in either direction, and inside frontiers as well, was a part of our heritage . . . travel within the country may be necessary for a livelihood."[41] "Freedom to travel is, indeed, an important aspect of the citizen's liberty . . . When activities . . . such as travel, are involved, we will construe narrowly all delegated powers that curtail or dilute them."[42]

As the Supreme Court noted in *Aptheker v. Secretary of State* in 1964, "freedom of travel is a constitutional liberty closely related to rights of speech and association." This ties together the sources of free speech and travel rights. The *Aptheker* Court, in declaring a section unconstitutional, reaffirmed that "a governmental purpose to control or prevent activities constitutionally subject to state regulation may not be achieved by means which sweep unnecessarily broadly and thereby invade the area of protected freedoms."[43] In 1965, *Zemel v. Rusk* reiterated from Kent (1958) that "the right to travel is part of the 'liberty' of which the citizen cannot be deprived."[44]

In 1966, in *United States v. Guest*, the Court rearticulated that the Constitution did not explicitly mention the right to travel because "a right so elementary was conceived from the beginning to be a necessary concomitant of the stronger Union the Constitution created . . . . The constitutional right to travel from one State to another . . . occupies a position so fundamental to the concept of our Federal Union. It is a right that has been firmly established and repeatedly recognized."[45] Indeed, *Guest* affirmed, "The constitutional right of interstate travel is virtually unqualified."[46] Today the travel right in its almost unqualified strength remains crucial to the formation and ongoing prosperity of the political union and common market.

The importance of such connectivity and liberty appears in *Shapiro v. Thompson* in 1969:[47] "This Court long ago recognized that the nature of our Federal Union and our constitutional concepts of personal liberty unite to require that all citizens be free to travel throughout the length and breadth of our land uninhibited by statutes, rules, or regulations which unreasonably burden or restrict this movement."[48] The decision highlighted that "[t]his constitutional right . . . is not a mere conditional liberty subject to regulation and control under conventional due process or equal protection standards."

Shapiro reaffirmed the right to travel as "a right broadly assertable against private interference as well as governmental action."[49] The right to travel is a "fundamental right" and personal liberty, which the government may not abridge. The protections against both public and private action empower the right and those availing themselves of its protection.

Quoting *Guest* in *Dunn v. Blumstein* in 1972, the Supreme Court ruled that "Freedom to travel throughout the U.S. has long been recognized as a basic right under the Constitution." The *Dunn* court held, "Since the right to travel was a constitutionally protected right, any classification which serves to penalize the exercise of the right . . . . is unconstitutional."[50]

In 1981, in *Jones v. Helms* (452 U.S. 412), the Court reiterated foundations of travel rights. In 1982, *Zobel v. Williams* held that the "article IV privileges and immunities clause has employed a long outreach of the right to travel and movement."[51] It holds that "[t]he right to travel ... and to move from one state to another has long been accepted" (*Zobel,* 9). Quoting *Shapiro v. Thompson* (1969),[52] it reiterated that "[t]he [constitutional] right to travel from one state to another ... occupies a position fundamental to the concept of our Federal Union. It is a right that has been firmly established and repeatedly recognized."

In 1999, the Court affirmed the fundamental constitutional right to travel in *Saenz v. Roe.* The components most relevant to interstate travel is: "citizens have the right to enter and leave another State."[53] The decision held unconstitutional a state welfare statute that discriminated against new residents. The ruling agreed with *Shapiro* in that "a classification that has the effect of imposing a penalty on the right to travel violates the Equal Protection Clause 'absent a compelling governmental interest.'"[54] While *Saenz* focused on state-to-state travel, the holding was not specific to states alone. Thus, the case features a travel right that extends across the states and the nation.

In 2015, in *Kerry v. Din,* Justice Scalia, referencing Blackstone, held that "personal liberty of individuals" protected under the Magna Carta "consists in the power of locomotion, of changing situation, or removing one's person to whatsoever place one's own inclinations may direct, without imprisonment or constraint."[55] Hence, the right to travel has a long running basis in American tradition and constitutional law.

THE RIGHT TO TRAVEL IN COMMERCE

As travel is also an instrumentality of commerce, Congress may regulate it in order to encourage commercial activities and intercourse. *Kent* established that the interstate commerce clause[56] protected interstate travel and its instrumentalities against governmental infringement.[57] *Guest* affirmed that "[t]he constitutional right to travel from one State to another, and necessarily to use the highways and other instrumentalities of interstate commerce in doing so, occupies a position fundamental to the concept of our Federal Union. It is a right that has been firmly established and repeatedly recognized."[58] The right to interstate commerce encompasses both the freedom of movement and the instrumentalities of transportation needed to do so.

Congress may not pass legislation that unreasonably burdens the right to travel, nor may the executive or its agencies create executive orders or agency rules that violate travel rights. The right may be exercised without governmental impediments. "One has the right, as against any prohibitory or other restrictive legislation, whether by Congress,[59] or by the States, to engage in the interstate or foreign commerce, that is, to transport persons or articles from State to State, or to or from a foreign country" (Cooke, 1910). Thus, Congress and administrative agencies may not infringe citizens' travel rights.

The travel right ensures the vitality of the government through the free movement of citizens in purposive travel. Specifically, the right preserves and facilitates citizens' ability to journey to their representative seats of government, both statewide and nationally, in order to petition under the First Amendment to have their grievances redressed. Foreclosing such a right would have offended the Founders in their suspicion of governmental overreaching into citizens' rights. The Founders therefore laid down protections for political speech and association inherent in the travel right. Even in the era of few travel modes besides walking, horse, and buggy, the Founders conceived of the travel right as broadly expansive and plenary.

Consequently, domestic requirements for passports, identification, or permit to citizen travel in the United States hamper exercising the right to interstate travel. They also invert the proper relationship between citizens and government (Sobel and Fennel, 2007). Government derives its "license" to operate from the people: when the government instead requires the people to obtain a license to travel, it abrogates foundational rights. Justice Brandeis concluded that the Fourteenth Amendment protects the right to travel: "the 14th amendment due process clause ... had to be applied ... to protect ... fundamental rights – speech, education, choice of profession, and the right to travel – none of which should be restricted except on showing of clear-and-present danger" (Urofsky, 2009, 619).[60] Justice Ruth Ginsburg stated in a public forum: "[t]here is a right to travel. We have had a common market in that respect from the very beginning. You can go from one state to another without any passport."[61]

While skeptical of using the Due Process Clause to strike down other substantive (vs. procedural) laws, Justice Brandeis held that "if his more conservative brethren intended to use the clause to protect property rights, then they ought to be willing to use it to protect other rights as well," including such "basic rights as travel" (Urofsky, 2009, 561–562). In short, Brandeis "would have preferred... the Fourteenth Amendment's Due Process Clause... to be applied and to protect what he considered fundamental rights, including the right to travel – none of which should be restricted except on a showing of clear-and-present danger" (Urofsky, 2009, 619). In the Brandeis–Frankfurther Conversations,[62] Brandeis noted on July 19, 1923, that if due process were to "be applied to substantive laws" for "things that are fundamental," these should include the "right to locomotion" (as well as choice of profession) (Urofksy, 1985, 320). By the right to locomotion he meant the right to travel.[63]

As noted in *Lawson v. Kolender* in 1981, "[t]he right of an individual wanderer to be free from the governmental intrusion of being required to furnish identification, however, is also substantial. The Supreme Court has extolled the freedom of locomotion."[64] Persons "wandering or strolling" from place to place have been extolled by poets from Walt Whitman to Vachel Lindsay. The qualification in laws about movement "without any lawful purpose or object" may be a trap for innocent acts.[65]

> These activities are historically part of the amenities of life ... though "not mentioned in the Constitution or in the Bill of Rights. These unwritten amenities have been in part responsible for giving our people the feeling of independence and self-confidence ... These amenities have dignified the right of dissent and encouraged ... high spirits rather than hushed, suffocating silence."[66]

As an example, Brandeis noted in *Buck v. Kuykendall* in 1925 that "the right to travel interstate by auto vehicle upon the public highways may be a privilege or immunity of citizens of the United States." He further explained that "[a] citizen may have, under the Fourteenth Amendment, the right to travel and transport his property upon them by auto vehicle."[67] While this and other early twentieth-century cases focused on the right to travel by what was then a relatively new technological innovation, the automobile, without licensing, it would apply equally well to more technologically sophisticated means of travel such as trains or planes under the *Beckman* doctrine of contemporary modes of transport.

The importance of *Kolender v. Lawson* lies in its underscoring freedom of movement that a person may walk wherever s/he pleases in lawful activities. The decisions like *Kolender* and *Hiibel* against imposing identification requirements typically involve aspects of the right to travel from walking to flying.

In short, because the right to travel preceded, yet is applicable to all modes, including modern means of transportation like trains and airplanes, it encompasses inherent liberty as an aspect of citizenship, personhood, and union. Just as the travel right was not originally linked to any particular instrumentalities for exercise of personal liberty, accordingly, the right to travel is not now tied to any specific mode of transportation. Consequently, it must encompass all means of travel, including rail and air.

THE MODERN EMBODIMENT OF THE RIGHT TO TRAVEL

As fundamental rights expand to encompass new technologies, constitutional case law evolves by retaining and applying the essence of the basic protections and principles to new situations (Breyer, 2005).

When the right to travel appeared in the Articles of Confederation, it preceded the formulation of the related rights to mobility and privacy or modern modes of transportation. Yet, the expansive nature of the travel right also drives the construction of privacy provisions. The evolution of privacy and other rights parallels the protections inherent in the right to travel and mobility. That evolution may not fundamentally alter the original rights.

INTERSECTION OF THE RIGHT TO TRAVEL AND THE RIGHT TO PRIVACY

In a parallel path to the travel right, the right to privacy has evolved from a focus on the protection of an individual's physical property[68] and personal body to encompass a broader swath of privacy safeguards, reliances, and expectations pertaining to an individual as a constitutionally protected person in both private and public.[69] The protections to privacy rights against intrusive searches and identification demands reside in the Fourth Amendment safeguards against unreasonable searches and seizures without probable cause.[70] These protections intersect with travel rights, particularly for citizens.

The *Kent* Court recognized that the application of these principles required it to consider the congressional purpose underlying the restrictions on the right to travel. Observing that the government has been allowed in times of war to exclude citizens from their homes and restrict their freedom of movement only upon a showing of "the gravest imminent danger to the public safety," the *Kent* Court reaffirmed that the fundamental right to privacy protects individuals' choices to conduct their personal lives free from governmental interference.[71] The right to privacy protects individuals engaging in private acts from government interference.[72] The "emanations" of several constitutional rights protect a range of privacy interests, personal privacy and autonomy.[73]

These constitutional rights also protect the right to privacy in travel (Sobel, 2014). The right to travel entails the right to privacy in its fundamental elements of individual choice regarding when, where, and how to move.[74] The intersection of the right to travel and the right to privacy as fundamental liberties allows individuals to engage in private and anonymous travel. Indeed, anonymous travel represents the concurrent exercise of these overlapping personal liberties.

The right to travel in anonymity, without having to identify oneself or carry identification documents, was articulated in *Kolender v. Lawson*.[75] There, Edward Kolender, an African American, frequently walked (traveled by foot) in white California neighborhoods where police repeatedly stopped him, asked for identification, and at times arrested him, even though he was pursuing legal activity.[76] In *Kolender*, the Court struck down as unconstitutional the California statute that required "persons who loiter or wander on the streets to provide a 'credible and reliable' identification and to account for their presence when requested by a peace officer."[77]

The Ninth Circuit held that the requirement to identify oneself "impermissibly intrudes upon the fourth amendment's proscription against unreasonable searches and seizures."[78] The circuit "agree[d] with the courts and commentators who have concluded that statutes . . . which require the production of identification, are in violation of the fourth amendment. The two reasons for this conclusion are that as a result of the demand for identification, the statutes bootstrap the authority to arrest on less than probable cause, and the serious intrusion on personal security outweighs the mere possibility that identification may provide a link leading to arrest."[79]

As *Kolender* classically noted, "The right of an individual wanderer to be free from the governmental intrusion of being required to furnish identification, however, is also substantial. The Supreme Court has extolled the freedom of locomotion."[80] This is the basis of the right to travel freely.

The Supreme Court invalidated the identification statute on the basis that it was "constitutionally vague within the meaning of the Due Process Clause of the Fourteenth Amendment by failing to clarify what is contemplated by the requirement that a suspect provide a 'credible and reliable' identification."[81]

In *Hiibel v. Nevada*, the Supreme Court reaffirmed that unless there is reasonable suspicion of a crime and a state law requiring identification under that circumstance, police may not require individuals to provide identification.[82] Like previous cases, where, for instance,

Kolender had simply been walking, Hiibel was a pedestrian at roadside when confronted by the officer, though first pursued under reasonable suspicion based on an informant's report that an alleged assault had been observed in a motor vehicle.[83] The Nevada statute, the Supreme Court ruled 5–4, only required *Hiibel* to disclose his name, but not to produce an identification document.[84]

As Machlin (1990, 1259) noted, "We have long enjoyed the liberty to walk the streets and move about the country free from arbitrary government intrusion. Freedom of travel, whether locally or between states, without having to either account for our presence or carry official papers, is one of the 'cherished liberties that distinguish this nation from so many others'" (Gomez, 1982, 143).[85] As Arizona Justice Feldman concurred, "The thought that an American can be compelled to 'show his papers' before exercising his right to walk the streets, drive the highways or board the trains is repugnant to American institutions and ideals." "A right to locomotion – the right to be left alone in public – is meaningless if police officials are free to board buses or trains and ask to see the identification of or search the luggage of, every passenger" (Machlin, 1990, 1335).

Thus, an individual moving around has the right to be private and anonymous in his or her affairs, free from government intrusion. Hence, the demand for identification, without probable cause that the individual is engaging in an illegal activity, interferes not only with privacy but also with travel rights. In short, the travel right not only entails the right to privacy but also encompasses freedom to travel anonymously and free from governmental infringement (Houseman, 1979, 43).

THE FAILINGS OF THE "SINGLE MODE DOCTRINE"

Historically, the fundamental right to travel in the United States is broad and encompasses all modes of transportation. As *Beckman v. Saratoga & Schenectady Railroad* underscores, the right applies to new modes of transportation. In contradiction, however, with the nature of this expansive travel right in a large union, some circuit courts have maintained that limitations on one mode of transportation do not implicate the right to travel. A modern construction that inaptly degrades the travel right, however, is the so-called "single mode doctrine," which maintains that if someone can travel by any mode of transportation, his right to travel is not abridged.[86]

In *Monarch Travel Services v. Associated Cultural Clubs* in 1972,[87] the Ninth Circuit ruled that the inability of a person to pay the fare of a common carrier in the form of charter flight fees was not an unconstitutional limitation of the person's travel rights, since there was no state action in government interference.[88] In 1999, in *Miller v. Reed,* the same circuit used the *Monarch* argument to construct what is now known as "the single mode doctrine."[89] The court asserted that "burdens on a single mode of transportation do not implicate the right to interstate travel."[90] Under the construction, for his refusal to provide a Social Security Number to get a driver's license, Miller was deprived of his "privilege" to operate a motor vehicle, but not the right to ride as a passenger or to travel by other means.[91] When the circuit court proffered its opinion, however, it created an unconstitutional limitation on the fundamental interstate travel right. The circuit's holding conflicted with the Supreme Court's emphasis in *Guest* that the right to travel is "virtually unqualified" and in *Shapiro* that the right to travel should be free of regulations that unreasonably burden or restrict it.[92]

If, instead, the single mode of air travel is blocked, citizens lose entirely their right to interstate travel. Especially in the noncontiguous United States, when a single mode like a plane becomes the sole mode of travel, a citizen's constitutional protections for travel are broadest. To be plenary and efficacious, the right to travel must include protections for using all possible modes of travel.

Indeed, the "single mode doctrine" is also inappropriate for travel within the contiguous United States because of limitations in national air transportation. The federal government has invested broadly in its responsibility for creating and maintaining the requisite air network. As Congress recognized through codification, there is a compelling public interest in maintaining a national air transportation network available to all citizens.[93] Therefore, as in *Beckman v. Saratoga,* the mandate that railroad common carrier services be available to all citizens analogously requires that US air transportation network and air common carrier services be available to all American citizens domestically, regardless of location.[94] The "single mode doctrine" also contravenes this congressional intent.

Air transportation is not only the most convenient method of even moderately distant interstate travel, but in many cases, it is the only feasible mode of interstate and in some cases of intrastate travel.[95] The Eighth Circuit held in *United States v. Kroll* that "flying may be the only practical means of transportation"; often when limited it deprives an individual of the right to travel.[96] Even if other modes of travel exist, the Second Circuit held in *United States v. Albarado*, it is not acceptable to force travelers to forego using air travel because "it would work a considerable hardship on many air travelers to be forced to utilize an alternate form of transportation, assuming one exists at all."[97]

A latter decision in *Mohamed v. Holder* (2014) reinforces that drastic nature of flight restrictions.

> The impact on a citizen who cannot use a commercial aircraft is profound. He is restricted in his practical ability to travel substantial distances within a short period of time, and the inability to fly to a significant extent defines the geographical area in which he may live his life.[98] An inability to travel by air also restricts one's ability to associate more generally, and effectively limits educational, employment and professional opportunities.[99]

In sum, contrary to the Ninth Circuit rulings in *Miller and Gilmore*, burdens on a single mode of transportation do implicate the right to interstate travel. This is clearest when there is only one mode of common carrier travel, such as flying by commercial airline, available between the two non-continental US locations, for instance, between the mainland and Hawaii. It is also an unconstitutional burden when there is only one practicable mode of travel for long distances. For example, the only way for John Gilmore to get to Washington, DC, from California to petition the federal government in a timely manner was to travel by air.[100]

For non-continental US travel, the only other hypothetical way to reach offshore locations is by ship, but commercial ship service by US carriers rarely exists as a realistic possibility.[101] Here, the "single mode doctrine" also proves deficient because of the burdens it imposes on individuals whose only alternative is not to travel by air.[102]

Passenger travel by airline constitutes the only mode for covering large distances in a timely manner within the continental United States. Citizens have responsibilities, and time is valuable. Jobs do not allow people to spend a great amount of time traveling.[103] Exercising constitutional rights requires timely access to travel great distances for citizens to petition the national government and exercise political liberties. An individual needing to reach the seat of the federal government in Washington, DC, or of the state government in Juneau to petition the government for redress of grievances, as guaranteed by the First Amendment, may require air traveling as the only available mode to reach the government in a timely manner (Sobel and Torres, 2013; Sobel, 2014).

Traveling long distances within the contiguous United States relies on only one mode of travel: commercial airlines. Therefore, restricting this single mode of travel, by air, abridges the right to travel and the right to exercise political and personal liberties. The single mode construction thus contravenes the right to travel within the US territory.[104]

By threatening to prevent the use of what is often the only viable method of transportation, airline travel, and by imposing chilling effects on citizens' right to seek redress from government, the "single mode doctrine" abridges the right to interstate travel and freedoms of expression and assembly. In doing so, it undermines the right to travel that is broadly empowered. The "single mode doctrine" fails historically and constitutionally. If any single mode is limited, the right to travel is abridged. Instead, the travel right is multi-modal and encompasses all forms of travel. In short, the unique nature of air travel is a necessarily accessible and protected mode of transportation under the constitutional travel right and federal law.

ABRIDGING THE RIGHT TO TRAVEL IN IDENTIFICATION REQUIREMENTS

The requirement to provide identification in order to fly on domestic airlines inhibits the right to travel, with ramifications for privacy.[105]

Prior to 1995, travel at most involved security procedures such as passing through metal detectors and screening of baggage. Requirements to provide identification in order to board an airline did not exist and have only been in place since 1996. They began after the TWA 800 crash in 1995 (shown to be an electrical malfunction). Initially, travelers without IDs could fly as "selectees" after undergoing a more intensive search such as a physical pat down. Since 1996, air passengers have faced the requirement to provide official identification in order to board aircraft, with the option of a search if they did not provide identification.

Between 1996 and 2008, a passenger without identification could fly by becoming "selectee" and undergoing a pat-down search. Thus, a "selectee" could fly without ID. Since 2008, there has been stronger identification requirement and more intensive search for those without identification (Holstege, 2005). Rules since then required that passengers have to identify themselves,[106] though it could be done without formal identification documents.

Since 2008, passengers must identify themselves, either from identification documents, matching informal IDs, or checking commercial databases. If the identification uses unofficial documents, the traveler is typically also searched. "Beginning Saturday, June 21, 2008 passengers that willfully refuse to provide identification at security checkpoint will be denied access to the secure area of airports. This change will apply *exclusively to individuals that simply refuse to provide any identification* or assist transportation security officers in ascertaining their identity."[107]

"NO-FLY" LISTS ABRIDGE TRAVEL RIGHTS

For many years, the government has accumulated a series of watch lists largely for those suspected of terrorist activities. A subset of the list involves the "Selectee" and "No-Fly List." The former requires heightened scrutiny at airports, while the latter prevents travel. The lists have been increasingly closely tied to airport profiling and pre-flight risk evaluations.

COMPUTER PROFILING, CAPPS, AND "SECURE FLIGHT"

Especially in the surveillance era after 9/11, federal impediments to domestic travel, particularly by air, have undermined and abridged the rights of millions of passengers. The major limitations on travel rights consist in developing identification and profiling requirements, as well as intrusive physical screening. These limitations involve official air identification requirements in order to fly, watch lists, "no-fly" designations, and passenger pre-screening schemes in order to get a reservation and board a flight. These essentially create an internal passport requirement to fly in the United States, abridging the right to move freely around the country.[108] As with universal E-Verify and worker ID requirements, profiling and air identification requirement also interfere with the exercise of citizens' rights to travel.

Since 1998, air travelers have also been increasingly subject to profiling under Computer Assisted Passenger Screening (CAPPS) based on information on flyer's travel patterns and outside information. That information has been the basis for pre-clearance for permissions to fly or not, and be issued a boarding pass. While these determinations had relied on information about travel patterns and behavior at the airports, the designations have increasingly become tied to matching of placement on government watch lists, such as the "No-Fly" and "Selectee" lists.

The original Computer-Assisted Passenger Prescreening System, CAPPS (I) in 1998, "was the first government-mandated airline passenger profiling system. It was developed by the Federal Aviation Administration (FAA) in the Department of Transportation, which was a regulatory agency that worked with the airline industry. "Beginning in 1998, the FAA required airlines to apply an undisclosed" CAPPS profiling algorithm to all passengers boarding flights in the United States, to decide which passengers to subject to more intrusive searches ('secondary screening')" (Papers, Please, 2015, 1).[109]

"CAPPS profiling was carried out by airlines, based on information contained in reservations ('Passenger Name Records' or PNRs) and/or on tickets. The simple original CAPPS profiling algorithm used data elements and criteria, so travelers were most likely to be subjected to secondary screening if they were traveling on one-way tickets purchased for cash at the last minute" (Papers Please, 2015, 2). The output of CAPPS profiling was a score designating normal screening or pat-down search.

During that period, airlines and their contractors carried out the "screening" of passengers, and baggage information from CAPPS profiling results were not routinely transferred to the government. When the Transportation Security Administration (TSA) was started after 9/11, one of its projects was developing an airline passenger profiling system, called "CAPPS II" (Papers Please, 2015, 2), without involvement of those with pre-9/11 aviation security experience.

"When TSA presented its CAPPS II plan to the airline industry in 2003, airlines did not routinely record passenger addresses, birth dates, phone numbers, and sometimes held group reservations, without even knowing passengers' names until they checked in" (Papers Please, 2015, 2).

At the point "civil libertarians, privacy advocates, and members of the traveling public complained about the proposed use of secret profiling and transfer of passenger data to the government as violation of travel and privacy rights." Responding to the objections, the TSA renamed CAPPS II "Secure Flight" and said CAPPS II had been "canceled" while still developing "essentially the same system" under the Secure Flight name (Papers Please, 2015, 2) (essentially CAPPS III). TSA postponed "Secure Flight" implementation until the information and reservation systems could collect and share the profiling data.

When Secure Flight began again, DHS required airlines to provide the TSA with more limited "Secure Flight Passenger Data" (SFPD) and other itinerary information for passengers on a domestic, rather than international, flight (Papers Please, 2015, 3). These and other government and commercial data are used for the profiling by TSA as part of "Secure Flight."

Under "Secure Flight," TSA took over "watchlist matching" from the airlines. "Because some of the data for CAPPS such as the form of payment for tickets, are not included in the Secure Flight, its profiling of domestic air travelers is not based on these factors." (Papers Please,

2015, 3). Since January 2009, Secure Flight has changed from identifying "high-risk" passengers by matching against the "No-Fly" or
"Selectee" list to assessing passengers' "risk" based on other data.
"Specifically, Secure Flight now identifies passengers as high risk" if
they match a list of "known or suspected terrorists" or "high-risk
criteria." Low-risk travelers can get expedited screening through
"TSA Pre-Check," a 2011 initiative that preapproves passengers for
faster screening. Yet "TSA lacks measures of whether 'Secure Flight'
profiling is effective in preventing terrorism and lacks oversight of
privacy protections" (Papers Please, 2014).

Since 2010, too, government rules for "Secure Flight" require that
passengers reveal birthdate and declare gender in order to get an airline
reservation and boarding pass within seventy-two hours of a flight.
Prior to the application of profiling under Secure Flight, there needs
to be an objective standard for applying potentially travel-denying
characterizations to the behavior of individuals involved in the legal
activities of air travel (EPIC, 2013b). Now the information on name,
gender, and birthdate is used to match (or in the vast majority of cases,
discover non-matches) to the No-Fly and Selectee lists.[110]

"By November 2010, TSA assumed the watch list matching function from aircraft operators and air carriers in Secure Flight. Since that
time, CAPPS has not been used to determine whether additional
screening is warranted for certain passengers" (Federal
Register, 2015; in Papers Please, 2015, 3). "This suggests TSA rea-
lized the use of cash to buy airline tickets, or the other CAPPS factors
not included in the [Secure Flight] dataset were not useful to indicate
intent to commit air terrorism" (Papers Please, 2015, 3).

> From May 2012 through July 2013, "TSA denied 1,384 individuals
> access to the sterile areas [of airports] as a result of identity checking
> procedures. These denials include travelers who did not appear to
> match the photo on their identification, who presented identifica-
> tion that appeared fraudulent or showed sign of tampering, and
> who were unwilling or unable to provide identifying information.
> (Government Accountability Office, 2014, 27)

Under provisions of Federal law for the CAPPS II passenger profiling program discontinued five years ago, and "applying the name of

that program and legal mandate to an entirely new scheme," TSA is adding passenger scrutiny to its profiling system for domestic flights (Papers Please, 2015, 1).

TSA-implemented new CAPPS was disclosed in a January 2015 posting on the DHS website and a Federal Register notice. "According to the documents, the new CAPPS scheme has been under development since 2013, in secret collaboration between the TSA, the National Counterterrorism Center (NCTC), airlines, and private contractors" (Papers Please, 2015, 1).

Nevertheless, according to the January 2015 notice, "TSA plans to incorporate a CAPPS assessment generated by aircraft operators into its Secure Flight risk-based analysis of passenger and other prescreening data ... [R]ecords containing assessments generated by aircraft operators under the Computer-Assisted Passenger Prescreening System (CAPPS)" will be passed on to the TSA along with the [Secure Flight] "dataset for each passenger on a domestic U.S. flight, and may be retained by the TSA in its Secure Flight records system" (TSA, January 2015).

If CAPPS was abandoned by the TSA since 2010, why was it revived in 2015? "In March 2014, the Homeland Security Studies Institute endorsed TSA's approach for conducting Secure Flight risk-based analysis and recommended TSA continue to strengthen the analysis by including CAPPS assessments. TSA reviewed its plans and refined the security value assigned to CAPPS data elements based on input from various offices" (TSA, 2015). "This effort resulted in refining CAPPS data elements," which appears to encompass new data to the basis for CAPPS profiling (TSA, 2015).

Rather than reinstating profiling based on the original CAPPS data elements like cash payment for tickets, "TSA wants to carry out more complex and intrusive profiling of domestic air travelers, using elements of PNR data not in the Secure Flight dataset. Imposing such a scheme requires legislation or regulations mandating that airlines either (a) provide additional data for domestic air travelers to the TSA or (b) carry out this profiling themselves." (Papers Please, 2015, 4)

And rather than ask Congress to pass new laws, TSA used a previous statutory mandate for airlines to use "CAPPS." Apparently, TSA interprets the law that if the TSA calls the new profiling scheme "CAPPS," airlines have to implement it. "This resembles TSA's claim that because air travelers are required to submit to 'screening,'" they are required to submit to whatever TSA decides constitutes "'screening'" (Papers Please, 2015, 4).

Under the system, the airline for domestic flights will profile and score each passenger. That score is passed on to TSA with the Secure Flight data. "Both the CAPPS score(s) and the Secure Flight data elements would be inputs to the TSA's second-stage profiling and scoring process, 'Secure Flight'" (Papers Please, 2015, 5). No longer using CAPPS II, Secure Flight is "CAPPS III" and this new scheme is "CAPPS IV."

TSA claims CAPPS IV is a "refinement" of the CAPPS system The addition of this new airline-operated layer to the TSA's passenger profiling scheme creates the possibility of misuse of data in Passenger Name Record and interference with the rights of travelers.

TSA, CAPPS, REAL ID AND PROFILING

According to the TSA, "Adult passengers 18 and over must show valid identification at the airport checkpoint in order to travel."[111] "Starting January 22, 2018, travelers who do not have a [REAL-ID] license from a compliant state or a state that has been granted an extension will be asked to provide alternate acceptable identification. If you cannot provide an acceptable form of identification, you will not be permitted through the security checkpoint. Starting October 1, 2020, every traveler will need to present a REAL ID-compliant license or another acceptable form of identification for domestic air travel."[112] In short, according to the TSA, if American citizens do not have "an acceptable form of identification" by 2018, and if citizens do not have a REAL ID by 2020, they cannot travel by air. CAPPS profiling in conjunction with REAL ID license requirements parallel the requirements for E-Verification and national identification system documents for employment.

Similar identification requirements to purchase Amtrak train tickets or to board interstate buses to travel domestically are equally detrimental and burdensome to the right to travel.[113] The ability to travel domestically without a passport is the hallmark of an open society. The proliferation of identification and background checking requirements to move around the country (and pursue employment) adds to the demeaning of citizenship and its inherent rights. The identification and profiling schemes set the foundation for an internal passport system to restrict movement and employment of citizens.[114] This development in profiling and identification requirements toward an internal passport system is largely unrecognized.

THE RIGHT TO TRAVEL ABRIDGED BY AIR IDENTIFICATION REQUIREMENTS

Just as the Supreme Court considers the right to travel fundamental and "virtually unqualified" in *Guest*, Americans take travel rights for granted. Travel freedom is essential for citizens wanting to live freely and discuss concerns with government leaders. Yet, Americans suffer restrictions on movement. The "right to be let alone" that Justice Brandeis coined in his famous legal writings is compromised by travel licenses.

In *The Right of Mobility*, Gerald Houseman identified how the right to travel is essential for the exercise of other fundamental rights, including employment and travel (1979, 86). "Mobility is a right which makes many other rights we hold dear both tenable and possible – the rights of association, privacy, and equality of opportunity, for example." He notes that a national identification system, including worker identification cards, constitutes an "internal passport" which he calls the "hallmark of repressive regimes such as [Apartheid] South Africa, the [former] Soviet Union, or Nazi Germany."[115]

Houseman identified the right to travel in mobility as integral for the exercise of other fundamental rights, in particular, employment. These restrictions extend beyond requirements to provide identification in order to travel by air or train to more general restrictions on various forms of mobility. In short, requiring identification to travel restricts occupation rights, too.

Like the requirement for government identification for citizen employment begun with the Immigration Reform and Control Act of 1986 by having to get official permission to take employment or travel citizens cease to have the right to take an occupation and exercise mobility. By being required first to provide identification, only then could they proceed to take a job or travel.

Having to prove citizenship to exercise freedom of travel undermines both the constitutional rights of citizenship and the travel right. Mobility-related decisions like *Kolender* and *Hiibel* make clear that the authorities may not demand identification from people for exercising constitutional liberties and doing nothing illegal. These decisions upholding the right to movement invoke the right to travel as a citizen right. The same principles that apply to pedestrians moving on a public street apply to passengers in cars and getting on airplanes. Acting legally does not need government permission.

Instead, under the "REAL ID" law the Secretary of the Department of Homeland Security takes the power to create the nationally computer-linked federal license for travel. Contrary to federalism, the law provides for minimal "consultation" with the states on the regulation, and no privacy protections. Under the REAL ID requirements, state driver's licenses become federal documents.

Under the proposed "Comprehensive Immigration Reform" (CIR), in order to work in the United States, American citizens would be required to have their biometric digital photograph in a government database at the Department of Homeland Security (DHS) and the image would have to be matched by a "photo tool" with a US passport or REAL ID compatible driver's license photo. Combined with security databases and facial recognition capacity (Myers, 2016), these identification systems could prevent anyone not only from getting a job but also from entering a subway or an airport (EPIC, 2013a). Hence, both in limiting mobility to take jobs and to enter transportation facilities or vehicles, the "comprehensive" parts of immigration reform, like photo-identification requirements to facilitate facial recognition technology (and creating a biometric Social Security card), deform citizens' and noncitizens' rights to travel.

A national driver's license, especially for "official purposes" (as defined by legislation or the Secretary of Homeland Security), contributes to a national identification system. It creates both a potential federal travel license and government benefits authorization card. If all states become "compliant" with the REAL ID law, a national driver's license could be needed for most travel. That could include requiring a national travel license for driving and for the "official purpose" to board planes at airports (or travel by Amtrak from train stations). It could potentially be required for taking the subway, buses, or commuter rail linked to a REAL ID. A REAL ID (as opposed to a simple driver's license) could be required to rent a car. Subway turnstiles, tied to REAL IDs and to facial recognition technology, could be programmed to stay shut if certain people on no-travel lists tried to enter them.

Requiring any single document or card, like a REAL ID, when only possessing and showing it can satisfy a demand, undermines the right to travel. Current air identification requirements can be met by a variety of documents (driver's licenses, passports), or none at all if identity on a boarding pass can be otherwise corroborated. But once only a single document, like a REAL ID, can satisfy the air travel requirements, then the right to travel is completely undermined and the foundations of an internal passport system enhanced.

The electronic transit pass systems could be reworked from permitting travel to denying travel to people without a REAL ID. Even travelers carrying cash could not travel without also carrying a license. Ostensibly, REAL ID creates a national driver's license by imposing federal "standards" on the states. Traditionally, under federalism, states have "police powers" to decide about licensing motorists. Instead, the electronic verification system along with REAL ID could function as an internal passport, limiting geographical and occupational mobility (Sobel, 2005a).

REAL ID would become the centerpiece of an internal passport system. As Massachusetts ACLU director, Carol Rose notes, echoing Houseman, "Historically, governments use national ID systems to control populations rather than to protect them ... Examples include the apartheid government in South Africa and the East German Stasi ... The phrase 'Your papers, please' is antithetical to traditional American values of privacy and freedom of travel." In a cashless society, electronic travel cards and a "REAL ID Card" could become required everywhere (Sobel, 2005a; Myers, 2016).[116] Tied to search of bags in transit system in New York, Boston, and Chicago, identification requirements raise that specter of nationalization of routine transit surveillance and searches for American citizens.[117]

And a national license could also be required "for official purposes" to receive a passport, enter a government building, or to get federal payments like social security or VA benefits. The demand for a national travel license by auto, air, and surface transportation could become as common as requests for credit cards.

Individuals and organizations across the political spectrum oppose the national driver's license and national identification because these types of internal passports undermine basic liberties to work and travel. These groups go beyond the ACLU to the American Conservative Union and Liberty Coalition. Coalition Director Michael Ostrolenk notes that the REAL ID could become "a law that 'federalizes' our state issued drivers licenses," creates interlinked national (and international) databases, and "turns our drivers licenses into an internal passport."[118] All of these, which are provisions within the REAL ID Act, place privacy, autonomy, and ultimately security in jeopardy.

In the concurrent (hybrid) exercise of two fundamental rights, one right, for example travel (or employment, often travel-related), may not be conditioned on abrogating another right like privacy.[119] Yet air identification rules, passenger profiling and intrusive searches abridge rights simultaneously. In summary, travel and privacy rights are intimately linked in their constitutional protections abridged by REAL ID restrictions.[120]

As *Shapiro* articulated, travel is a "fundamental right" guaranteed by the Constitution.[121] "An individual's liberty may be harmed by an act that causes or reasonably threatens a loss of physical locomotion or bodily control" (Foley, 2006). As *Guest* found, the interstate travel right is "virtually unqualified."[122]

The provisions of the Comprehensive Immigration Reform bill for a biometric identification and Social Security card parallels what Houseman foresaw in the 1970s in Congress's considering establishing a system of "forgery-proof" Social Security cards, complete with photographs and plastic lamination, for everyone entitled to have one. Houseman identified this Social Security card as a "national passport – internal passport – by acting as a work ID . . . Any potential employer must then refuse to hire anyone who fails to produce this card" (Houseman, 1979, 42). While its sponsors denied "that this could easily be turned into a national identification system, it is not difficult to imagine this being done in the name of bureaucratic efficiency, national security, or . . . to snoop and perhaps to limit mobility" (17).

AIR IDENTIFICATION REQUIREMENTS IMPEDE THE RIGHT TO TRAVEL: GILMORE AND MOCEK

In 2006, *Gilmore v. Gonzales* challenged the air identification requirement for domestic travel as a violation of the right to travel, and especially to travel to the seat of government to seek redress of grievances under the First Amendment.[123] On July 4, 2004, John Gilmore attempted to fly from San Francisco and Oakland, California to Washington, DC, to petition against the air identification requirement. Gilmore's refusal to submit to an identification or search requirement in order to fly from California to the seat of government in Washington, DC, led to being denied boarding. In *Gilmore*, the government revealed that identification was not required in order to fly. "The identification policy requires that airline passengers either prevent identification or be subjected to a more extensive search."[124] While not stating that there is a right to travel, the government held that identification was not required. Although in *Gilmore* the government revealed that identification was not absolutely required in order to fly, TSA has subsequently restricted the alternatives in which a traveler can fly without ID. In *Gilmore*, the Ninth Circuit "recognized the fundamental right to interstate travel" but inappropriately relied on the "single mode doctrine" in restricting freedom of movement.[125]

In 2012, Philip Mocek declined to provide identification to fly in Albuquerque International Airport and was arrested for the refusal while photographing the TSA's response. He attempted to fly without identification under the right to travel, and when questioned by a TSA agent, he began to videotape the encounter. When Mocek refused to stop, the TSA agent called the local police, and an officer subsequently arrested Mocek on a series of charges of refusing to provide identification. In the jury trial acquitting him on all charges, the government also acknowledged that people can fly on commercial airlines without providing identification.[126]

In testimony, a TSA agent responded to Mocek's asserting his right to fly without ID: "You are correct . . . You do not have to have an ID to get on a plane . . . If you do not bring your photo ID to the airport, there is a procedure . . . You can still get on a plane."[127]

Commentary on the Mocek case asking, "Do you have a right to travel by air?" responds that the answer is "Yes." The Airline Deregulation Act of 1978 guarantees the "public right of freedom of transit" by air, and that's the right to travel.[128] Because airlines are common carriers, Mocek's attempted trip was an exercise of "the right peaceably to assemble" as guaranteed by the First Amendment of the US Constitution.[129]

CONSTITUTIONAL INFIRMITIES OF AIR ID REQUIREMENTS AND THE "NO-FLY" LISTINGS

In two recent decisions, judges have rejected or expressed skepticism about the government's arguments for secrecy and against meaningful process for challenging inclusion on the watch lists that ban travel to or from the United States or over American airspace. These decisions include an August 2013 ruling in *Latif v. Holder*, in which a court found preliminarily that ability to fly internationally is protected by the Constitution.

A federal court took a step toward placing a check on the government's secret No-Fly List.[130] In a ruling in the *Latif* challenge to the No-Fly List, US District Court Judge Anna Brown recognized that the Constitution applies when the government bans Americans from the skies. Latif filed in June 2010 on behalf of thirteen US citizens, including four military veterans, who were barred from flying to, from, or within the United States because of their apparent placement on the No-Fly List. The judge added that "[t]he realistic implications of being on the No-Fly List are potentially far-reaching" and can prevent a listed person from traveling by air, sea, or land (*Latif*, 2013, 25).

The No-Fly List violates the Constitution because it deprives those who are on it of their ability to travel without any notice, stated reasons, or a hearing to challenge the denial of their rights (Handeyside, 2014).[131]

In *Latif* judge Brown noted, "Here it is undisputed that inclusion on the No-Fly List completely bans listed persons from boarding commercial flights to or from the United States or over United States air space" (*Latif*, 2013, 25). Thus, plaintiffs have shown their placement on the No-Fly List has and will severely restrict plaintiffs' ability to travel internationally.

Moreover, the *Latif* judge noted,

> The implications of being on the No-Fly List are potentially far-reaching. For example, the source of the No-Fly list in Terrorist Screening Center shares watchlist information with 22 foreign governments and United States Customs and Border Protection makes recommendations to ship captains as to whether a passenger poses a risk to transportation security. This can result in further interference with an individual's ability to travel as they attempt to travel abroad by boat and land and were either turned away or completed their journey only after an extraordinary amount of time, expense, and difficulty. Accordingly, the Court concludes on this record that Plaintiffs have a constitutionally-protected liberty interest in traveling internationally by air, which is affected by being placed on the list. (*Latif*, 25–26)

Similarly, in *Mohamed v. Holder* (2014), US District Court judge Anthony Trenga ruled on right to travel issues. Noting that "[t]he impact on a citizen who cannot use a commercial aircraft is profound. He is restricted in his practical ability to travel substantial distances within a short period of time, and the inability to fly to a significant extent defines the geographical area in which he may live his life." The judge went on to note that "[a]s a practical matter, an affected person is restricted in his ability to visit family and friends located in relatively distant areas of the country or abroad, which through flight can be reached within a matter of hours but would otherwise take days, if not weeks, to access"(528).

His most telling point was that[132] "[a]n inability to travel by air also restricts one's ability to associate more generally, and effectively limits

educational, employment and professional opportunities. It is difficult
to think of many job categories of any substance where an inability to fly
would not affect the prospects for employment or advancement; one
need only reflect on how an employer would view the desirability of an
employee who could not travel by air. An inability to fly likewise affects
the possibility of recreational and religious travel, given the time periods usually available to people, particularly those who are
employed."[133] In short, the opinion ties limitation on the right to travel
to limitations on employment opportunities.

Plaintiffs claimed a Fifth Amendment "liberty interest ... in air
traveling" (*Mohamed*, 2014, 537) The court further found "the substantial liberty interest in freedom of movement possessed by every
citizen" (*Mohamed*, 2014, 532).

In *Mohamed*, the district court addressed the deficiencies of the
"single mode doctrine," particularly when a citizen needs to travel
between the contiguous and the noncontiguous United States.[134]
Travelers have a "liberty interest in ... traveling by air like other
American citizens."[135] Commercial air service is the only mode of
passenger transportation available between many US locations, especially American states and territories outside the continental union.
Particularly, for non-continental interstate travel, where the only viable
means of travel is by airplane, the "single mode doctrine" imposes on
citizens an onerous, unreasonable, and unjustified burden (Sobel and
Torres, 2013). It cannot withstand constitutional scrutiny.

Judge Trenga's ruling in January 2014 rejected the government's
request to dismiss a case brought by a US citizen alleging he was
prevented from returning to the United States because he appeared
on the No-Fly List. Judge Trenga described the consequences of
inclusion on the No-Fly List: "The impact on a citizen who cannot
use a commercial aircraft is profound" as "placement on the No Fly
List is life defining and life restricting across a range of constitutionally
protected activities and aspirations." In short, "a No Fly List designation transforms a person into a second class citizen, or worse"
(*Mohamed*, 2014, 529).

The court's opinion recognizes that inclusion on the No-Fly List
severely impacts peoples' constitutionally protected liberties. It rejected
the government's argument that No-Fly list placement was merely

a restriction on the most "convenient" means of international travel as in the single mode doctrine. As the Supreme Court noted in *Kent*, "We must remember that we are dealing with citizens who have neither been accused of crimes nor found guilty" (*Mohamed*, 2014, 529).

"In sum," Judge Trenga noted, "the No Fly List assumes that there are some American citizens who are simply too dangerous to be permitted to fly, no matter the level of pre-flight screening or on-flight surveillance and restraint, even though those citizens cannot legally be arrested, detained, or otherwise restricted in their movements or conduct" (*Mohamed*, 2014, 532).

The *Mohamed* ruling noted that "when the basic principles [associated with rights of association and freedom of speech] discussed in *Kent* and *Aptheker* are applied to the No Fly List, substantial constitutional issues are immediately apparent" (531). "[T]he constitutional issues presented by the No Fly List, as it applies to American citizens, go far beyond any claimed right to travel by the most convenient means. In any event, in none of the cases the defendants cited was the plaintiff deprived entirely of the right to travel by air" (*Mohamed*, 2014, n. 22). "The general right of free movement is a long recognized, fundamental liberty" (*Mohamed*, 2015, 4).[136]

As noted in *Mohamed*, "This type of distribution, of course, only compounds the restrictions on travel and other effects placement in the TSDB [Transportation Security Database] has on an American citizen" (*Mohamed*, 2014, n.11).[137] Similar restrictions could be imposed on rail or bus travel. The recognition of the abridgement of travel rights makes the restrictions ripe to challenge.

Intrusive Airport Searches also Abridge Travel Rights

Along with identification demands, intrusive scanners and physical searches at airports burden citizens' rights to travel and to privacy. These involve whole body scanning and "enhanced" pat-down searches. As noted in *Kolender*, "the pat down can be a degrading experience, especially when conducted in public view" (*Lawson v. Kolender*, 1981, 1367–1368). Together, intrusive identification demands and searches abrogate citizens' rights without materially improving security procedures beyond what less invasive ones can accomplish.

Invasive airport scans and searches also violate the fundamentals of the Fourth Amendment and the right to privacy. As the Ninth Circuit noted in *United States v. Davis*, in 1973 the "election to submit to a search is essentially a 'consent' granting the government a license to do what it would otherwise be barred from doing by the Fourth Amendment"(913). These intrusions function as mass searches without even the "protection" of the general warrants and writs that motivated the Founding Fathers to rebellion. During a trial challenging the use of writs of assistance in the pre-Revolutionary colonies, James Otis "attacked the Writ of Assistance because its use placed the liberty of every man in the hands of every petty officer" (*Frank v. State of Md.*, 359 U.S. 360, 364 (1959)). Historically through today, invasive general search schemes conjure up again Otis's concerns about liberty and privacy lost in the hands of petty officers, and they directly contradict the underpinning of the Fourth Amendment in the unconstitutionality of airport body scans and searches (Sobel and Torres, 2013; Sobel, 2014).[138] There are constitutional and less intrusive alternatives that the government can employ to preserve travel and privacy rights.[139]

The intrusiveness of recent airport searches is currently sanctioned by another questionable doctrine of "administrative searches" (Primus, 2011) that further erodes Fourth Amendment protections. The administrative search construction, particularly in conjunction with the questionable "single mode doctrine," permits searches without particular suspicion, undermining travel rights and degrading the Fourth Amendment protections by resurrecting the equivalent of governmental use of general warrants.[140] The impact on the society and body politic as a whole of having to submit to across the board violations of privacy deserves significant scrutiny.[141]

UNDERMINING RELIGIOUS FREEDOM AND TRAVEL

Like the effects of identification requirements for work in undermining the right to travel, the requirement for identification, digital photographs, and searches to work or travel, including facial recognition and body scanning, undermines religious freedom through travel licenses and intrusions. Religious groups like the Amish and many Fundamentalist Christians eschew photos and identification numbers on licenses (R. Smith, 1997, 504, 644; Lerner, 2015). Many states accommodate these beliefs with non-photo and non-Social Security Number licenses. But REAL ID would destroy these freedoms and accommodations.

Though the search for religious freedom created this country and is protected in the First Amendment of the Bill of Rights, REAL ID and comprehensive electronic verification remove the religious accommodations that twenty states offer in the form of driver's licenses without photographs or Social Security Numbers for reasons of religious faith. Currently, drivers in those states can get valid licenses without photographs and in some cases without Social Security numbers for religious reasons.[142] By removing the religious accommodation, Comprehensive Immigration Reform, E-Verify, and REAL ID undermine religious freedom for millions of the faithful who oppose mandatory biometrics like digital photos on their licenses as contrary to Scripture. The objections of religious believers reveal the perils to the wider citizenry.

These religious exemptions follow the Supreme Court's upholding under the First Amendment of a Nebraska woman of Christian faith's observance of the Second Commandment prohibition against images (other religions may also qualify). *Quaring v. Jensen* creates the religious exemption from a photograph on a driver's license, which twenty states still honor for reasons of religious faith.[143]

A previous attempt to create a national identification through immigration reform and control in 1981 was derailed during a cabinet meeting when Hoover senior fellow Martin Anderson reminded President Reagan of the religious ramifications of the misguided effort.[144] The Secretary of the Interior then noted that "it sounds [like] you are talking about the mark of the Beast" (M. Anderson, 1990, 276), the Biblical representation of numbering on every individual. That led to Reagan's tabling of the discussion and national ID proposal.

The nature of digital photography and airport scanning, as based on numeric technologies, contradicts their religious beliefs against personal enumeration. If mandatory digital photos, biometric identifications like REAL ID licenses, and body scanners at airports are forced on religious believers, many hold that they will face everlasting condemnation. At a time when states are providing driver's licenses without Social Security Numbers for undocumented residents, REAL ID and Comprehensive Immigration Reform would remove the non-photo license and Social Security Number religious exemptions in states for a range of denominational adherents, many of whom believe that the Biblical punishment for biometric enrollment is eternal damnation. Religious objections particularly to biometric identification systems are the more acute recognition that identification regimes *per se* in their repressive natures undermine travel rights of citizens.

IN CONCLUSION: THE RIGHT TO TRAVEL REMAINS FUNDAMENTAL

The joint nature of citizenship and travel freedom means citizens have a right to travel without abridgement and need not prove citizenship or identity, for instance, to travel by air. They can simply fly after properly screening. The burden of any question about citizenship or identity remains on officials. Having to provide a license or passport to travel domestically undermines the constitutional right founded strongly in *Guest, Shapiro,* and *Kolender.*[145]

In short, travel, like voting and employment, is fundamental as a constitutional right. Its roots derive from the Magna Carta and Articles of Confederation. Its reach extends to all forms of transportation. It is a right exercisable without government permission. Restricting travel rights and requiring government identification also retard employment rights. Hence, no identification requirements, system of pre-travel profiling, intrusive airport screening, or system of employment verification can precondition and prevent exercising the right to travel. Like E-Verification, programs of air identification requirements, No-Fly Lists and Secure Flight profiling undermine the right to travel without a passport in the domestic United States.

Because of the strength and breadth of the right to travel and the right to privacy in a federal union, the burden falls on the government to facilitate travel by its citizens. It must provide means to travel without identification and with constitutionally proper screening. The American government is constitutionally required to find ways for people to travel without identification and without intrusive scanning or searches. The procedural and technical possibilities exist for unabridged travel rights within the current technology and need to be applied across its range lest a system of internal passports undermine the right to travel as well as the right to work here. These points need to be recognized and explained in larger public discussions.

Indeed, the fundamental rights to vote, employment, and travel face threats from profiling and identification schemes. Identification regimes contract the nature and scope of the polity, union, and citizenship. The exploration of the reasons why such identification schemes may not abridge these rights underscores both the nature of fundamental citizen rights and ID threats to their strength.

When the rights to vote, to work, and to travel are each restricted by apparently different identification requirements, it begins to become clear that citizens' rights need to be preserved and promoted because identification requirements and ID systems are as such threats to citizens and their rights. These seemingly separate, yet linked, forms of abridgement by identification systems in the political, occupational, and travel arenas provide initial warnings of what more careful examinations of other nations' identification systems demonstrate about the larger perils of national identification schemes.

6 THREATS TO CITIZENSHIP RIGHTS IN IDENTIFICATION REGIMES

The civic arguments about the nature of American citizenship and its accompanying rights in voting, work, and travel are powerful foundations for preserving and protecting the rights of citizens and others. Close examination and explanations of citizen rights are missing from current debates about citizenship, immigration, and national security. Because the failure to recognize the essential nature of fundamental rights of citizenship and the eroding of those rights by identification systems undermines citizenship itself, the absence of citizen issues in political debates has political consequences in degrading citizen rights. The empowerments through argument and in policy of the exercise of rights *per force* of citizenship and to be immune from identification demands strengthen citizenship as a foundation of rights.

Once the American Revolution rejected British authority, "sovereignty had shifted from a monarchy claiming to derive its authority from God to a legislature claiming to derive its authority from the people." Political power flowed not downward from the heavens but upward from the citizenry. Indeed, this was the fundamental change that made the war for independence a revolution (Ellis, 2015, 133). Then began the question: "How could a republic bottomed on the principle of popular sovereignty be structured in such a way to manage the inevitable excess of democracy and best serve the long-term public interest?" (86).[1]

This country was founded on the principle structured constitutionally into the polity and policy that democratic government is accountable to its citizens. The federal government was created by and derives its powers from the people and the states. The unique history of the country involves the creation of a federal government by the people through the states. That creation of republican government occurred under the process of integration up from decentralization. The failings of the first attempt at a general government under the Articles of Confederation required reformulation into a more perfect union under the US Constitution (Ellis, 2015). As the Constitution explicitly guarantees to each state a republican government and to citizens its privileges and immunities, adherence to the constitutional structure itself assures the federal government remains republican and democratic. Yet, the imperial imperatives revealed in British mercantilism forcing the colonies into serving the mother country reassert themselves in identification regimes servicing the national state.

The rights to life, liberty, and pursuit of happiness precede the Constitution in their fundamental locations in the Declaration of Independence and Articles of Confederation. Contrarily, the absence of recognizing the empowering conceptions of citizenship abets the idea that identification requirements and regimes may be imposed on the United States. Failing to realize that identification demands suspend rights as ID demands become ubiquitous and thereby demean citizenship and citizen rights leads to the consequence of desensitizing people to the harm of being constantly "proofed." Rights thereby become alienated and unexercisable prior to "verification." This sundering of citizenship from its constitutional prerogatives undermines the rights of citizens and noncitizens alike anti-constitutionally in identification regimes. Philosophical explanations of rights against identification requirement as detrimental to the polity, on the other hand, abet the preservation of citizenship rights. As Justice Stephen Breyer notes, "If [a basic constitutional] principle is theoretical, it ... reflects a theory that most Americans ... believe important" (2015, 145).

Identification regimes impose removable pseudo-identities on citizens. National identification regimes undermine the constitutional structure of government because identification requirements reverse the proper relationship of citizen to government articulated in the Declaration about inalienable rights and consent, and in the Preamble about the People "secur[ing] the blessings of liberty." Invocations to secure these "to ourselves and our posterity" appear at the very start of the constitutional document to alert citizens and leaders upfront to guard against degradations and inversions. Contrary to the pursuit of liberty's blessings, a national identification system represents a fundamental constitutional violation.[2]

A national identification system substitutes, in place of the proper consent relationship, a bureaucratic regime based on constructed privileges and constricted procedures. In particular, demands for citizens to prove citizenship, especially to exercise a constitutional right like voting, working, or traveling, constructively denaturalizes the citizens. In other words, the burdens remove citizenship and its accompanying rights. Demands to present proof of citizenship and not just provide a name to vote; to demonstrate citizenship and not just show competence to work; or to prove citizenship and identity to travel, including to get a driver's license, reverse the presumptions of citizenship that citizens have and can exercise rights because they are citizens.[3] Moreover, demanding identification without probable cause reverses the assumptions that distinguish our legal system presuming innocence to one in which whoever does not provide identification becomes assumed guilty. For instance, under identification requirements in the Immigration Reform and Control Act of 1986 or the Illegal Immigration Reform and Immigrant Responsibility Act of 1996, citizens are presumed to be "illegal aliens" until proven otherwise. In short, the assumptions behind ID regimes reverse the presumptions of innocence, freedom, and privacy.[4] Who asks identification negates fundamental rights.

Essential constitutional protections lie in the rights and presumptions of citizenship and personhood. The privileges and immunities clause of Article IV assures the right to employment and travel. The Fifth and Fourteenth Amendments prohibit the deprivation of liberty, property, and franchise absent due process. Instead, a national identification system removes and suspends a person's identity and citizenship rights and transfers them to cards, numbers, and databanks.[5] Consequently, identity exists in tokens or objects rather than in a person, as people become paper, plastic, or electronic subjects.[6] Thus, not appearing in a databank in a national identification system risks losing one's rights, livelihood, identity, and liberty.

The requirement to have a national identification system shifts the balance of power toward the government and public officials, which undermines the rights and powers of citizenship. National identification regimes upset proper surveillance of relationships: rather than citizens "proofing" government, the state proofs subjects.

Here, the people are vigilant against abuses of state power by being wary of what the government does and does not do. "The legitimate role of a government in a free society is properly limited to those functions necessary to protect rights. Government must be monitored by citizens rather than the other way around" (Crews, 2002). National identification systems form a surveillance web by the government on its citizens and residents. They constitute the basis for a universal tracking system and chill debate, dissent, and freedom of association and movement.

A national identification system has myriad constitutional infirmities. The privileges and immunities clause in Article IV and the First, Third, Fourth, Fifth, Ninth, and Fourteenth Amendments' liberty provisions require the government to leave constitutionally protected citizens alone. The Fourth Amendment protects individuals against unreasonable search and seizure without particularized suspicion of illegal activity. The combination of the rights to remain silent in the First and Fifth Amendments intersects with the prohibition against unreasonable search in the Fourth Amendment mandate against requirements for possessing and presenting identification. A national identification system circumvents the Fourth Amendment by rendering it technologically easy for officials to demand people provide identification or undergo facial recognition. It captures and exposes information that would have previously required physical searches and judicial authorization. National identification systems also violate unenumerated rights and reserved powers under the Ninth and Tenth Amendments.

Conversely, there is no constitutional basis for a national identification system since it is not among the enumerated powers in the Constitution (Miller and Moore, 1995). Nor is it necessary and proper for carrying out an enumerated power. As Stephen Moore noted, "Nowhere in the Constitution is the federal government conferred authority to establish a computer registry, to compel citizens to obtain a national ID card, or to involve itself this intimately in the everyday business decisions of employers" (Miller and Moore, 1995; Miller 1997).

A National Research Council study noted that "[t]he constitutional limitations on an agent's ability to require presentation of IDs, along with limitations on the ability of Congress to enact a nationwide identity system, should be explored before any such enactment to avert the costs of imposing the system and then having to revise or abandon it in the face of its unconstitutionality, to say nothing of its effects on civil liberties" (National Research Council, 2002, 29). As the Electronic Privacy Information Center concludes, "the combination of technical concerns and prevalent American constitutional values protecting freedom of movement, privacy, and anonymity strongly suggest that any national identification schemes must be rejected" (EPIC, 2002, 7, 16).

A Congressional Research Service (CRS) Report discussing Legal, Regulatory, and Implementation Issues on the REAL ID Act of 2005 found that

> There have been four main constitutional arguments made against REAL ID. First, because REAL ID cannot be premised on Congress's power to regulate interstate commerce, it is a violation of states' rights as protected by the Tenth Amendment. Second, the requirement that REAL IDs be used to board federally regulated aircraft impermissibly encroaches on citizen's right to travel. Third, specific requirements such as the digital photograph potentially violate the Free Exercise Clause of the First Amendment. Finally, REAL ID infringes upon a citizen's right under the First Amendment to freely assemble, associate, and petition the government. (CRS, 6)

The Report raises issues of federalism in REAL ID appropriating state licensing powers.

> [B]ecause the issuance of drivers' licenses remains a function of state law, the minimum issuance and verification requirements established by the act, even if limited to federal agency acceptance, constitute an effective commandeering by Congress of the state process, or a conscription of the state and local officials who issue the licenses. (CRS, 8)

The CRS also considers how travel rights conflict with REAL ID:

> The Court has declared that the constitutional right to travel consists of three different components: first, it protects the right of

a citizen of one state to enter and to leave another state ... Given that the airlines are seemingly authorized to refuse service to anyone who fails to present proper identification, ... a strong argument can be made that REAL ID imposes an additional burden on citizens who wish to travel by federally regulated aircraft. (CRS, 10)

In sum, a national identification system contradicts American principles, values, and freedoms. The Constitution and the Bill of Rights afford protections for individuals against the arbitrary exercise of governmental power. This scheme of protection encompasses federalism as the division of power among different levels of local, state, and national governments. It also includes a separation of powers that divides authority, thereby incorporating checks and balances among the legislative, executive, and judicial branches. An essential purpose of both federalism and separation of powers is the barrier against the threat to democracy posed by centralized power (Silverstein, 1996 30–31). These structural provisions of governance consciously privilege liberty over efficiency. "The American political system was set up to be inefficient, to divide power ... What ID numbers [cards and systems] do is centralize power, and in a time when knowledge is power, then centralized information is centralized power."[7] National identification regimes are foreign to the United States.

IDENTIFICATION REQUIREMENTS CONTRADICT CITIZENSHIP AND DEMOCRATIC GOVERNMENT

In reversing the presumptions of citizenship and innocence, identification regimes obscure the meaning of "security" from the right of the people to be secure against government intrusions to one in which the government intrudes on these rights. Rather than the Fourth Amendment protection of the "right of the people to be secure in their persons, houses, papers and effects, against unreasonable search and seizures," security becomes defined as invading of exactly these rights. The tendency to diminish the right to be left alone or to give up liberty for "security" contributes to erosion of sentiments that reinforce freedom while moving toward a willingness to become dependents of the government. As Bernard Baruch once said, "We must remember that the peoples do not belong to the government but the governments belong to the peoples" (Baruch, 1960, 369).[8] Moreover, like employee IDs that say they are "property of" the issuing business, national IDs and their related identities become forms of government property.[9]

Rather than fostering a "new birth of freedom," identification regimes debilitate liberties. Identification demands erode the right to vote, work or travel and to simply move around without government documents. The requirement means that somebody not carrying identification or not revealing one's name risks losing his or her legal identity or being arrested. A national identification scheme creates an internal passport system. It sets the foundations for a "Hukou" system as in China, where government permission and documents are required to move and settle.[10] Rather than the exercise of rights inhering in citizenship, a national identity regime instills no rights – no vote, no work, no travel – as the default.

UNDEMOCRATIC INVERSIONS IN IDENTIFICATION REGIMES

The fundamental problem with identification regimes lies in their reversal of the upward democratic creation into a downward authoritarian imposition. In that way, such a reversal under a national identification card and system undermines the proper consenting relationship between citizens and the state from one in which the government operates by the consent of the governed. Identification regimes invert governing relations and presumptions and create permanent bureaucratic and surveillance systems that pervade less free countries, and that emerging democracies have been abandoning. Under inversion of identification regimes, the government bestows and withholds consent from citizens as subjects who might be permitted to exercise privileges.

The American government was created by and derives its powers from popular consent. Under a national identification system, the government creates and denies identities, and thereby expands its powers. Identification regimes invert the constitutional relationship by enabling the goverment to employ the political and legal force of law to compel citizens to give information to the state. This confronts citizens with a state that can intrude ever further on their constitutional rights.

Constitutional protections like free speech and privileges against self-incrimination do not require citizens to provide identification or justification first before the government lets them exercise rights. Placing a duty on citizens to disclose their identities hinders free speech under the First Amendment's freedom of expression and the right to silence and the Fifth Amendment's prohibitions against self-incrimination. Government officials may not ask citizens their identities unless the state has satisfied its burden of proof that the individual represents a threat.

A national identification system turns citizens into charges of the government. It reverses the nature of democratic government from consent and unlinks citizenship from its foundation in the Fourteenth Amendment to dependency on government permission. Because consent of the governed undergirds active citizenship, the government assuming power under a national identification system to give or take away identities destroys the proper relationship of government to the citizenry. Government issuing or denying national identification cards effectively owns, and "consents" to, or withholds, people's identities. The proper balance of citizen and government becomes distorted when the government bestows and deprives identity through documents, numbers, technologies, or databanks.

Citizens do not have to justify themselves to the democratic state, and government cannot take action against them without compelling justification. From silence alone the government may not infer probable cause for an arrest or guilt. From lack of identification, the government officials may not assume someone is a threat.

Indeed, the problem with identification regimes begins, in Friedman's formulation, with the registration requirements that precede identification systems. "It is important to distinguish three different levels of control: first, registration; second, certification; and third, licensing" (1962, 2002, 149). "By registration, I mean an arrangement under which individuals are required to list their names on some official register if they engage in certain kinds of activities" (144). "He may be charged a fee ... as a scheme of taxation" (144). "Even registration has significant social costs. It is an important first step in the direction of a system in which every individual has to carry an identity card, every individual has to inform authorities what he plans to do before he does it" (149). When identification becomes a license to vote, work, or travel, the control mechanism becomes systemically intertwined.

The related forms of this inversion lie in identification requirements for politics, work, and movement. The cumulative inversion lies in creating a national identification system like REAL ID in which citizens cannot exercise rights without government verification and permission. This is especially so when both a technologically sophisticated identification card and facial recognition capacity are required. People no longer have rights by personhood, citizenship, or presumption, and they may only exercise privileges when their pseudo-personhood or citizenship is validated by documentation. These erase citizens' personhood and substitute instead digital representations or avatars. In embodying fundamental citizenship and human rights, the freedoms are with the people, and the burdens fall on the state. Otherwise pseudo-personhood and -citizenship prevail, where one's digitized persona replaces the real one. Rather than citizens having rights against government powers, states under identification systems subsume personal rights and leave individuals powerless.

Each demand for identification is an imposition writ small. Universal Electronic Verification under REAL ID or Comprehensive Immigration Reform (CIR) represents an authoritarian system writ large. As in the theory of colonialism, which the American Revolution fought against, rather than serving the people who create them, national governments require the people to serve them.

In sum, like voter IDs, worker IDs, and travel IDs, a national identification regime is foreign to our nation and system of government. As Houseman notes, employment IDs become travel IDs. Even after Judge Posner recognized IDs are not so ubiquitously required as supposed,[11] mandating their presentation becomes increasingly pervasive.

FUNDAMENTAL CRITIQUE OF A NATIONAL IDENTIFICATION

Both a national ID and a national identification system demean personhood and identity (Sobel, 2001, 2002), and alter citizenship in conflicts with American principles and practices into foreign forms (R.E. Smith, 1991, 4; 1997). The federal government was created by and derives its powers from the people. Under a national identification system, the government's creation of identities expands its powers. While the federal government may not remove citizenship, yet identification regimes constructively suspend it and withhold rights until identification documents are produced. The existence of a universal identification regime functions as a nationwide general warrant.

Similarly, the presumptions of individual rights that are protected by the political buffer around citizenship clash with a national identification system (Pollmann, 2001). Privileges and immunities are embodied in the rights of citizenship, under which the burden of proof is on the state, and the presumption of innocence, the prohibition of unreasonable search and the privilege against self-incrimination protect the individual.[12] These rights exist because the nature of personhood and citizenship under the Constitution are protected from arbitrary and unrestricted governmental action. On the other hand, inherent qualities in personhood and citizenship become degraded when citizens may only exercise rights by having an identification card, number, or location in a databank. In short, because political rights and personhood exist inherently in a free society, they are not subject to identification checks before they can be exercised. In the same sense, citizenship and citizen rights are not subject to modification or suspension by prior governmental permission or action.

These conflicts with American principles and practice make a national identification system and card fundamentally foreign here (R. E. Smith, 1991, 4). National identification documents with facial recognition capacities become the predicate for nationwide general warrants. Increased requests for identification diminish the security owed to Americans in their persons, papers, and effects. Ubiquitous checkpoints and handheld devices with facial displays elude the protection provided by citizens' constitutional rights and options to resist identification demands by not showing ID.

No matter how stringent the standards before checking identification, the existence of national identification documents like REAL IDs expands their uses. This increases the likelihood that the IDs will be used for surveillance of individuals even though public opinion opposes random searches of citizens.[13] Moreover, under current Supreme Court Fourth and Fifth Amendment doctrines that are not always followed, and even more so under "justifiable reliance" (Sobel, Horowitz, and Jenkins, 2013), the police may only ask for identification when there is at least reasonable suspicion of criminal activity.[14] Ultimately, not having identification makes people free, not suspect.

Centralization of extensive information and surveillance systems makes abuse likely because the government possesses the power to coerce through the courts, police, and the military. Like the assurances that Social Security Numbers would only be used for tracking pension account payments, promises of limitations on national identity cards or facial recognition technology are compromised by expanding the number of agencies with access to the technologies and data (Rosen, 2000, 46). This movement toward centralization has been set in motion by regulations that allow law enforcement and national security agencies access to personal and medical information under HIPAA.[15] The Patriot Act also permitted law enforcement to access medical, education, and financial information without procedural safeguards.[16]

As Justice Brandeis famously noted, "[the makers of our Constitution] conferred, against the government, the right to be let alone – the most comprehensive of rights and the right most valued by civilized men."[17] Requirements for photo identification to vote, work, or fly destroy basic freedoms accorded by the Constitution: the right to be left alone in privacy and anonymity unless there is a particularly compelling reason for intrusion.[18]

The spontaneity of human life disappears in the requirement to constantly carry and show "papers."[19] Simply entering a voting booth, getting a new job, or boarding an airplane becomes impossible without government identification.

Maintaining an open society requires the realization that a national ID and national identification system, integrated with law enforcement, and national security databanks, imperils rights. In essence, because a national identification system itself is a bureaucratic mechanism utilized to collect and control private and public information, it cannot be adequately safeguarded to prevent privacy invasions and abuses of personhood and citizens' rights. As such a system is fundamentally flawed and expansive; any national identification system ultimately intrudes on fundamental citizen rights.

A NATIONAL IDENTIFICATION SYSTEM UNDERMINES FEDERALISM

The structure of a national identification system also threatens the principle of federalism embodied in the Constitution, Ninth and Tenth Amendments. There, powers not delegated to the federal government are reserved to the states and people in order to prevent concentration and centralization of power in the national government.[20] Under police power, only states have the authority to set their requirements for law enforcement and licensing. The federal government has no police power. However, under a national identification system like "REAL ID" driver's license, an ID would become a national document. The imposition of federal standards on state identification circumvents the states' police power and discretion under constitutional federalism.

Moreover, in conjunction with REAL ID and E-Verify, Comprehensive Immigration Reform (CIR) undermines federalism by imposing on all states identification provisions that many states have rejected. Not only does CIR mandate "E-Verify" as a national verification system for employment for the twenty-seven states in 2016 that have not joined in compliance (four totally noncomplying), the bill also revives the REAL ID requirement for sharing of digital license photos among the states and federal government, which half the states opposed by law or resolution. In short, less than half the states are in compliance and several actively opposed the law.[21]

National identification systems undermine federalism, too, by imposing E-Verify and REAL ID on the states that have refused to participate in either or both programs. Illinois outlawed the use of E-Verify until the federal government sued to overturn it.[22] Like the standalone E-Verify bills, "The Legal Workforce Act," and "Pass-ID" proposals to replace REAL ID, CIR resurrects these two identification systems many states have rejected. Similar to the expansive provisions in the Patriot Act, NSA surveillance, and TSA background "pre-checking," E-Verify undergoes mission creep into a bureaucratic web for verifying or denying work and other rights.[23]

National identification systems are also broadly unconstitutional by violating the principle of "anti-commandeering" (J. P. Steven, 2014). Identification regimes essentially command states and state officials to follow the requirements of the federal government against constitutional stricture preventing the states from becoming administrative units of the national government.

The constitutional principles under federalism prohibit the national government, particularly as a form of "commandeering," from requiring state and local officials (other than judges) to perform tasks for official purposes. As Tushnet notes, the anti-commandeering principle "barred the national government from dragooning state legislatures and executive officials into doing Congress's bidding" (2005, 271–273). Under a federal system, states are not administrative units of the national government, but other sovereign entities. The national government may not enforce its provisions on the states except through the courts. It may not force state and local officials to do anything without their consent. That is the essence of a federal and decentralized system of democracy as opposed to a centralized and authoritarian government, in which states and localities are administrative conduits for national orders.

SYSTEMIC PROBLEMS WITH NATIONAL IDENTIFICATION SCHEMES

A national identification system is prone to arbitrariness, mistakes, and hacking produces consequences that could be devastating ranging from lost jobs to lost freedom. Once in place, such a system becomes almost impossible to dismantle, while the imperatives of scale and wider use expand its reach.

Specific aspects of national identification systems are particularly troublesome. For example, capturing and collecting biometrics, like digital images and fingerprints in a national identification databanks, themselves invade privacy. This occurs because the process of developing biometrics requires the "capture" or seizure of a person's features. Taking biometric representations of those features implies criminal behavior. Biometrics as digitial representations can be counterfeited to make it appear someone was where she was not. Centralized in a national databank, biometric data can be inappropriately accessed and reproduced.[24]

Similarly, national identification systems presuppose the government power to scrutinize and track citizenry in ordinary circumstances. They imply criminalization of law-abiding citizens and justification for suspicion and intrusion on broad segments of the public. Mass surveillance diverts attention and resources from appropriately investigating particular threats.[25]

National identification systems risk having one's identity denied or revoked accidentally or purposefully. A person becomes presumed not to be oneself without positive proof; persons become suspect without ID. Errors in the database deny individuals their jobs or freedom. Incorrect information in a large databank is very difficult to correct. Losing a national ID is risking losing one's identity, livelihood, and liberty. Not showing up in the database, refusing facial recognition technology, or not carrying national identification at a crucial time, such as at a job check, border crossing, or traffic stop, could mean unemployment, detention, or arrest. The expectation of carrying an ID or submitting to facial recognition increases the official exercise of arbitrary discretion on encountering someone without a card.[26]

National identification systems have not solved problems like terrorism elsewhere. The Soviet Union ID and South African pass systems did not stop terrorism or illegal immigration. Israel's identification system has not prevented terror. On the other hand, governments in transition to democracy have modified or abandoned the types of surveillance systems the United States is constructing. Moreover, institutions like prisons where everyone is constantly monitored and identified are filled with crime and violence. No identification system is foolproof or particularly effective (R.E. Smith, 2002, 6).[27]

A national identification and nationalized driver's license like a REAL ID becomes, as Houseman foresaw, a license to travel and an internal passport. Similarly, too great of a focus on IDs removes attention from other potential weak points subject to attack (Mayer-Schoenberger, 2002). Requirements for a national identification or

REAL ID licenses will not make air travel safer than nonintrusive and physical solutions that do not undermine travel rights.[28]

Terrorism is only the most recent justification for a national identification card, periodically proposed to stop threats ranging from communism to fascism to illegal immigration to identity theft. In the 1930s, national identification would save the nation from fascist infiltration; in the 1950s, from communists; and in the 2000s, from terrorists (Sobel, 2003). A national identification system is most simply a means of keeping track of and controlling people that magnifies the power of governments and officials.

Because there is no database of all terrorists, international and domestic, whose number is relatively small, databanks soon include lesser suspects or criminals. This leads to a national system that detains travelers or denies travel. A nationalized driver's license system like REAL ID, where driver's license numbers are replaced by Social Security Numbers as another national identification enumerator, moves beyond the license as a credential to drive into a *de facto* national identification card, making it a de jure one.

Requirements for presenting any identification should remain limited in uses under constitutional standards (EPIC, 2002, 7).[29] Suggestions that a national ID might be voluntary or that only terrorists' fingerprints or facial scans would be kept in a national database like the FBI's Next Generation system conflict with mission-creep imperatives. The cards become mandatory and the information gathered used repeatedly and routinely.

With full imposition of a national identification system, a combination of REAL ID, mandatory E-verification, and Comprehensive Immigration Reform systems, US citizens could be required to carry and produce identification and submit to facial recognition on official demand at the workplace, checkpoints, and traffic stops. The proliferation of databases with biometric image capacities at checkpoints, kiosks, human resources computers, and hand-held devices with facial recognition technology enables a national identification system to exist without identification cards. The repeated imposition of such procedures, in effect, makes a police demand for identification routine and "reasonable," but not justifiable (Sobel, Horwitz and Jenkins, 2013). Collectively, they diminish a reasonable expectation of privacy, if not justifiable reliance on constitutional rights. While the words of the Fourth and Fifth Amendments sustain a justifiable reliance on their protections, identification regimes in practice erode constitutional protections (Spencer, 2002a, 2002b; Sobel, Horwitz and Jenkins, 2013).). The interconnections of various identification systems create a constant surveillance network.

As Justice John Marshall Harlan dissented in *United States v. White* in 1971, the constant surveillance that a national identification system represents destroys freedom and spontaneity (Sobel, Horwitz and Jenkins, 2013). National identification systems make dossier creation, surveillance, location tracking, and invasions of privacy simple and pervasive. As occurred in post–World War II Britain when rationing cards became national ID cards, the consequences of police demand for names and identification make them more frequent and increase pressures for a national identification scheme. Yet the Constitution's system of enumerated powers and reserved rights instead require public officials to address problems like crime or terrorism without undermining basic freedoms.

Many conservatives and liberals consider national identification anathema for political and religious reasons. The Bush administration did not press for a national ID even after September 11. Bush's cybersecurity chief, Richard Clarke, did "not think a [national ID] is a very smart idea" (O'Harrow and Krim, 2001, A1). Despite the disavowal of a national ID in the enabling legislation, Homeland Security Head Tom Ridge "work[e'd] quietly with the state motor vehicle official and the staff of the [National Governors Association] to help standardize the process by which people provide their identities in order to obtain licenses" (Brill, 2002, 48). With the implementation of a nationalized driver's license in a "REAL ID," the motor vehicles "registry" that is the source of frustration as a "time tax" takes on a more onerous meaning. The facetious phrase, "Your papers, please," about old European impositions now takes on increasingly ominous implications.

An era of "the 24/7 digital footprint" erodes past protections. In previous times, a person normally would only come into contact with law enforcement if she witnessed or was a victim of a crime, or committed a traffic offense or a more serious crime. As a result of national identification systems like REAL ID, individuals come into contact with law enforcement, knowingly or not, nearly all the time when they are in public. This contact can be because of automatic license plate readers, video surveillance cameras (closed-circuit TV–CCTV), police body cameras, drones, smartphones, and other invasive technologies. When facial recognition software is used, people are identified and can be tracked continually. As additional video surveillance cameras and drones are deployed, the digital footprint grows. This may be the goal of law enforcement; in a 24/7 digital footprint the individual gains knowledge of the contact only when and if government decides to inform them. "With the ever increasing use of smart appliances, a smart grid, and connectivity to the Internet the footprint can and will include when individuals are at home, or other buildings."[30] This is particularly invasive when the video surveillance cameras not only collect images but are connected to facial recognition technology that may identify people without reasonable suspicion of law violation or their consent, thus undermining the protections for law abiding activities in *Kolendar* and *Hiibel*.

In writing about wartime civil liberties, former chief justice William Rehnquist noted that "it is all too easy to slide from a case of genuine military necessity ... to one where the threat is not critical and the power either dubious or nonexistent" (2000, 234). Homeland Security Head Tom Ridge noted, "We should be distrustful of government's reach when it comes to civil liberties and privacy ... It is in the midst of extraordinary times that America will be judged" (Ridge, 2009, 108, 145). Benjamin Franklin's warning remains true that during perilous times, giving up liberty for a little security preserves neither.

IS THERE A DEMOCRATIC ID OR IDENTIFICATION SYSTEM?

Is there such a thing as a democratic ID, particularly for citizens? There is not. This is because having no identification is the most supportive of liberty in a democracy. One's presence, personhood, citizenship, and their presumptions of rights are the bases for individuals' exercising rights. They serve as the best buffers against government violations of the right to be let alone. Everyone has rights because she or he is a person. Additionally, citizens have rights because of their citizenship as the basis for exercising political rights. Personhood and citizenship protect against demands for identification. Persons can move about as with a common carrier ticket without a name on it. Hence, no identification is the most democratic "ID."

Less democratic though still simple is asserting one's citizenship, without identifying oneself: "I am a citizen." Less democratic is having the lowest complexity, substitutable, and unlinked type of identification possible. This might include a piece of mail, a bank statement, or a utility bill used to satisfy for some voter identification requirements. A voter registration card without a photo is also relatively democratic. In the sense that identification be substitutable, multiple IDs have the added feature that they are not unitary and their matching names indicate likely possession of their owners.[31] As EPIC noted, "Privacy and security interests are best protected by documents serving limited purposes and by relying on multiple and decentralized systems of identification in cases where there is a genuine need to establish identity" (EPIC, 2002, 4).

No photo identification or biometric identification can be democratic because their creation and application involves invasion of privacy and denial of personhood by presumptions. In fact, the proper scale for identification systems is more or less authoritarian, rather than relatively democratic, because identification systems are inherently schemes of social and population control.

In fact, the most authoritarian identification system is a different type with no-ID card, which does not require identification documents, because the system identifies people through facial recognition at checkpoints, kiosks, or in public without consent or procedural safeguards. Such identification systems undermine the court decisions in *Kolender* and *Hiibel* – official demands, e.g., by police require probable cause or reasonable suspicion of criminal behavior. In short, facial recognition systems undermine the principle that police may not identify people unless they have done something wrong.

Most authoritarian then is the system, without cards, where one's digital photograph or other biometrics are available or retrievable at kiosks, workstations, or handheld devices by authorities like police that can be called up and facially matched to individuals. Here the government can impose a national identification system on people without requiring individuals to carry identification (which people could refuse to carry or show). Such systems based on facial (or gait) recognition are even more detrimental as they require no direct contact or standards.

Next most authoritarian are single, national, interconnected IDs, based on biometrics. These are the sole documents (or "tokens") that may be used for multiple purposes, e.g., for voting, working, and travel. A final authoritarian feature is unforgiving IDs which must be used and cannot be substituted by a combination of lower-tech ones. The REAL ID nationalized driver's license is such a feature since without a REAL ID, and only a REAL ID (or passport), it may not be possible to fly or enter government buildings under "official purposes." Only slightly less authoritarian are a series of separate high-tech photo IDs needed, e.g., for work, voting, and travel.

In short, there is no democratic document or liberty-respecting identification system. The best system is one without identification in which one's personhood or citizenship prevails and does not require identification. There one may live without being subject to identification or facial recognition. The turn to national identification regimes here is both a sign and means of the increasingly authoritarian nature of US politics and culture in the post-September 11 world.

THE EXERCISE OF CITIZEN RIGHTS

Instead, the government needs to facilitate the exercise of citizens' rights. The government needs to protect and foster the exercise of those rights without IDs. When citizen rights, like voting, working, or traveling, are involved, the government needs to assist citizens in exercising them and minimizing burdens. The burden is on the government to find clearly constitutional ways for citizens to exercise their rights. For instance, election judges need to facilitate voting and TSA agents need to make sure everyone gets on airplanes safely with or without ID.

Because the norm of not requiring proof of citizenship in order to exercise citizens' rights needs to prevail, there can be few valid requirements to prove identity or citizenship. When there is a constitutional basis for identification, it needs to start with the minimum possible, and most easily met, requirement. This begins in simple attestation of citizenship, for instance, for voting or work. At most, citizens need to state that they are citizens and sign a form to that effect in order to work. Similarly, for voting, citizens need at most to state their name and address in order to get a ballot. They need a reservation and boarding pass in their name without ID. Credible and reliable identification means simply providing one's name and address verbally.

In sum, the arguments about the nature of citizenship and its rights and about why identification requirements are detrimental to the polity are instead powerful foundations for preserving and protecting the rights of citizens and others. Citizen rights are missing from current security and immigration debates. Their absence has political consequences in the failure to recognize the fundamental rights of citizenship; it reinforces the acceptance that identification requirements and regimes may be imposed. Empowerment lies instead in the exercise of rights *per force* of citizenship and immunity from identification demands. When identification demands become ubiquitous, they routinize the harm of being constantly "proofed" and demean citizenship and citizens. Rights become alienated and unexercisable prior to "verification." This sundering of citizenship from its constitutional perquisites undermines the rights of citizens and noncitizens alike.

Identification regimes degrade democratic government. They invert the proper relation of citizens to government from one in which the government draws its powers from consent of the people as sovereign to government giving and withholding permission for citizen subjects to exercise rights. They undermine sovereignty in democracy. As Joseph Ellis noted, "A bill of rights was so important to Jefferson because its essential function was to define what government could NOT do, creating a political zone where individual rights were free to roam beyond the surveillance and restrictions of kings courts, legislatures, and judges" (Ellis, 2015, 203).

The ultimate inversion is a national identification system in which citizens may not exercise rights without government permission or verification. People there no longer have rights by personhood, presumption, or citizenship, and they are permitted to exercise privileges only when pseudo-personhood and diminished citizenship are verified by documentation. There citizenship and personhood are deleted and replaced by digital designations. The system in which citizen's images are centralized to be recallable for facial recognition at checkpoints and through handheld devices exceeds even the regime in which everyone has to carry and show national identification. The combination of requirements for E-Verification with those for REAL ID sets the basis for an internal passport system in the United States.

Finally, because this country was founded on bottom-up democracy, and the principle that government has to justify itself to the citizens, and identification regimes invert this relationship, national identification schemes are fundamentally foreign here. Like voter IDs for elections, worker IDs for employment, and travel IDs for flying, a national identification regime is alien to our nation and system of government. It institutionalizes the inversion of the proper governing relations and presumptions and the intrusions inherent in identification checks. It creates permanent bureaucratic and surveillance systems that pervade less free countries and does not solve problems addressable in constitutionally and fiscally sound ways. To remain democratic and free, the government must reaffirm that rights inhere in citizenship and personhood. And its Meaning for American is to abandon and prevent the recrudescence of a comprehensive national identification system.

IN CONCLUSION: IDENTIFICATION REGIMES UNDERMINE CITIZENSHIP

National identification schemes are inherently constitutionally deficient in a democratic system of consent and citizenship rights. REAL ID violates the anti-commandeering requirements of federalism that the national government may not require the states to administer its policies where the federal government has no power to carry them out at the national level. This is exactly because the national government may not itself create a national identification system that attempts to impose such a requirement on the states or people. This structure of constitutionalism embodied in Article IV and Fourteenth Amendment privileges and immunities and the Ninth and Tenth Amendments' reserved rights and powers contradicts the imperative to create national and international systems that identify everyone.

The pervasive identification demands a national identification scheme creates also violate the Fourth and Fifth Amendments' protections for individual privacy and autonomy. They also undermine the rights to be let alone and personal autonomy of an open society. Demands to prove citizenship and identity violate the protections and presumptions of citizenship that citizens have certain rights, especially to vote, work, and travel as aspects of citizenship itself. Amid discussion of immigration and national security issues here debate needs to recognize and highlight the empowerment of citizenship as well as immigrant rights and the creeping expansion and corrosion of bureaucratic control under national identification systems, like E-Verify and REAL ID.

In sum, a national identification regime in the United States suspends citizens' rights and undermines basic freedoms in a democracy by inverting the proper relationship of citizens and states. It undermines basic American political values and federal protections by degrading the separation of powers under federalism. It creates the basis for an internal passport system. It removes rights of citizenship protected by the Bill of Rights.

A national identification system also fails to solve the problems better addressed in constitutionally sound and effective ways. The far-reaching ramifications of national identification demean the liberties that enrich citizenship and rights. Experiences elsewhere warn Americans, unfamiliar with national identification regimes of how their pervasive nature can soon demean democracy here and elsewhere.

7 OTHER COUNTRIES' SYSTEMS CONSTITUTE WARNINGS

The nature and development of the United States from a voluntary confederation of sovereign states and peoples create the exceptional nature of US history, politics, and society. Because of the differences in the nature of other governments and their relationships to their citizens and subjects, the argument that people in other democratic countries have to carry and show identification does not support the proposition that this should occur here. Those countries and governments developed from autocratic and authoritarian origins different from the American nation. In fact, the requirements for national identification systems in foreign countries argue and provide reasons against one in America.[1]

Some democratic countries, typically outside of the British Commonwealth, have national identification systems. "In Germany, for instance, all citizens over age sixteen must carry a passport or an identification card bearing a photograph, date and place of birth, address and signature. France and Denmark use similar systems" (Etzioni, 1999, 126). "In Spain, an ID card is mandatory for all citizens older than 14, and they are required for many government programs. Argentineans must get a card when they turn 8 and re-register at 17" (O'Harrow and Krim, 2001, A18).

"Belgium first used ID cards during the German occupation in World War I. Today every citizen older than 15 has to carry one" (O'Harrow and Krim, 2001). Belgian and German former colonies like Rwanda still impose derivative identification regimes.[2] Kenya, with a history of internment (Elkins, 2005), requires its citizens to carry an ID at all times (O'Harrow and Krim, 2001, A1). The colonial administration of Kenya adopted regulations in the 1920s requiring adult men to carry a registration certificate (Longman, 2001, 348).

Moreover, other democracies like France, Germany, and Spain that have such cards exemplify why the very different kind of democracy in the United States should not have one. European national developments from monarchical autocratic and authoritarian regimes led to governments bestowing rights and taking them away from their subjects. As Ellis explained, "[t]he trouble with most Europeans [Jefferson] observed, was that they were bred to prefer 'a government [they] can feel'" (Ellis, 2015, 203).

In the United States, where citizens in the states created the nation and national government, the Constitution reserves rights to citizens and states. The Constitution enumerates and limits government powers. Here the people are sovereign as sovereignty resides in them, and hence the burden of proof is on the government. Identification systems are, instead, part of social control in which the compelled production of documents is a characteristic feature of the state's dominant relationship to its citizens.

THE FRENCH STATE ID POLICY

In France, for instance, citizens and nationals carry "a Carte Nationale d'Identite" as an identification document as part of identity "control" to maintain public order. French newborns are registered with the government at birth and receive ID cards as teenagers.[3] Police can ask for identification in public places, within twenty kilometers of the borders and during emergency periods, as a general requirement for verification of identity. Residents over age thirteen must carry identification, and those not "voluntarily" carrying a national or other identification can be detained, fined, and potentially arrested for not possessing an identity document. Without a *Carte*, citizens may not vote, acquire a business, or obtain a professional license.

France has a unitary national state and an inquisitorial system of justice distinctly different from the United States. In France, those arrested face the burden of proving they are not guilty rather than the American presumption of innocence. The philosophy of the French republic is that the state is right. "In its long history as a unified state, France has always maintained a strict separation between the state and the people. The traditional 'raison d'etat' allowed the state to develop and pursue ... policies outside and independent of public opinion. Even today, compared to other ... advanced democracies, France has a reputation of having a political elite ... that is largely insulated from public pressures" (Howard and Howard, 2003, 107).[4]

As former French General become President Charles de Gaulle proclaimed, "There could be no France without the state ... Nothing is of capital importance save the legitimacy, the institutions and the functioning of the state."[5] The French approach of assuming that an individual may be "illegal" or someone else until an identity document indicates otherwise parallels the legal assumption of "guilty until proven innocent." It represents a social situation in which citizens are more subjects of the state and where the burden of proof is not on the government but on the individuals. These run counter to American principles.

In essence, the rights and opportunities of individuals may be subordinated to the French State. As French sociologist Raymond Aron advised in 1970, "[a] greater concern for efficiency than for constitutional principles? This is the case in France, not in the United States" (Aron, 1970, 133). As the *Wall Street Journal* opined, "[t]he specter of a national ID card sends shivers down liberty-loving spines. It conjures up images ... of French bureaucrats imagining they're some kind of Napoleon every time they ask to see our papers."[6] *Liberte, Equalite, et Fraternite* imply more collective ideals than "Life, Liberty, and the Pursuit of Happiness."

BRITAIN'S DETRIMENTAL EXPERIENCE RESCINDED

Around the two world wars, Britain developed the equivalents of national identification systems. The earlier one began in 1915 as part of developing a National Register (NR) listing the names and addresses of the population available for "industrial purposes" and "military and naval purposes" (Agar, 2001, 104). National registration included all men and women aged 15–65. After completing a local registration authority card, a certificate was issued as "the first general identity card" in Britain (104) and had to be updated if the person moved or lost the card. This "Prussianizing" institution of "universal registration," "encapsulate[ing] undue interference by government in everyday life" (103), was also used for conscription, and shared for employment and school (106). These identity cards developed "parasitic vitality" from connections to other systems such as food rationing (102). The First Great War period generated "debate about identity cards [on] the distinctiveness of a British 'character,' as opposed to various European models" of "Prussification" (100–101). It raised the concern for "data creep" in National Registration (114) against "an inalienable right to privacy" (116).

The successor national identity system was created "temporarily" in Britain by the 1939 National Registration Act. The second UK national identification was established for mobilization and manpower controls and potential rationing during World War II (Anton, 1996). It remained in place thirteen years, seven beyond the war's end in 1945 until 1952. This prolongation occurred because "when Parliament is confronted with an emergency that may justify the introduction of identity cards, it virtually abandons its roles as the protector of the citizens against the executive and as the scrutinizer of legislation" (Identity Cards in UK, 2005). This version of a national identity card, which did not include a "photographic portrait" (109), was also developed for its connection to other social functions such as food rationing and avoiding "double identities" around bigamy (116).

The police regularly demanded this national identification card for other law enforcement purposes.[7] Once national identification was in use, the temptation for police to demand it rose substantially.[8] "Identity cards have put another weapon into the hands of many minor officials to badger the innocent public" (Agar, 2001, 110). "It turns every village policeman into a Gestapo agent" (Agar, 2001, 110). In "round ups" at railways stations "the absence of a registration certificate was the badge of outlawry" (112). Its abandonment occurred in reaction to increasing police demands for the cards for identification.[9]

In 1947, Member of Parliament (MP) Aneurin Bevan noted in the House of Commons, "I believe that the requirement of an internal passport is more objectionable than an external passport, and that citizens ought to be allowed to move about freely without running the risk of being accosted by a policeman or anyone else, and asked to produce proof of identity."[10] The supposed justification of an internal security document like an identification card is particularly offensive in a nation that objected to imposing a European currency on the British economy[11] and voted to exit the European Union.

That lingering identification regime into the 1950s became objectionable because the police continued to demand the card and identity information from citizens who could be fined or jailed for failing to produce identification then or shortly afterward. Even five years after the war's end, in 1950, 500 people were still being charged annually under the act. It was only abandoned after the test case of *Willcock v. Muckle* (1951),[12] when a motorist refused to provide identification after being stopped by police. "Because the police have powers, it does not follow that they ought to exercise them on all occasions as a matter of routine .... The police now, as a matter of routine, demand the production of a National Registration Card whenever they stop or interrogate a motorist for whatever cause ... This Act was passed for security purposes: it was never intended for the purposes for which it is now being used."[13] Partly because of protests over these frequently occurring identification checks, the national identification was discarded after 1952 when rationing ended by court order (Seaman, 1994, 61). After twelve years of operation, "British identity cards collapsed for a second time in 1952. By experience, cards were only kept when they were given a vampyric 'parasitic vitality' through attachment to something valued by the public, in particular food supply" (Agar, 2001, 119).

By the early 2000s, there were calls again for a national ID in Britain in order to "combat perceived threats to the social order – most recently, football hooliganism, underage drinking and benefits fraud" (101). "Frauds of the double life" (113) led again to calls for a national identity card to stop "Bigamy: Double Identities [in] the Social Order" (115). "Bigamy, which struck at the foundation of the social order, was the recurrent – and imaginary – opponent" (120).

The more recently proposed British national identity system was advanced in 2001 as a post-9/11 security measures. By becoming law in 2006, it would have become compulsory to carry and produce ID on official demand. It likely would have repeated and exacerbated these problems of police and private entities' regularly demanding the cards and imposed a financial burden on citizens required to pay for their IDs.[14] Touted as a security measure, it would have returned the continually expanding "function creep" and negative consequences for those failing to comply. The House of Lords, as defender of British liberties, opposed the plan as a violation of human rights. At first, the Liberal government evaded the Lords' power by initiating the program based on House of Commons support. The plan was abandoned when the Conservatives came back into power in 2009. The Conservative government reversed the compulsory proposals to a "voluntary" one.[15]

The detrimental British experiences with a national identification card around the world wars reveal reasons for finally ridding the country of its imposition and prohibiting its recurrence. The nation that wisely chose to end the identification would wisely not repeat the mistakes in a sophisticated national identification system.[16] In short, a UK national identification undermined fundamental English liberties back to the Magna Carta and up to the Universal Declaration of Human Rights.[17] A national identification card in Britain violated the historic rights of English heritage won eight centuries before from King John under the Magna Carta. This was two centuries after the Doomsday Book became the predecessor of the National Register on which a UK national identification system would be based now. A national ID embodied the government's imposition of a bureaucratic system to provide and remove the identities of its subjects. Yet, since British sovereignty resides in the parliament rather than the people, this contrasts with the US political system in which the citizenry create the government and its legitimacy.

Moreover, major British Commonwealth countries, including Ireland and Scotland, Canada, Australia,[18] and New Zealand do not have national IDs. Attempts to impose national IDs on New Zealand or Australia by the government have been vociferously opposed (R.E. Smith, 1991, 1, 2, 36). In fact, numerous other countries from Sweden to Norway to South Korea do not have national IDs.[19]

SINGAPORE STRAITS

Singapore provides another cautionary tale about a national identification system. Singapore's government epitomizes efficiency, and as an authoritarian system closely monitors its citizens and visitors. The use of IDs and a national database comprise parts of the Singapore's social control.

An island city-state of five million people at the end of the Malaysian peninsula, Singapore has taken a very different path from the United States. A British colony after 1867, it gained independence in 1958 and left Malaysia in 1965.[20] Government policies "stressed economic development, government management of economy and society, firm government with little tolerance for dissent" (Federal Research Division, 1989). There is only a national government (no state or local level) and a single-chamber legislature. There is compulsory voting and no trial by jury. Though courts have been relatively independent, the government has "intimidated and imprisoned its political opponents, [but] always followed legal forms and procedures."[21] The power structure is "extremely centralized." Its political culture is "centralized authoritarian, and statist."[22]

Despite elections, there is no "tradition of civil liberties or of limits on state power" or presumption of innocence. In addition to capital punishment, there was "mandatory beating with a cane and imprisonment . . . for most serious crimes." "Government operates radio and television and supervises newspapers." College-educated women have been "especially encouraged by exhortations and incentives to marry and have children."[23] The police keep records of people registering for "speakers corner,"[24] and the national database stores all medical records.[25] Freedom House rates Singapore as "partly free."[26]

Singaporeans must carry identity cards, containing a universal identity number, a picture, fingerprint, and date of birth. Citizens must get national identification at fifteen and reregister at thirty. Anyone changing residences must report the new address and phone numbers to the police.[27] Citizens can be fined for not carrying the card. Under the National Registration Act, anyone who gives their identification to another person may be fined $10,000 and imprisoned for ten years.[28] The police routinely ask people to produce their papers.

Singapore's Land Transport Authority uses locational technology to regulate traffic and parking through a nationwide vehicle tracking system. The system works like toll-road technology where scanners read signals from transponders in passing vehicles. Electronic systems can locate every vehicle or person equipped with mandatory transponders (Brzezinski, 2003).[29]

HISTORICAL ABUSES THROUGH IDENTIFICATION SYSTEMS AND DOCUMENTS

Identity systems and documents have a long history of use for discrimination and social control. Through the American Civil War, slaves were required to carry passes in order to travel away from plantations. "Of course, not *all* Americans have been able to move freely about the country. In many parts of colonial America, both North and South, Negroes were required to carry 'passes' (Machlin, 1990, 1260, emphasis in original, citing Higginbotham, 1978, 171). Both before and after the Civil War, blacks – free and slave – were restricted in their freedom of movement in parts of the North and South. Prior to the war, both antislavery and white supremacist feelings led Iowa, Illinois, Indiana and Oregon to bar blacks from entering the state" (citing Foner, 1988, 26). The pass system did not end with the Thirteenth Amendment's abolition of slavery and involuntary servitude in 1865 for sharecroppers even after they were emancipated and became citizens by virtue of their birth in the United States under the Fourteenth Amendment in 1868.

Other forms of identification have been used for population control. Fingerprints have been used to track and control increasingly mobile, diverse populations.[30] Fingerprint identification offered a way to discriminate among ethnic minorities, particularly African and Asian Americans, as "White America" feared that they all look alike.[31]

The development of passports as an identity document has followed a similar course in the United States. Under the Passport Act of 1926,[32] the secretary of state has wide discretion to grant or withhold passports.[33] The act states that "no passport shall be granted or issued to or verified for any other persons than those owing allegiance, whether citizens or not, to the United States" (Hilberg, 1985).[34] This discretion led to discriminatory laws and practices barring members of communist organizations from applying for or renewing their passports, and from using or attempting to use their passports. The Secretary Of State used this statute to deny passports to individuals deemed to be communists, a practice subsequently found unconstitutional by the Supreme Court.[35] The Court has held, however, that the State Department may prevent individuals from traveling to certain countries with which the United States has broken diplomatic ties.[36] The secretary's discretion in the denying and granting of passports led to discriminatory restrictions on the rights of individuals to travel. The use of passports became a method of suppressing dissent and controlling citizens' travel as abridging the due process clause of the Fifth Amendment.[37]

NAZI GERMANY IDENTIFICATION REGIMES

National identification cards and systems in Nazi Germany enabled rounding up, controlling, and eliminating unpopular minority populations. The use of cards in those countries makes clear how they can be used initially for purposes of societal control that can easily turn into abuse.[38] The examples of expansive use of identity cards for social and population control raise serious questions here.

A system of identity cards was employed by the Nazi regime "to isolate and gather Jews in Germany and other Nazi-occupied territories prior to and during World War II." German Jews had to apply for these cards by December 31, 1938 (Hilberg, 1985, 344).

The Holocaust began with censuses for the purpose of identification.[39] As Edwin Black notes in *IBM and the Holocaust*, "on October 28, 1939, for the Jewish people of Warsaw, everything stopped. That day they were counted" (2001, 190). As journalist Chaim Kaplan in Warsaw remarked of the effects of a forthcoming census, "[t]oday, notices informed the Jewish population of Warsaw that next Saturday there will be a census of the Jewish inhabitants . . . . Our hearts tell us of evil – some catastrophe for the Jews of Warsaw lies in this census" (189). The Nazis conducted two censuses to identify

Jews. The first in Germany in 1933 identified practicing Jews (Black, 2001, 55–56). The second census in the Greater Reich, including Germany, Austria, the Sudetenland, and the Saar in 1939, identified "racial Jews by ancestry" (169). German Jews were required to carry IDs, and their passports and ration cards were stamped with a red "J."[40]

As Black noted further in *IBM and the Holocaust*:

> Whenever Jewish persecution was reported, the media invariably reported the incessant registrations and censuses as Nazidom's initial step .... For example, a March 2 [*sic*], 1940, *New York Times* article, entitled "Jews in Cracow Move to Ghettos," described how 80,000 Jews had been herded into overcrowded flats in a squalid urban district devoid of resources. "A common sight," the report asserted, is the white armband with the blue Star of David, which all Jews must wear by government decree ... [signifying] their registration in the government card file. (Black, 2001, 201)

Furthermore, the processing of the information by IBM's German subsidiary Dehomag helped to combine pseudo-science and official racial and religious persecution.[41] "Racial hygiene, race politics, and a constellation of related anti-Semitic disciplines were just talk in the absence of genuine statistics. Now a lightning storm of anti-Jewish legislation and decrees restricting Jews from all phases of academic, professional, governmental, and commercial life would be empowered by the ability to target the Jews by individual name" (Black, 2001, 59).[42] Germany depended on "IBM technology for its totalitarian vision of the future" (Urekew, 2002, 84–85).

The identification system "was a powerful weapon in the hands of the police ... It enabled police to pick up any Jew, anywhere, anytime ... Identification had a paralyzing effect on its victims. The system induced the Jews to be even more docile ..." (Hilberg, 1985, nn.155, 158). The punch card technology enabled the identification system.

As Black noted, "Jews could not hide from punch cards thudding through Hollerith machines, comparing names across generations, address changes across regions, family trees and personal data across unending registries ... Even as Hitler's fanatic followers thunder-marched through Nuremberg, Hollerith machines in Berlin were dispassionately clicking and rattling through stacks of punch cards slapping into hoppers to identify the enemy for the next drastic measures" (Black, 2001, 107, n. 156).[43] "The degraded situation appears in how the political and civil rights, including the liberty to practice their professions, of Jews were denied when the Nuremberg laws stripped away their citizenship and they were impelled into anomie as displaced persons after the Nazi overthrow" (Sobel, 2007, 242).

It was a situation from which "no one would escape. This was something new for mankind. Never before had so many people been identified so precisely, so silently, so quickly and with such far-reaching consequences. The dawn of the Information Age began at the sunset of human decency" (Black, 2001, 104, n.156). In the aggregate, "by early 1942 . . . Nazi Germany no longer killed just Jewish people. It killed Jewish populations. This was the data-driven denouement of Hitler's war against the Jews" (Black, 2001, 365). The technology enabled oppression and ultimately genocide.

Similarly, when the German Army invaded Denmark, Norway, the Netherlands, Belgium, Luxembourg, and France in 1940, officers examined birth, voting, and business records to identify Jews and members of other "undesirable" groups to be rounded up by the Gestapo and sent to concentration camps (Madsen, 1992, 22–23). The Dutch Census Bureau expressed gratitude for the German requirement to register all Jews, because it created "an untold administrative simplification and a saving of tens of thousands [of guilders] for the country" (Presser, 1969, 37). The registration and documentation of Dutch Jews developed with limited suspicion of the approaching genocide. The East German *stasi* imposed similar policies.

SOVIET INTERNAL PASSPORT CONTROLS

Since the Russian Revolution in 1917 and the establishment of the Soviet Union in 1922, Russian and Soviet citizens or subjects carried internal or domestic passports to travel within the country, and for those privileged to travel abroad, external or international passports. The foundation of the passport system was the "*Metrika*," birth, marriage and divorce, and death documentation. By 1923, urban populations had to obtain identification cards from the local *militsiya* (police) departments, and rural residents from the *volost* (governmental offices). Originally, "[t]hey could have a photo pasted on. Neither photos nor identification cards were obligatory" ("Passport System", 2016, 2). At that point, registration, then known as *propiska*, differed from the later residential permit system also known as *propiska*. The purpose of the "Passport System," was to provide a "police supervision and taxation systems" (2).

In 1932, the Soviet Union began requiring citizens to carry internal passports in order to travel around the country or relocate to different cities. It established "the Unified Passport System within the USSR and the Obligatory Propiska of Passports." The Soviet police, or *militsiya*, maintained the system of passport provision and control. Virtually everyone over the age of sixteen was required to have one. The system generally applied to urban residents as a form of permission to live and work in the major cities. Moreover, rural residents did not have passports and thus could not move out of their towns. By 1933, all citizens sixteen years and older near the major cities needed to have a passport with *propiska* (residence permit). The *propiska* was a stamp put in a Soviet internal passport to indicate the city or town of official residence. "All Soviet citizens were required to carry internal passports" (Filipov, 1997).[44]

This "surveillance order" was formed for the Soviet practice of "classifying, monitoring and controlling place of residence, career trajectory, and officially designated nationality" as well as economic, social, and political problems faced by the USSR (Garcelon, 2001, 83). "A centralized system of internal passports formed the administrative fulcrum of this surveillance order, for the residential housing permit (*propiska*) needed to secure a legal domicile and the work books (*trudovye knizhki*) required to secure employment were issued only with the presentation and registration of a valid [internal] passport at a local policy office" (Garcelon, 2001, 83).

"Since 1937 all passports had a photo headshot of the owner" (Passport, 2015). In 1953, the USSR Council of Ministers made passports mandatory for all citizens over sixteen in nonrural settlements. Rural residents could not leave their residence for more than thirty days and needed a permit to do so. The temporary *propiska* was issued for work-related reasons and for study elsewhere. By the 1970s new rules were propagated, and "blanket passportization" was completed in the early 1980s (Filipov, 1997; "Passport System," 3).

The extensive information on the passports included age, marital status, nationality, religion, employer's name, employment beginning and end dates, and criminal record (Hingley, 1971; Knight, 1990). Soviet and Eastern bloc citizens were required to have both internal passports, and for those permitted to travel abroad, external passports.

"The Soviet internal passport was," as Garcelon notes, "much closer to the notorious pass documents used by the apartheid regime in South Africa to dominate the African population" (Garcelon, 2001, 84). As in the South African case, the genealogy of the Soviet internal passport maps a distinctive Soviet pattern of "internal colonialism" (84), such that "internal colonialism entails 'administrative differentiation' such that there are both citizens and subjects" (84), separating the party members (*apparat*) and "the nominal citizen of the Soviet Union" (84). The system subordinated the rural peasants, the vast majority denied passports (95), to the urban workers. "The internal passport stood as the principal instrument of controlling the agrarian population" (86). Under the *rezhim* [regime], there was a "passportization" of the closed Soviet cities (87). This system was "at the heart of police power in the USSR" (88).

"Each Citizen feels that without a passport he will be unable to travel anywhere, that the single document confirming his identity is the passport" (Garcelon, 2001, 89). "The mandatory inclusion of photographs in each passport in 1937, at the height of the Great Terror, further strengthened internal passports as the principal administrative element of control over internal movement under Soviet socialism" (97). "In effect, citizenship had been transformed into an administrative mechanism for putting a colonized populace under surveillance" (98). In short, "a comprehensive apparatus of document-based control" controlled "movement, labor and housing" (100).

Since the end of the Soviet Union, the internal and external passport systems, though formally abolished, have been maintained, especially in Moscow. Citizen passports replace Soviet ones, though the purposes remain similar. However, in 1998, the Constitutional Court ruled that citizens may not be required to produce a resident permit to receive an international passport (Immigration and Refugee Board, 1998, 5). Still citizens moving to a new city without a valid residency permit may not be legally employed and cannot receive social benefits (5–6). Now all citizens over fourteen must possess an internal passport. These passports no longer require declarations of "nationality," typically religion, though some minorities protest this exclusion as part of "russification" (Immigration and Refugee Board, 8).

Without a valid internal passport, "a peculiar document that may be the most significant vestige of the U.S.S.R," a citizen is "an undocumented person in my own country" and cannot open or close a bank account, receive medical care at a public clinic, buy a cell phone, or enter into a contract (Gessen, 2012). The passport contains name, date and place of birth, legal right to reside at an address, military duty, marital status, including children under fourteen, foreign travel passport, and optionally, blood type. One gets his first internal passport at fourteen, a new one at twenty, and "in case one reaches the age" at forty-five. Then the passport is expected to be carried for the rest of one's life (Gessen, 2012).

THE CHINESE HUKUO RESIDENCY REGISTRATION SYSTEM

The "Hukuo" system in the People's Republic of China is one in which government permission and documents are required to live in and move residence. Hukou as a system of household registration records name, birth, residence, parents, and spouse. Similarly, a "hukou" permit is issued per family, including marriage, divorces, and moves of all family members. It derives from an ancient Chinese system of household registration. Its original purposes included taxation, conscription, and social control ("Hukou System," 2015, 2). In 1958, the "Communist government officially promulgated the family register system to control the movement of people between urban and rural areas," when individuals were urban or rural workers. Few workers were allowed to move from country to city, and without permits they could not get rations, employer-provided housing, or health care and were restricted in education, employment, and marriage.

From 1953 to 1976, police periodically "rounded up those who were without valid residence permits, placed them in detention centres, and expelled them from cities" ("Hukou System," 2015, 3). In 1982, police were authorized to detain and repatriate people to the permanent residences. After economic reform, it has become easier to unofficially migrate and get a job without a permit (3). During the mass famine of the Great Leap Forward from 1958 to 1960, "having an urban versus a rural hukou could mean the difference between life and death" (4). The hukuo system has "a less well-known but very powerful role of social control" of "targeted people" to be monitored and controlled for their "different political opinions" (4).

Those Chinese living outside of their officially registered area are less eligible for education and government services, "living therefore in a condition similar ... to that of illegal immigrants" ("Hukou System," 2015, 5). The children of farm workers are not permitted to enroll in city schools. Since the 1990s, rural residents may sometimes buy temporary urban residency permits, so by 2004, over 100 million rural citizens work in cities, but "have not fundamentally changed the hukou system" (6). In 2013, plans for a national system of residence permits was proposed for a "unified national residence permit system" as part of a decade-long urbanization plan (Ruwitch and Li, 2013). In 2014, proposals were drafted to abolish the hukou system in small cities, but retain it in larger ones ("Hukou System," 2015, 6). "Scholars have argued that the hukou system works in tandem with cultural distinctions which perpetuate and evolve the structure of inequality, despite institutional reforms" (6).

SOUTH AFRICAN PASS SYSTEM

Identity documentation in Southern Africa was a common practice in colonial government as part of controlling the supply of labor (Longman, 2001, 347). The first laws requiring the carrying of passes were adopted in the 1700s to maintain control over slave labor. When the British took control of South Africa in the 1800s, they expanded the pass laws "as parts of efforts to force Africans into the labor market" (347). By 1896, Africans entering the mining areas had to have passes to authorize them to seek employment. Hindering the free movement of black Africans "helped to guarantee cheap labor for the mines and plantations" (347). As Barnes noted, "a fully developed pass control system minimized workers' freedom and maximized the control that capital and the state could exercise over the physical movements and economic options" (348). Pass violations were the largest category of criminal prosecutions among men.

For over forty years, beginning in 1958 for men and in 1963 for women, the South African apartheid government required blacks to carry passbooks that prohibited their moving freely about the country (Omond, 1986, 122). The green reference books that all black citizens were required to carry regulated where they could travel and work in the country (122). The official purpose of the pass was to prove that a South African black had the right to be present in a specific area (122)

In 1985, a new law decreed that all South Africans carry identification cards (123). In reality, it only applied to the black majority population. Yet, over a ten-year period, blacks were arrested 637,584 times under the new law, whereas no whites were arrested under the law (123). The system of pass laws was repealed in 1986 as the movement toward ending apartheid in 1994 developed ("Pass Laws," 2016).

ABETTING THE RWANDAN GENOCIDE THROUGH ID SYSTEMS

A system of identity cards applied to other African countries, typically as vestiges of the colonial past. Descending from the Belgian and German colonial heritages was the identification system in Rwanda that distinguished Hutus from Tutsis and contributed to the genocidal killings there in the 1990s. "In Rwanda, the Belgians 'instituted a system of rigid ethnic classifications, involving such 'modern scientific' methods as measurement of noses and skull sizes, and the attribution of obligatory identity papers stating one's ethnicity.'" Students of Rwandan history commonly trace the roots of the 1994 genocide to official colonial policies that fixed group identities, arranged in a hierarchy, and instilled in the Rwandan groups a hatred and distrust of one another." "Postcolonial policies maintained the official registration of ethnic identities and reinforced group divisions" (Longman, 2001, 347). "In part because of the issuance of identity cards, most Rwandans today, unlike in pre-colonial times, believe that ethnicity is a fixed trait of individuals" (347). "The implementation of forms of identity documentation was common practice for colonial governments in Africa, usually as part of efforts to regulate the supply of labor" (347).

"Belgian administration first issued identity cards as part of the effort to implement indirect rule" through Tutsi chiefs over Hutu subjects. "The issuance of identity cards in Ruanda-Urundi in the 1930s seems to have been an extension of the policy of issuing identity papers implemented in Belgium during the interwar years" (352). By 1994, plans were in place for "a massive slaughter" of Tutsis and moderate Hutus at the behest of Hutu extremists. "Identity cards became an important tool during the genocide, because they were an easy way to identify Tutsi. Since every Rwandan was required to carry an identity card, people who guarded barricades demanded that everyone show their cards before being allowed to pass" (355). Those with cards showing Tutsi were generally killed on the spot. Those without cards were temporarily spared but suspected of being Tutsi, and usually killed (355).

In remarks at Kigali Airport, on March 25, 1998, about the genocide in Rwanda,[45] President Bill Clinton criticized the West for moving too slowly in responding to the massacres whose scope and procedures echoed the Holocaust. "And when they were found, the old and the sick, women and children alike, they were killed – killed because their identity card said they were Tutsi."[46]

Identification cards were essential to carrying out the genocide because "[i]t's so difficult to tell them apart that even the Tutsis and Hutus can struggle" (Gwinn, 2014). "One of the first things the post-genocide government did was to eliminate the ethnic designation on national identity cards, which were manipulated by the Belgians after World War I to divide the population and keep it subjugated" (Gwinn, 2014).

JAPANESE-AMERICAN INTERNMENT

The lower likelihood of such abuses with identification documents in the United States does not remove the possibility of bureaucratic and discriminatory misuses of identity badges and numbers here.

In fact, enumeration without observance of strict privacy protection has also led to dangers here. The US Census, conducted every ten years under constitutional mandate, is currently the only complete enumeration of the population.[47] US census information is to be kept secret by statute for seventy-two years,[48] with felony penalties for violations.[49] Even more than educational information, census information may only be used for its statistical purposes and may not be published in any way in which individuals could be identified.[50] This protection rests partly on recognizing that the social system as a whole may benefit from the census, but individuals may be at risk by providing such information.[51]

Yet even before the Japanese attack on Pearl Harbor in December 1941, President Franklin Roosevelt ignored these protections and ordered the Census Bureau to collect information on "American-born and foreign-born Japanese" from the census data lists. Information from the 1930 and 1940 censuses on all Japanese-Americans was quickly gathered and distributed to the FBI, the governors, and the top military officials in western states.[52] Its use led to the internment of almost 110,000 Japanese-Americans on the West Coast, two-thirds US citizens.[53] A Japanese-American faced with internment, Toyosaburo (Fred) Korematsu, sued claiming violation of due process and deprivation of liberty and property. The Supreme Court found for the government that the internments were constitutional under the war powers of Congress and the Executive, as justified by military necessity. As Justice Francis Murphy's dissenting opinion illuminated, the internment of Japanese based on their ethnicity goes beyond military necessity and "falls into the ugly abyss of racism."[54]

The gathering of census information on race and ancestry shows how easily even the most tightly drawn statutory and constitutional rights can be violated during periods of crisis and fear.[55] Racial profiling, particularly tied to computerized identification systems and documents, raises these issues anew. With a computerized national identification system, the efforts to identify and locate citizens and other persons, dangerous or not, can be made much easier. In short, identification systems abet repressive governmental actions.

IN CONCLUSION: HEED CAUTIONARY TALES LEST THEY HAPPEN HERE

Because of the differences in the natures of other governments and the relationship of their citizens to government, the argument that residents of other democratic countries have to carry and show identification does not support, and in fact opposes, the proposition that this should occur here. Because those countries and governments developed from autocratic and authoritarian origins different from the American nation, the requirements for national identification systems in foreign countries argue against one in America. Even if some democratic countries, typically outside of the British Commonwealth, have national identification systems, the experience in France shows that identification checks become ubiquitous. Belgian use of identification cards during the German occupation in World War I continued into their colonies in Africa, so that their former possessions like Rwanda still imposed derivative identification regimes. That contributed to the Hutu genocide against the Tutsi there in the 1990s.

Moreover, other democracies like France and Germany exemplify why the very different kind of democracy in the United States should not have a national identification scheme. European nations' development from autocratic governments, which granted privileges and took away rights of their subjects, leaves identification schemes as vestiges of systems of rank and social control. Echoing Houseman's concerns, *hukou* and *propiska* systems of movement control can become pervasive in other countries as well as embedded here.

National identification systems are integral parts of social and population control in which the compelled production of documents becomes an acculturating and indoctrinating feature of the state. As the examples elsewhere suggest, seemingly neutral administrative systems turn into instruments of repression. Besides eroding the rights and presumptions of citizenship, the beginnings in Air Identification requirements, Worker ID systems, and REAL ID create the infrastructure for an internal passport and population registration system here. Under such a foreign system the decisions where to live, work, and travel are made and denied by the government.

Widespread and constant surveillance schemes create, a national identification network. As a result of the national identification systems like REAL ID, individuals come into contact with law enforcement, knowingly or not, nearly all the time when they are in public. When facial recognition software is used, people are identified and can be tracked continually." The specific systems and cumulative combination of identification requirements that Voter ID, E-Verify, REAL ID, Comprehensive Immigration Reform, Air Identification, and "Secure Flight" constitute create an "iron cage" of surveillance networks (Lerner, 2016). As Bruce Schneier concluded, "[i]t is poor civic hygiene to install technologies that could someday facilitate a police state" (Schneier, 2000, 53). Because of American ingenuity and technological sophistication, an American National Identification Scheme could dwarf those of previous repressive regimes.

The experiences of autocracies and other democracies provide cautionary tales for democratic and struggling governments around the world about why not to develop national and international identification systems. "It can happen here"(Lewis, 2005). The Triumph of the Will to Identify can precede the degradation of citizenship rights. Wider discussion in immigration and national security debates of the benefits of empowering citizen rights and detriments from " real " identification systems reflect these warnings from other countries' experiences: that may mean brighter rights or darker regimes.

8 CONCLUSIONS: SUSTAINING EMPOWERING CITIZENSHIP

Citizenship as Foundation of Rights explores the unique constitutional and political empowerments of American citizenship. It explicates the "thick" nature, foundations, meanings, powers, ramifications, and consequences of American citizenship particularly in the rights for politics, work, and travel. The foundational nature of United States citizenship and the rights flowing from it constitute the bedrocks of American democracy in identification schemes.

This book holds that American citizenship is constituted in fundamentally empowering political and related rights. Those rights are exercisable *per force* of citizenship, and government must abet and not abridge their exercise in identification schemes.

Citizenship as Foundation of Rights expounds on the meanings and policy ramifications of American citizenship for political, work, and travel rights. It explicates inviolate and empowering political citizenship rights. It extends and deepens the discussion of the right to vote in constitutional and political elements. It reveals the foundational bases of the right to employment. It develops the right to travel in historical, economic, political, and constitutional dimensions.

The debates around citizenship, immigration, national security, and national identification often neglect the nature of citizenship as a source of empowerment for citizens and aspiring citizens. Most debates about security and immigration neglect the corrosive effects of those immigration "reforms" that undermine citizenship and rights by imposing identification regimes on the exercise of rights to work and travel. Restrictions, for instance, on citizens' political, work, and travel rights by identification requirements undermine the foundations and meaning of citizenship and democracy. "Thick" empowerment of strong citizenship rights benefits all persons, including noncitizens, beyond what personhood sustains.

"Citizenship talk" is in the air today as a theme in American politics and society. But the meaning of American citizenship at its most empowering levels needs more thorough airing to inform both the scholarly and policy discussions. Approaches to citizenship that emphasize benefits, responsibilities, human rights, or global reach complement the conceptions here around rights and empowerment of citizenship.

"The opening proclamation of *The Adventures of Augie March* – 'I am an American, Chicago born' – explains the predominant character of U.S. citizenship (Bellow, 2006). By its very nature, citizenship by birth embodies distinctive qualities that anchor citizens and others' rights in fundamental protections. These extend to the rights of other natural born citizens, naturalized citizens, and, to some extent, even non-citizens" (Sobel, 2008, 237). Denying birthright citizenship would "mean that a society could freely denationalize citizens against their will . . . perhaps even leaving them stateless" (Schuck and Smith, 1985, 37). The consequences of stateless status become dramatically clearer in cashiered army lieutenant Philip Nolan's water exile in *The Man Without a Country* (Hale, 1888, 31) and common sailor Gerard Gale's demise of citizenship rights abroad from loss of his seaman's card on *The Death Ship* (Traven, 1940, 197, 239). "The pursuit by aspirants of citizens' rights would prove as meaningless as seeking Citizen Kane's Rosebud if birthright and naturalized rights were fungible" (Sobel, 2008, 257).

THE CONTEMPORARY COMPONENTS OF CITIZENSHIP

The dimensions of "the most basic institution of our public life" in American citizenship include political rights like voting, jury service, militia service, and office-holding that are part of the "formal bundle of rights" of citizenship. While the political rights are most tightly held, citizenship empowers other rights. The fundamental natures both of the US polity and basic rights require that natural-born and naturalized

American citizenship and concomitant rights are unassailable. By common law "native birth conferred a natural political membership" (R. Smith, 1997, 175).

After the Civil War, the Fourteenth Amendment overturned *Dred Scott* and it fundamentally recognized citizenship for all persons born here. Citizen rights are firmly anchored lest government may take them away. These protections are intrinsically intertwined with the Thirteenth Amendment's abolition of slavery and involuntary servitude and the Fourteenth Amendment's protections of the rights of citizenship. Citizenship is a bulwark against government and state actors' reimposing subservience. Only citizenship as a natural right, as Shklar noted, "bears a promise of equal political standing in a democracy."

Citizenship is fundamentally about fully belonging to the body politic and community. It encompasses "an ensemble of rights enjoyed" for formal members of the community. "Citizenship remains," in Bosniak's terms, "a binding relationship between the individual and the political community." As Thompson noted, citizenship is a "precondition" for influence in political processes and institutions because "citizens without citizenship" are not free.

Here as Sassen revealed, sovereignty and the people commingle. Indeed, Lincoln's Attorney General Bates' reminder to that president reveals that it was not the Constitution itself that makes the citizens, but it is "in fact, made of them." The generative nature of American citizenship in the people's sovereignty bulwarks it for rights protection against the state and temporary majorities.

Full privileges and immunities are anchored for citizens. The most completely grounded citizenship rights for native-born citizens in the United States are founded in birthplace here (*jus soli*). The children of US citizens born abroad are also native citizens (by *jus sanguinis*), when properly recorded. Validly naturalized citizens have similar rights but for presidential aspiration.

The distinctiveness of citizenship is maintained because birthright citizenship exists separately from governmental action, while fundamental rights to be free and sovereign flow from citizenships. A citizen may not lose natural-born citizenship by any governmental act, even for treason. Only illegally obtained naturalized citizenship is revocable.

Citizens may only shed their standing by voluntary renunciation. Denying birthright citizenship, as Schuck and Smiths noted, would mean a government could "denationalize citizens" and leave them "stateless." Birthright citizenship must remain an asymmetric relationship. Citizenship is not 'subject,' in Schuck and Smith's felicitous phrase, "to the whims and prejudices of transient majorities."

EXTENDING THE EXPOSITIONS OF EMPOWERING CITIZENSHIP

The foundations, sovereignty, presumptions, and empowerments of citizenship rest on the basis that citizens by citizenship have political and related rights. Citizenship ultimately encompasses the rights and requisites to determine the nature of society and government. Citizens may exercise rights *per force* by the empowerment in citizenship. These rights exceed the protections of persons and human rights. While rights in the US Constitution reserved to citizens alone include federal offices, jury duty, and diversity suits, citizens' political rights like voting provide the clearest demonstration of reserved prerogatives.

Identification regimes, on the other hand, threaten the sovereignty of citizenship. Requiring proof of citizenship or identification to exercise rights debases citizenship and those rights. Underestimating the relative burden obscures the reality that restrictions *per se* on a right like voting abridge a fundamental right of citizenship. The policy consequences of making citizen voting rights contingent, for instance, on proof of citizenship or identification documents effectuate disenfranchisement and denaturalization by choosing which citizens can participate in elections.

Requirements to prove citizenship or produce government identification before exercising basic rights undermine the foundations of citizenship. Rights that exist by citizenship may not be impeded by the prerequisite to prove citizenship or identity through official documents. Both the right to vote and the right to employment are political in exercising authoritative actions essential to the polity.

Requirements to show identification in order to exercise basic rights transform and invert government by consent of the people into a regime of citizens praying for privileges by "consent" of the government. This inversion of the proper relation of citizens to state undermines the natures of democratic and republican politics and government. Clarifying the debilitating nature of a national identification regime for citizenship (Sobel, 2002a, 2002b) constructs the basis for policies and mobilizations to enhance citizens' rights protections and reverse this inversion. Three clear examples of threats to citizen rights occur in politics, work, and travel.

THE RIGHT TO VOTE

Voting as a fundamental constitutional right of citizenship may not be abridged. That right inheres in the nature of a constitutional republican democracy. The right is contradicted by administrative regime that privileges procedure over substance. Legislative impositions burden the exercise of the franchise by requiring official photo identification requirements to vote. Instead, seeing the franchise as part of citizenship strengthens voting rights.

THE RIGHT TO EMPLOYMENT

Likewise, the right to take employment has long been part of fundamental both privileges and immunities for citizens. From the early republic to the civil rights era, Court decisions from *Corfield* (1823) to *Roth* (1972) recognize employment as a foundational citizenship right. The right to earn a living, as Shklar revealed, parallels suffrage. Citizens are guaranteed the right to take employment, though they are not promised a job.

THE RIGHT TO TRAVEL

The right to travel is a further privilege and immunity of citizens in a broad federal republic and commercial union as guaranteed in Article IV of the Articles of Confederation and the Constitution. From *Corfield* (1823) to *Saenz* (1999), courts have recognized how the right to travel perfects the union and sustains Americans to pursue happiness. Identification restrictions tether travel rights. Requirements to show IDs like driver's license or passport for domestic travel impede the fundamental right of free movement here.

Voter, worker, and travel identification requirements undermine citizen rights. Voter identification laws are relatively recent spillovers of contested elections. Citizen employment has been restricted since 1986 by the Immigration Reform and Control Act, which requires citizens to produce government IDs to take employment. Prior restraint on exercising a basic occupational right of citizens constructively severs citizenship from employment and limits mobility. More recent air identification requirements have restricted travel rights.

Recurrent proposals since the 1980s to require a national "worker" ID reinforce the barrier to a directly exercisable employment right. Requiring that national identification include a fingerprint, digital photograph, or DNA sample in a government database and on identification cards like a REAL ID in order to be "official" (or "documented") compounds the separation of citizen rights from their political and economic exercise.

In the 1970s, Houseman's *Right to Mobility* identified how Congress considered establishing "a system of 'forgery-proof' Social Security cards, complete with photographs . . . as a national passport – internal passport – acting as a work ID." "Any potential employer must then refuse to hire anyone who fails to produce this card." His prophesy has turned disturbingly prescient.

Mandatory biometrics such as digital photographs turn people's physical bodies against them, their personhood, and their citizenship. Personal data obtained from identification demands, centrally stored in national databanks, and implanted in worker identification cards with digital photographs separate persons from personhood. "Eligibility" to get a national worker identity document like a "REAL ID" undercuts the foundation that citizenship confers employment rights and does not require proof for citizens. Mandatory digital photographs along with facial recognition technology further extend the threats of identification regimes in their automatic and autocratic imposition.

Immigration and other social policy reforms have to respect the rights of citizens and immigrants. Citizens do not need to prove citizenship or be "documented." Citizenship carries with it presumptive protections. Citizens are citizens with rights prior to and without government identification. The burden of proof is on the state to demonstrate that someone is not a citizen. No identification demand is justified for citizens and others engaging in law abiding activities.

Requirements to provide identification in order to board an airline since 1996, more stringent provisions since 2008, and demands to declare birth date and gender to get an airline reservation and board a plane since 2010 also interfere with the exercise of citizens' rights to travel. Similar identification requirements to purchase train or bus tickets extend the regime. The ability to travel domestically without a passport is the hallmark of a free society. That hallmark is being sullied by identification schemes.

The proliferation of identification requirements and systems like E-Verify REAL ID or "Secure Flight" to move around the country add to the degradation of citizenship and its rights. They set the foundation for an internal passport system. It is because the national government is created from the sovereignty of the individual citizens and states that it requires the consent of the governed and may not require its consent for citizens' identities and rights.

These philosophical arguments about the nature of citizenship and ensuing rights, as well as explanations of why identification requirements are detrimental to the polity, are powerful intellectual foundations for sustaining and protecting the rights of citizens and others. The absence of these arguments has telling political consequences, because the failure to recognize the fundamental rights of citizenship – the empowerment to exercise rights and to be immune from identification demands – fosters more frequent impositions of identification requirements. When identification demands become ubiquitous, they desensitize people to the harm of constant "proofing," which demeans citizenship and citizens. Rights become alien and unexercisable prior to "verification." Separating citizenships from its constitutional perquisites undermines the rights of citizens and noncitizens.

Protecting citizenship rights protects the rights of others. Maintaining citizen rights assures the goal of many noncitizens – to become full citizens – is not destroyed in allegedly defending it. Preserving and protecting the continuity of citizen rights make citizenship more inclusive. Undercutting citizens' rights to regulate or punish "illegals" degrades citizens and citizenship. The exercise of those rights by citizens must be protected for current and future practitioners. As McPherson noted about the ongoing relevance of the Civil War legacy (2015, 170), protecting citizen rights today secures the blessings of liberty to ourselves and our posterity and maintains the bedrock of citizenship for practicing and aspiring Americans.

PROTECTING CITIZENSHIP RIGHTS PROTECTS HUMAN RIGHTS

Protecting citizenship rights protects the rights of more than citizens (Nickel, 1978, 149). It also protects the rights of others, including noncitizens. Solidifying citizens' rights enhances the human rights protections for noncitizens. Protecting citizen rights also protects personhood rights, natural rights, and human rights. Citizen rights at their best are the high points of aspirations and norms for other rights protections. (Appiah, 2014) Maintaining citizen rights assures the vitality of full citizenship, lest it becomes degraded in its supposed defense. Preserving and protecting the nature and continuity of citizen rights make citizenship ultimately more inclusive than exclusive. "The revitalization of the idea of constitutional citizenship need not, in principle," as Bosniak warns, "result in a total diminution of rights of aliens" (2006, 100).

Conversely, undercutting citizens' rights in order to punish terrorist or "illegals" degrades citizens and citizenship. While there can be penalties for noncitizens attempting to exercise citizens' rights, the rightful exercise of those rights by citizens must be protected for current and future practitioners. The rights of citizens and noncitizens need to be protected intensely.

Beyond the dozen rights reserved to citizens in the Constitution, most of the rights in the founding document protect persons and personhood (see R. Smith, 1997, 534). These include citizens, permanent resident nationals, immigrants, visitors, and unauthorized immigrants. The vigorous enforcement of citizens' rights often spills over into support for personhood rights and human rights.

There overlapping hierarchies of fundamental rights filter down to others. Citizenship rights are the firmest, followed by personhood, common law court decisions, and international compacts such as the Universal Declaration of Human Rights.

The issues of requiring identification documents and documentation need to become more prominent issues on the human rights agenda (Sobel, 2006, 121). Many other countries prevent citizens from leaving (internal exile) or entering (exile) due to denial of identification, from passport to visas. Identification systems are not neutral. They are often sources of repression and oppression, and their political implications need to be more thoroughly investigated.

"In terms of emerging human rights norms, particularly noteworthy are the subsidiary issues of the denial, and granting of passports and visas as political tools and sources of repression (Klinghoffer and Klinghoffer, 2002, 123–125, 149–158, 179). This is especially pertinent in terms of applying human rights norms now when there are increasing pressures for imposing national ID cards and surveillance systems in Great Britain and the United States. Similarly, the norms apply to the US practices of fingerprinting and photographing all foreign visitors (US-VISIT, mimicked in retaliation by Brazil) as if they were all potential criminals or terrorists" (Sobel, 2006, 121).

As perspective on the ramification of identification systems suggests, "[i]n considering the extension of the International Criminal Court and international citizens' tribunals, institutional norms and mechanisms are needed to challenge widespread and spreading violations of human rights that take place in public areas but are hidden from human rights scrutiny under guise of security. In their more sterile and efficient forms, it is possible to forget the more egregious uses of ID systems in Nazi Germany, the USSR, South Africa and Rwanda" (Sobel, 2006, 121).

"Americans should recognize . . . and take responsibility . . . in ways that express what seem on reflection to be their finest principles and purposes . . . They must embrace purposes and institution embodying the liberal democratic commitment to preserving and expanding the practical enjoyment of freedom by all citizens, and insofar as possible by others as well" (R. Smith, 1997, 497).

Moreover, international human rights bestow rights on citizens and noncitizens alike. The Universal Declaration of Human Rights and common law imply rights to vote, to work, and to travel. Many constitutionals grant these and other rights to their citizens, though often not to citizens of other countries. Even stateless people can demonstrate the need for citizenship and the standards by which their treatment needs to be measured.

IN RETROSPECT AND PROSPECT

Citizenship as Foundation of Rights has provided a parsimonious statement of the empowering nature of citizenship, its meaning, and its concomitants. It explains the nature of citizenship and its ensuing rights. "Empowering Citizenship" identifies the nature of American citizenship against limiting alternative conceptions and introduces citizens' political, occupational, and travel rights. "The Nature of American Citizenship as the Foundation of Rights" explains the essence of American citizenship.

The nature of citizenship undergirds the rights to vote, take employment, and travel. "The Right to Vote" develops much more fully the nexus between citizenship and the voting franchise. "The Right to Employment" explains how taking employment is enmeshed as a constitutional privilege and immunity of citizenship. Similarly, "The Right to Travel" explains the nature of travel rights in citizenship and their constitutional foundations.

"Threats to Citizenship Rights in Identification Regimes" reveals how identification requirements undermine citizenship and rights. Its explanation synthesizes and extends the analysis of problems identification requirements create for exercising fundamental rights. "Other Countries' Systems Constitute Warnings" distinguishes the lesser foundations of citizens' rights in other even democratic regimes and warns that national identification systems can readily turn into infrastructures of oppression even here.

"Sustaining Empowering Citizenship" provides insights into citizenship and the empowerment possibilities by maintaining foundational citizen rights. "Protecting Citizenship Rights Protects Human Rights" explains how reinstating the fundamental nature of citizenship empowers citizens and others.

As citizenship rights are stronger than personhood, common law (R. Smith, 1997, 406), and natural and human rights, this strength can empower the protections of other rights. American citizenship is an expansive force that supports rights for those aspiring to its protections. Protecting citizenship rights for straightforward exercise and against identification restrictions ultimately empowers all who attain the title of citizen of the United States. This is the Meaning for America.

CONCLUSION: CITIZENSHIP AS EMPOWERING

In short, *Citizenship as Foundation of Rights: Meaning for America* provokes insights into the empowering character of American citizenship. It reveals the constitutional foundations of citizenship itself, particularly for political, employment, and travel rights. The philosophical, policy, and worldly debates around the consequences of strengthening citizenship rights in these arenas against identification demands and systems – that by their very nature IDs undermine citizenship and those rights – are fundamental to sustaining democratic governance. The wider recognition that identification burdens become threats that cannot be allowed to compromise citizens' constitutional and foundational rights strengthens those basic rights for citizens and others.

Public awareness of the issues around citizenship, immigration, national security, and national identification solidifies the recognition of the essential nature of citizenship and citizen rights most pervasively in politics, work, and travel. *Citizenship as Foundation of Rights'* exposition of the unassailable nature of citizenship supports the foundation of rights for the healthy body politic against identification injury.

Bringing these perspectives prominently to public forums reveals and enhances the understanding of their significance and reverses the perils in the erosion of citizenship under a national identification regime. In myriad ways, *Citizenship as Foundation of Rights* fires the imagination, fortifies freedoms, and energizes debates across the nations.

NOTES

2. THE NATURE OF AMERICAN CITIZENSHIP AS THE FOUNDATION OF RIGHTS

1. See J. P. Stevens (2014, 8) for the misconception that the Fourteenth Amendment "granted" citizenship, and McPherson (2015, 5) that it "conferred," rather than declared citizenship.

2. The unclear relationship between state and national citizenship in the antebellum Republic created questions around whether free Negroes (and corporations) were citizens enough to be covered in the diversity-citizenship clause (Fehrenbacher, 2001, 277). This was a question in *Dred Scott v. Sandford*, though for jurisdictional purposes a US citizen was also a citizen of the state (406). Under the Articles of Confederation, free Negroes in five New England states were citizens there and hence of the United States (407).

3. Schall (2006, 69, n. 166) notes that the "republican perspective emphasizes 'civic bonds.' In fact, the line between communitarianism and republicanism is fuzzy, if existent at all."

4. *Zobel v. Willians* , 457 U.S. 55 (1982), footnote 3/9.

5. *Hicklish v. Orbec*, 437 U.S. 518 (1979), quoting *Austin v. New Hampshire* (1975).

6. *United States v. Lopez-Mendoza*, 468 U.S. 1032, 1050–51 (1984).

7. Fundamental Right (Cornell, 2015); "Fundamental Rights," Cornell Law School, 2015; "Fundamental Rights" (Case Briefs), (2015); see also "What are Fundamental Rights" and "Fundamental Rights" (The Constitutional Society), (2015).

8. *Palko v. Connecticut*, 302 U.S. 319, 325, 1937.

9. *Palko*, 319.

10. "Substantive Due Process – Fundamental Rights," 2015.

11. *Washington v. Glucksberg*, 521 U.S. 702, 719 (1997).
12. "Substantive Due Process – Fundamental Rights," 2015.
13. *Collins v. City of Harker Heights*, 503 U.S. 115, 125 (1992).
14. See *Palko v. Connecticut* (1937) on rights for ordered liberty in relation to basic governmental and social natures, functions, protections, and foundations. See R. Smith (1997, 534, n. 37) for an enumeration of the twenty-one references in the Constitution to person or persons. A related concept is "denizens" (1997, 46, 56, 280), an "intermediate status that provides rights of 'subject-ship' except inheritance and eligibility to sit in parliament" (1997, 46). The amendments in the Bill of Rights "invariably referred to the rights of persons, not citizens" (1997, 135).
15. In *Luis v. United States* (No. 14–419, March 30, 2016), Justice Thomas concurred that "constitutional rights necessarily protect the prerequisites of their exercise" (1) "The authorization of an act also authorizes a necessary predicate act." As Justice Scalia noted in *Reading Law*, (2012) "where a power is conferred or duty enjoyed, every particular power necessary for the exercise of the one or the performance of the other is also conferred" (3). "Constitutional rights thus implicitly protect those closely related acts necessary for their exercise" (3). "Justice Clarence Thomas voted with the plurality, but did not adopt what he called its balancing approach. If the right to counsel is a fundamental constitutional guarantee, he said, it cannot be weighed against other interests" (Liptak, 2016).
16. One of the basic distinctions between the rights of citizens and the rights of non-citizens is that the US Constitution enshrines civil and political rights for citizens and mainly provides more general protections for other persons, which includes aliens who are either authorized or unauthorized. These dozen amendments specify through out the provisions of the Constitution the rights and powers. of citizens and citizenship. Protections for non-citizens reside mainly in the Bill of Rights.
17. *Sugarman v. Dougall*, 413 U.S. 634 (1973) (Rehnquist, dissenting).
18. The dozen mentions of citizens' rights in the US Constitution include (1) Article I, Section 2.2, (2) Section 3.8; (3) Article II, Section 1.5; (4) Article III (4–7); (5) Article IV, Section 2.1; (6) Eleventh Amendment; (7) Fourteenth Amendment 14, Section 1; (8) Fourteenth Amendment 14, Section 2; (9) Fifteenth Amendment; (10) Nineteenth Amendment; (11) Twenty-fourth Amendment; and (12) Twenty-sixth Amendment. A total of twelve separate amendments (here in parentheses) or sections include sixteen mentions of citizens (numbered here in brackets).
19. The second sections of the Thirteenth, Fourteenth, Fifteenth, Nineteenth, and Twenty-fourth Amendments state that "[t]he Congress shall have power to enforce this article by appropriate legislation." This means that the laws for enforcing these articles are not simple legislation but also have constitutional force.

20. Fundamental rights generally need to be constitutionally-based. Hence, most statutory citizen rights, such as social welfare benefits, are not fundamental. Privileges and immunities, unenumerated rights, and rights to enter, live in, and leave the U.S. are fundamental.
21. "What are the Benefits and Responsibilities of Citizenship?" 2015.
22. *Corfield v. Coryell*, 6 Fed. Cas. 546 (1823).
23. *Palko v. Connecticut*, 302 U.S. 319 (1823).
24. Similarly, there is no list of unenumerated rights protected by the Ninth or undelegated powers under the Tenth Amendments. For a partial list that includes the rights to travel, privacy, autonomy, and dignity, see "Unenumerated Rights," 2015.
25. *Logan v. United States*, 144 U.S. 263, 293–294 (1892).
26. "'Does the president have the authority to use a weaponized drone to kill an American not engaged in combat on American soil?' After Senator Rand Paul's filibuster, presidential spokesman Carney announced, 'The answer to that question is no ... The president has not and would not use drone strikes against Americans citizens on American soil.'"
27. See also *Hamdi v. Rumsfeld*, Scalia dissent, 542 U.S. 577. *Mohamed v. Holder*, 2014.
28. *Newton v. INS*, 736 F.2nd 336, 343, 6th Cir, 1984.
29. *Ibid.* Taranovsky (2003). See also *Mohamed v. Holder* (2014) on "Violation of U.S. Citizens Right to Reside in the United States and to Reenter the United States from Abroad" (25).
30. *Ng Fung Ho v. White*, 276 U.S. 276, 284 (1922).
31. At least 4,000 deportees in 2010 were citizens (J. Stevens, 2011, 608). See Table 1, p. 622, that 1 percent of detained deportees turned out to be US citizens. See also Bhandari (2013). "Although it's difficult to obtain an exact number of Americans illegally detained by ICE, Jacqueline Stevens, a political science professor at Northwestern University estimates that over 4,000 U.S. citizens were detained or deported in 2010 alone. According to a study published by Stevens last spring, this raises the total number of American citizens detained or deported since 2003 to well over 20,000" (Khalek, 2011). If there were felony penalties for deportation citizens (cf. R. Smith, 1997, 44, 361), they would spill over onto stronger protections for noncitizen rights. These would be similar to the impact in some states before the Civil War of personal liberty laws of severe penalties for seizing free blacks (R. Smith, 1997, 261). This exemplifies how stronger protections for citizens spill over into stronger protections for noncitizens.
32. Papers, Please, "Does a U.S. Citizen Need the Government's Permission to Return to the U.S.?" (April 1, 2014). "Article 12, section 4 of the ICCPR (a treaty ratified by and binding on the US) provides that 'No one shall be arbitrarily deprived of the right to enter his own country.' Though the government has a form, Authorization To Transport United States Citizen To The

United States both with no-fly message and a yes-fly message, it cannot apply to citizens. 'The U.S. government seems to think that even US citizens need the government's permission to travel to the US. The CBP [Customs and Boarder Control] didn't issue a reminder to airlines or other common carriers of their general obligation to transport all qualified would-be passengers, or sanction the airline for denying boarding to US birth and US citizenship.'"

33. Committee on Foreign Affairs, 1966.

34. 394 U.S. 618 (1969); *Corfield v. Coryell* (1823) and *Saenz v. Roe* (1999) uphold freedom to travel fundamental based on privileges and immunities (fn 40). See Chapter 5 here for a discussion of the bases of travel rights.

35. Papers Please, "No-fly Trial," 2014.

36. Foreign Affairs Manual, 2015. www.state.gov/documents/organization/86556.pdf.

37. United States Code (USC) TITLE 10, ARMED FORCES, Section 311.

38. This conception supports the conclusion that the right to bear arms is not an individual right under the Second Amendment because at issue is the militia right rather than the putative right of persons to own a gun. It is not a right of citizens versus rights of persons. The Supreme Court now defines the right to own a gun as an individual right (*District of Columbia v. Heller*, 2008), but not just for citizens. If, however, the right is attached to the military clause, as earlier Supreme Court decisions defined it (*United States v. Miller*, 1939), and only citizens can join a militia, the Second Amendment right becomes solely a collective one for the militia and not an individual right (of citizens or other persons) to own guns. In short, the right to receive militia training and serve in the militia is a citizens' right, but there is not an individual right to bear arms separate from the militia service. As Ellis (2015, 211–212) notes, the Second Amendment was meant as a "prohibition of a standing army" as a "threat to republican values," and as an assurance that "the defense of the United States would depend on state militias rather than a professional, federal army." In Madison's formulation, "the right to bear arms was not inherent but derivative, depending on service in the militia," and Heller is "clearly at odds with Madison's original intentions" (Ellis, 2015).

39. Most jobs with federal government agencies require US citizenship ("What are the Benefits and Responsibilities of Citizenship?" 2015). Jobs that involve "the political function exception" (such as police and probation officers "that exercise and, therefore, symbolize [the] political power of the community" may be restricted to citizens (Bosniak, 2006, 61). See also *Foley v. Connelie* 435 U.S. 295 (1978).

40. This provision provided the bases for presidential candidate John McCain to run in 2008 as a "natural born" citizen born in the Panama Canal Zone. (Mitt Romney's father George, a presidential candidate in 1968, was born in Mexico to US citizen parents). Though he was born in Hawaii, presidential candidate Barrack Obama, though a natural-born citizen, was accused of not being eligible to run in 2008. The eligibility of presidential candidate Ted

Cruz, born in Canada to an American mother, was also questioned in 2016 by McCain (Zezima, 2006). Katyall and Clement (2015) hold that birthright citizenship is citizenship at birth, without need for naturalization, including for citizens' children of born abroad.

41. See also *Mohamed v. Holder* (995 F. Supp. 2nd, 502; 2014) on "Violation of U.S. Citizens Right to Reside in the United States and to Reenter the United States from Abroad."

42. The right to bring noncitizen family members to the United States is a statutory but not fundamental right of citizens. The 1965 Immigration Act gave higher preference to the relatives of American citizens. The preference system for visa admissions became (1) unmarried adult sons and daughters of US citizens, (2) married children of US citizens, and (3) brothers and sisters of US citizens over age 21. While not a constitutional right and hence not fundamental for citizens, it derives from immigration legislation related to the constitutional power to naturalize in Article I, Section 8, Clause 4.

43. Among other essential rights that are not reserved to citizenship is the right to medical privacy that belongs to all persons. See Sobel (2005) and Program in Psychiatry and the Law (PIPATL) amicus (2006).

44. See "Fundamental Rights" (Freedictonary), 2015. The right to education and to attend public schools is also a fundamental right but not just of citizens. Powell (2004, 997) holds education is another citizen right. *San Antonio Independent School District. Rodriquez*, 411 U.S. 1 (1973) held education as fundamental for all people. In 1875, President Ulysses S. Grant proposed an amendment to the US Constitution providing free education to all Americans (R. Smith, 1997, 321). *Plyler v. Doe*, 457 U.S. 202 (1982), states that the Fourteenth Amendment rights apply "to anyone, citizen or stranger" and that undocumented immigrant children also have the right to free public schooling. Under the Fifth and Fourteenth Amendments liberty interests include education.

45. Laws and penalties may prohibit the false claims of citizenship, or exercising citizen rights illegally. But this must be a knowing process of claiming one is a citizen when one is not. Yet, there are also citizens who do not claim they are citizens (for instance, when citizens face deportation) for fear of retaliation and may end up being illegally deported (see J. Stevens, 2011b. 608; see note 31 above).

3. THE RIGHT TO VOTE

1. See also "Fundamental Rights" (Fordham, MIT), 2015.

2. Occasionally, after formally declaring their intention to become citizens, immigrant aliens have become eligible to vote. Before about the 1850s, after filing a declaration of intent aliens could vote in seventeen states (CT, DL, IL,

KY, MD, MA, NH, NJ, NY, NC, OH, PA, RI, SC, TN, VT, VA). After the Civil War through the end of that century and as late as World War I, aliens filling a declaration of intent could vote in twenty-two states (AL, AR, CO, FL, GA, ID, IN, KA, LO, MI, MN, MI, MO, MT, NE, NV, ND, OK, OR, SD, TX, WI). Regardless, there had to be a close tie to citizenship for those voting in state and federal elections. Around the American Revolution, free Black men could vote in NJ, NY, PA, CT; and ten states only had property requirements for voting (CT, DL, RI, VA, MD, NJ, NC, NY, MA, SC). More recently, in local or special elections in fourteen states, "non-residents," who could potentially include noncitizen landholders, have been eligible (CT, DL, NM, AZ, AR, CA, CO, DL, MT, NE, NM, OR, TN, WY, and Chicago). Before the Civil War, free Black men were allowed to vote as citizens in six mainly New England states (MA, ME, NH, RI, VT, NY, and also NJ, PA) (R. Smith, 1997, 214, 384, 568, 587, 630, 616) and for a while in NC (257, 283, 345). Black voters were largely disenfranchised during the 1890s to 1905 until the 1960s (363). Before the American Revolution, women could vote in NY, MA, NH, and NJ. From 1870 to 1887, women voted in Utah territory. In the two decades before the Nineteenth Amendment in 1920, women could vote in state, local, and federal elections (553) in a few mainly western states like ID, WA, CA, OR, AZ, KA, AL, ND, IN, NB, MI, NY, SD, OK, CO, ID, WA) (R. Smith, 1997, 338–39, 457).

3. "Permanent Residence v. Citizenship," 2014. See Schall, 2006, 57 on "The notion of voting as a natural right was asserted among the former colonists who had recently revolted on the basis of such Lockean principles" (Keyssar, 2000, 9–11).

4. See *Veasey v. Perry*, 135 U.S. 9 (2014); see also Sobel (2009; 2014).

5. *Ex Parte Yarbrough* (110 U.S. 651).

6. *Yick Wo*, 118 U.S. 356, 370 (1886).

7. *Guinn & Beal v. United States*, 238 U.S. 347. (1915).

8. *United States v. Bathgate*, 226 U.S. 200 (1918).

9. Giving the same interpretation to the like phrase 'rights … secured by the Constitution' appearing in § 1 of the Civil Rights Act of 1871, 17 Stat. 13 *U.S. v. Classic*, 313 U.S. 299 (1941). See also *Ex Parte Yarbrough*, 110 U.S. 651 (1884); *United States v. Mosley*, 238 U.S. 383 (1915). And see *Hague v. CIO*, 307 U.S. 496 (1939). Also, *Wiley v. Sinkler*, 179 U.S. 58 (1900) *Swasord v. Templeton*, 185 U.S. 497 (1902) *United States v. Mosley*, 238 U.S. 383 (1915), *Ex parte Siebold*, 100 U.S. 371 (1879); *In re Coy,127 U.S. 731* (1881); *Logan v. United States*, 144 U.S. 263 (1892).

10. *Harper v. Virginia State Bd of Education*, 383 U.S. 663 (1966).

11. *Harper*, 667.

12. *Lubin v. Panish*, 415 U.S. 709 (1974).

13. *Wright v. Mahan*, 478 F. Supp. 468 (E.D. Va 1979).

14. *Burdick v. Takushi*, 504 U.S. 428, 433, 1992.

15. *McCutcheon v. FEC*, 134 U.S. 1434, 2014.
16. *Shelby County v. Holder*, 570 U.S. 1 (2013).
17. *Crawford v Marion County Election Board*, 42 F.3d 436, 438, (2007b).
18. *Crawford v. Marion County Election Board*, 128 U.S. 1610 (2008).
19. *League of Women Voters of Wisconsin v. Walker*, 834 NW 2d. 393 (2014).
20. *League of Women Voters of Wisconsin v. Walker*, 5.
21. Though seen as routine today, voter registration requirements are another impediment to voting. Their implementation last century significantly lowered the levels of turnout. While some requirements are not particularly burdensome, they still impose costs on voters that could be avoided by same-day registration, with affidavit requirements. See Keysaar (2000) and Minnette (2010) on identifying how registration requirements restrict the franchise more than serving good government purposes: "The notion that registration-in-advance is simply a good government reform that protects the integrity of the ballot, not a mechanism for shaping the electorate, is the one that prevails today ... For others, voter registration rules, because they establish the gateway to the ballot, are a battleground where Americans continue to fight over the right to vote – what it is, what it should be, and who should have it. For them, the registration process should impose no undue burden on this right" (Minnette, 2010, 25; Nowak and Rotunda, 1991; see also James, 1987, 1619 n. 21) (suggesting that the fundamental right to vote could be grounded in various provisions of the Constitution).
22. Civil Rights Act of 1964 and Voting Rights Act of 1965 outlaw discriminatory registration requirements.
23. *Hynes v. Mayor and City of Oradell*, 425 U.S. 610, 1976.
24. See *Elrod v. Burns* (1976); *CSLNAACP v. McCrory* (2015), p. 29.
25. See note 36 for the impact of voter ID laws in diminishing turnout. See also Sobel, 2014, on the cost of a "free" voter ID, and the North Carolina exemption for "a reasonable impediment" to providing an ID (except from principled opposition to ID requirements to vote).
26. *League of Women Voters*, 5.
27. *Lawson*, at 1367. *Hiibel* and *Kolender* both agree that one may not be asked for identification absent at least reasonable suspicion of criminal activity. As opposed to *Kolender*, the demand in *Hiibel* to produce a name as identification contradicts the now-famous principles in *Miranda v. Arizona* and a series of cases of strong dicta that protect the right to remain silent against identification demands (see note 30).
28. *Kolender v. Lawson*, 461 U.S. 352, 355 (1983).
29. *Kolender*, 363.
30. See Sobel and Fennel, 2007 (617, 628) (discussing the dicta on the right to remain silent), and how the swing vote, Justice Kennedy, missed the fact that *Hiibel* violated Fifth Amendment prohibitions against self-incrimination by having to reveal a name that triggered automatic arrest under Nevada's

domestic violence law. For decisions against compelled identification largely under the Fourth Amendment, see *Terry v. Ohio*, 34 (1968) (White, J., concurring) ("the person may be briefly detained against his will while pertinent questions are directed to him. Of course, the person stopped is not obliged to answer, answers may not be compelled, and refusal to answer furnishes no basis for an arrest"); *Kolender*, 461 U.S. at 365 (a *Terry* suspect "must be free to leave after a short time and to decline to answer the questions put to him") (Brennan, J., concurring); *Berkemer v. McCarty*, 439–440 (1984) (the "officer may ask the ... detainee a moderate number of questions to determine his identity and to try to obtain information confirming or dispelling the officer's suspicions. But the detainee is not obliged to respond"); *Illinois v. Wardlow*, 125 (2000) (stopping a fleeing suspect "is quite consistent with the individual's right to go about his business or to stay put and remain silent in the face of police questioning"). See also Machlin (1990).

31. *Kolender*, 362 (Brennan, J., concurring).
32. *Kolender*, 362 (Brennan, J., concurring).
33. *Hiibel v. Nevada*, 542 U.S. 177, 187–189 (2004).
34. See Sobel and Fennel (2007), for the constitutional problems with requiring identification in light of Fifth Amendment protections.
35. *League of Women Voters of Wisconsin v. Walker*, 2, 6–7, 2014. Other voter suppression measures are reduction of early voting and removing same-day registration (*NC NAACP v. McGrory*, 2016).
36. Nationally, in the 2004 election, voter turnout declined 3 percent (6% for African Americans; 10% for Hispanic Americans) in states that imposed identification requirements (Drew 2007). The General Accountability Office (2014) similarly found a 2–3 percent reduction from voter identification laws. If voter identification requirements reduce overall turnout by 3 percent, with, for instance, approximately 4.5 million eligible voters in Indiana (www.census .gov), about 135,000 potential voters may have been deterred from voting by identification rules. Although there was no evidence of even one instance of in-person fraud in recent Indiana history (*Crawford*, 2007a, 954; 2007b), a significant group of otherwise eligible Indiana voters would likely be deterred by voter ID requirements. In short, a 10 percent abridgement of voting would reduce congressional representation by 10 percent. A different approach to a similar proportion focuses on disparate impacts on minority population (though the Fourteenth Amendment does not require discrimination, only abridgement). Indiana's 2,000 voting age population (VAP) was 4,407,679 (www.census.gov). The Voting Age Populations (VAP) of African Americans and Hispanics, two groups most disadvantaged by the voter ID law, were 342,087 and 136,266, respectively (with an additional 45,200 considering themselves of two or more races). The total of these identifiable minority groups is 523,553, or 11.6 percent (one-ninth), of Indiana's VAP, and a basis for reduction in representation. The proportion whose voting rights

are abridged is larger by accounting for other groups facing discrimination. These include women as half the population and elderly as about one-eighth (12 percent). While Section 2 of the Fourteenth Amendment refers only to male citizens twenty-one years and older, the Nineteenth (women's suffrage) and Twenty-sixth (18-year-old vote) Amendments, respectively, invalidate such limitation (see Amar, 2005, 392–394).

37. See, e.g., *Brief for Petitioners Indiana Democratic Party*, 2007, 2; also Amar (2006, 205); Karlan (2008, 46–47).

38. As "history demonstrates," to Justice Thomas in dissent, "the most significant effect of election reform has been not to purify public service, but to protect incumbents and increase the influence of special interest groups." *Colorado Republican Federal Campaign Committee v. FEC*; 518 U.S. 644, 1996.

39. Illinois voters in 2014 passed a constitutional amendment by referendum that prohibits the type of discrimination that voter identification laws generate (see Nelson, 2014).

4. THE RIGHT TO EMPLOYMENT

1. See Sobel (1989, chapter 6) and Sobel (1994) on the correspondence between work and politics as parallel authority structures. It is in part because participation in work contributes to participation in politics that the right to employment needs to be sustained for a vital polity. See also Sobel (1986) for early arguments against the requirements for worker to provide IDs in order to take employment.

2. See also Nickel (1978–1979) on the human right to employment. Citizens' right to take employment differs from the right to be guaranteed a job. See note 4.

3. John Powell (2004), who holds voting and education as citizen rights (997), also notes that "personhood became a presumption bestowed to all citizens at birth" and "the rise the nation-states" created a new political space for personhood (and membership) rooted in citizenship that had the effect "to limit personhood to citizens" (987). See Chapter 2 on the rights to travel unconditionally into one's country and not to be deported. See also *Shapiro v. Thompson* (1969) and *Saenz v. Roe* (1999) about freedom to travel fundamentally based on privileges and immunities.

4. The citizen's right to employment is the right to take a job offered. This "right to follow an occupation" (Bienen, personal communication, July 24, 2007) means that a citizen may take a job offered, without the burden of requirements for proof such as identification. It is not a right to a guaranteed job to anyone or to protect groups against discrimination. Whether everyone has a right or guarantee to a job, as human rights advocates maintain, is a question of

social policy. The right to employment also differs from economic due process that applies to all persons, not just citizens.

5. Whether a corporation can be a person (R. Smith, 1997, 406, 615), or citizen (557–558), is not addressed here that focuses on natural, not artificial, persons like corporations (406, 615). In the notes to 1886 *Santa Clara Country* dicta, corporations are considered persons. See *Paul v. Virginia*, 75 U.S. 168 (1869). See also Fehrenbacher (2001, 71, 277) on Taney's conception of whether corporations are citizens for diversity jurisdiction. Lockean consent and Lockean labor theory contradict Lochnerian contract liberty.

6. *Corfield v. Coryell*, 6 Fed. Cas. 546 (1823).

7. *Butchers' Union Co. v. Crescent City Co*, 111 U.S. 746, 757 (1884). Quoting Adam Smith, the opinion continues: "It has been well said that 'the property which every man has in his own labor, as it is the original foundation of all other property, so it is the most sacred and inviolable. ... It is a manifest encroachment upon the just liberty both of the workman and of those who might be disposed to employ him. As it hinders the one from working at what he thinks proper, so it hinders the others from employing whom they think proper.'" Adam Smith, *Wealth of Nations*. bk. 1, *c.* 10. This is similar to Lockean consent and labor theory around employment discussed above.

8. For the citizen right to vocation, see Rogers Smith (1997, 276, 339, 575, 588, 592, 615).

9. "Right to Employment," Legal Dictionary, 2015.

10. *Butchers Union Co.* 111 U.S. 756. See Sobel (2008, 2013a, 2013b).

11. See Sobel and Fennel (2007, 617, 625) on dicta about the right to remain silent, and notes 27 and 30 in Chapter 3 as it relates to voter and national identification systems.

12. For information on the right to work for citizens and noncitizens alike in the Universal Declaration of Human Rights and other documents, see "Right to Work" (Wikipedia), 2015: "the right of everyone to the opportunity to gain his living by work." This is related to the right to property wherein "property owners ... were initially granted civil and political rights, such as the right to vote." The Friedmans in 1980 in *Free to Choose* held that the choice of profession should be free "without first getting a permit or license from a government official" (p. 2). "[An] essential part of economic freedom is freedom to use the resources we possess in accordance with our own values – freedom to enter any occupation, engage in any business enterprise, buy from and sell to anyone else, so long as we do so on a strictly voluntary basis and do not resort to force in order to coerce others" (p. 66). See Institute for Justice, "Economic Liberty" on constitutional court cases. These rights are not limited to citizens but reinforce citizen rights.

13. The early verification procedures were tempered by Citizen Attestation programs that permitted citizens simply to claim citizenships. See "Citizen Attestation Employment Pilot Program." Under its provisions, "an employee

who attests to U.S. Citizenship or nationality ... does not have to present any documentation." "Employers verify employment eligibility only for all newly hired alien employees." See also "U.S. Citizenship Attestation Form," www .cityofomaha.org/planning/hcd/images/stories/attestation%20form.pdf Similar straightforward provisions such as checking previous addresses were considered by Senators for Comprehensive Immigration Reform, but ignored (Yadron, 2013).

14. The term "illegal immigrant" does not imply immunity from the laws. "As James Madison himself argued, those subject to the obligations of our legal system ought to be entitled to its protections: [I]t does not follow, because aliens are not parties to the Constitution, as citizens are parties to it, that whilst they actually conform to it, they have no right to its protection. Aliens are not more parties to the laws, than they are parties to the Constitution; yet it will not be disputed, that as they owe, on one hand, a temporary obedience, they are entitled, in return, to their protection and advantage" (Cole, 2003, 371). The obligation to the laws also explains why birthright citizenship applies to the children of so-called illegals because both are "subject to the jurisdiction thereof" (Fourteenth Amendment).

15. The United States has agreements with over seventy-five countries for "interoperable" data sharing (Harper, 2009). For the expansion of collection of biometric data, including digital photographs for citizens not suspected of crime, see "EPIC Files" (2013) about the FBI's "Next Gen" system for biometrics.

16. Digital photographs as a form of biometrics in the Homeland Security databank can be the source for matching anyone anywhere using facial recognition surveillance technology. Because the digital photo standards are cross-national and the government exchanges information with over seventy-five governments and global organizations, the digital photos can be obtained by foreign and international intelligence services and police agencies.

17. Immigrant and permanent resident employees as well as permanent residents would have to get biometric (based on body measurements like fingerprint scans and digital images) worker identification cards. Another provision requires immigrants and permanent residents to submit additional biometrics to the Homeland Security databank.

18. While sponsors of the Social Security card denied "that this could easily be turned into a national identification system, it is not difficult to imagine this being done in the name of bureaucratic efficiency, national security, or ... to snoop and perhaps to limit mobility" (Houseman, 1979, 17).

19. Public Law 109–103.

20. The Immigration Reform and Control Act of 1986 included a provision for expedited repeal if it could be shown that implementing employers sanction (mandating ID checks) caused "widespread discrimination" in hiring. The GAO reported that about one in five (20 percent) new hires experienced

discriminating yet Congress refused to repeal the law. Workplace regulations need to be implemented in nondiscriminatory ways that also do not undermine citizen's right to employment without identification (Dillin, 1990; Isikoff, 1990; Pear, 1990).

21. See "Citizen Attestation Employment Pilot Program" and "U.S. Citizenship Attestation Form," www.cityofomaha.org/planning/hcd/images/stories/attes tation%20form.pdf.

5. THE RIGHT TO TRAVEL

1. See Magna Carta, 2015, Clause 41.
2. Cited in *Kerry v. Din*, 135 S.Ct. 2128, 2133 (2015) and *Mohamed v. Holder* (2015). Blackstone's *Commentaries on the Law*, 1769.
3. Articles of Confederation, Article IV.
4. Freedom of movement within a country is also internationally recognized as a right. The right to travel is embodied in national constitutions, most pertinently in the Mexican Constitution's (1917) guarantee in Article 11 of the right of "everyone ... to enter and leave the Republic, to travel through its territory and to change his residence without necessity of a letter of security, passport, safe-conduct or any other similar requirement." The German Basic Law (1949), Indian Constitution (1949), Argentinean (1994), Spanish (1978), Romanian (1991), Croatian 1990), Turkish (1982), and South African (1996) constitutions mention the right to move freely within the country. Travel is defined as fundamental by international governmental organizations in international treaties: the American Declaration of the Rights and Duties of Man (ADRD)(1948), adopted by the Ninth International Conference of American States (1948), in *Basic Documents Pertaining to Human Rights in the Inter-American System*, OAS/Ser.L/V/I.4 Rev. 9 (2003), (1949); the Universal Declaration of Human Rights (UDHR) (1948), particularly Article XII, Universal Declaration of Human Rights, G.A. Res. 217A(III), U.N. Doc. A/810 (1948); Convention for the Protection of Human Rights and Fundamental Freedoms (1953), Convention for the Protection of Human Rights and Fundamental Freedoms, September 3, 1953; the Helsinki Act (1975), Conference on Security and Co-operation in Europe Final Act [OSCE Final Act], Helsinki 1975, August 1, 1974, www.osce.org/item/4046.html (to which the US and thirty-five countries are signatories); African Charter on Human and Peoples' Rights, October 21, 1986, and the "International Covenant on Civil and Political Rights (ICCPR)," March 23, 1976, which codifies the Universal Declaration.
5. See Chafee (1956); Schroeder (1975), 117–120; Baker (1975).

6. *Paul v. Virginia*, 75 U.S. 168, 180 (1869). See also Sotomayor (1979). See also her comments at Northwestern Law School on March 7, 2011, distinguishing travel rights for constitutional versus statutory citizenship (see Pat Vaughn Tremmel, 2011). "Long Way Up to Highest Court of the Land" (not discussing the distinction). http://www.northwestern.edu/newscenter/stories/2011/03/sotomayor-trienens-judicial-scholar.html.

7. *U.S. v. Wheeler*, 254 U.S. 294 (1920), as quoted in *Zobel v. Williams* (1982).

8. "Fundamental Rights," (Case Briefs) 2015.

9. *Paul v. Virginia*, 75 U.S. at 180 (1869).

10. *Zobel v. Williams*, 457 U.S. 55 (1982).

11. Article 1, § 8.3 of the U.S. Constitution enumerates the powers of Congress to regulate interstate commerced among Nations, states and tribes.

12. Article I, § 9.6 enumerates the powers of Congress to regulate state ports and prohibit duties.

13. Even before adoption of the Articles, a few of the Chapter Colonies explicitly protected freedom of movement. The Rhode Island Carter gave members of that Colony the right to "passe and repass with freedome, into and through the rest of the English Colonies, upon their lawful and civil occasions." "Massachusetts showed some of the same liberality to foreigners entering the Colony" (*Zobel v. Wiliams*, 1982, 24–25).

14. See also Case Briefs, "Fundamental Rights," 2015: "The right to travel within the United States is guaranteed to all persons by the federal system of government."

15. *Corfield v. Coryell* (1823).

16. U.S. Const. art. IV, § 2.

17. *Corfield*, 552.

18. *Corfield* (citing Articles of Confederation art. IV).

19. *Gibbons v. Ogden*, 22 U.S. 1 (1824).

20. *Beckman*, 3 Paige Ch. 75 (1831). See also Torres, 2012, and Sobel and Torres, 2013, on common carriers.

21. *Beckman v. Sarasotu*, 45.

22. *Beckman*, 75.

23. *The Passenger Cases*, 48 U.S. 283 (1849).

24. Congress may impose taxes on common carriers and ports only if these taxes are regulated and uniform throughout the nation since "all duties, imposts and excises shall be uniform throughout the United States." U.S. Const. art. 2, § 8, cl.1.

25. *The Passenger Cases*, 48 U.S. at 492 (Chief Justice dissenting).

26. *Griswold v. Connecticut*, 381 U.S. 479, 493 (1964) (citing *Snyder v. Massachusetts*, 291 U.S. 97, 105 (1934)).

27. *Crandall v. Nevada*, 73 U.S. 35, 49 (1867).

28. *Crandall*, 35.

29. The court described the tax power as "being in its nature unlimited," and interfering with powers of the federal government. See *Crandall*, at 36, 46–48. The power to tax is the power to destroy. An identification requirement serving as a tax on exercise of a right destroys the right. "Licenses are a mode of taxation upon certain business and occupations" (*Ward v. Maryland*, 1870). See also Friedman (1962, 2002, 149) on registration and identification as taxes.

30. *Crandall v. Nevada*, 49.

31. *Crandall*, 43–44.

32. *Paul*, 75 U.S. 168, 171.

33. *Ward v. Maryland*, 79 U.S. (12 Wall.) 418, 430 (1871).

34. *The Slaughterhouse Cases*, 83 U.S. 36, 79 (1873).

35. *Ibid.*, at 75.

36. Reaffirmed in *Ward v. Maryland*, 79 U.S. 418 (1870) and *Hoxie v. New York, N.H. & H.R. Co.*, 82 Conn. 352 (1909).

37. *Williams v. Fears*, 179 U.S. 270 (1900), quoted in *Schactman v. Dulles*, 925 F. 2d. 938 (1955). See also on "freedom of locomotion," *Papachristou v. City of Jacksonville*, 405 U.S. 154, 164 (1972).

38. *Buck v. Kuykendall*, 267 U.S. 307 (1925)

39. See, e.g., *United States v. Guest*, 383 U.S. 745, 759 n. 17 (1966); *Kent*, 257 U.S. 125 (1958).

40. *Edwards v. California*, 314 U.S. 160 (1941).

41. *Kent v. Dulles*, 357 U.S. 116, 125 (1958); *Zemel v. Rusk*, 381 U.S. 1, 15 (1965). See Chafee (1956), 171–181, on "how deeply engrained in our history this freedom of movement is … Our nation has thrived on the principle that … every American is left to … go where he pleases."

42. *Kent*, 128–129.

43. *Aptheker v. Secretary of State* 508, 517 (1964). Quoting *NAACP v. Alabama*, 371 U.S. 307 (1964).

44. *Zemel v. Rusk*, 381 U.S. 1, 15 (1965)

45. *Guest*, 383 U.S. 745, 758 (1966). *Ibid.*, 757.

46. *Guest*, 757–758. See also *Haig v. Agee*, 453 U.S. 280, 306–307 (1981) on the right to interstate travel as "virtually unqualified."

47. *Shapiro*, 394 U.S. 618 (1969).

48. *Shapiro*, 629.

49. *Shapiro*, 630–631.

50. *Guest*, 745; *Dunn v. Blumstein* 405 U.S. 330, 338 (1972) (striking down a residency requirement restricting voting rights).

51. See, e.g., *Zobel v. Williams*, 455 U.S. 55 (1982) 185; Note, Hastings, 1975, 858–859 (1975); Schroeder 1975, 117, 119–120, n. 14 (1975); Baker 1975, 1129, 1130, n. 7 (1975).

52. *Shapiro*, 618, 630.

53. *Saenz v. Roe*, 526 U.S. 498, 500 (1999).

54. *Saenz*, 490.
55. *Kerry v. Din*, 135 S. Ct., 2128, 2123 (2015), from Blackstone, 1769, Plurality Opinion, cited in *Mohamed v. Holder* (2015).
56. U.S. Const., art. I, § 8, cl. 3. Farber, 1981, 263–287.
57. President Woodrow Wilson would not abridge American citizens' rights to travel and engage in commerce, even during wartime. Responding to Sen. W. J. Stone suggesting that "this government tak[e] definite steps toward preventing American citizens from embarking upon armed merchant vessels," Wilson wrote, "... I cannot consent to any abridgement of the rights of American citizens in any respect ... To forbid our people to exercise their rights for fear we might be called upon to vindicate them would be a deep humiliation indeed." "President Wilson's Letter," 1916.
58. *Guest*, 757.
59. "Congress can set the regulations, conditions, or prohibitions regarding the permissibility of interstate travel or shipments if the law does not contravene a specific constitutional guarantee" (Nowark and Rotunda, 1991; 2007).
60. Urofsky, 2009, 561–562. Coauthor of "The Right to Privacy," in *Harvard Law Review*. 1890 and the privacy dissent in *Olmstead* (1928), Justice Louis Brandeis held in *Buck v. Kuykendall* (1925) that "the right to travel interstate ... may be a privilege or immunity of citizens of the United States."
61. Associate Justice Ruth Bader Ginsburg responding in a public discussion to a question by Dr. Richard Sobel, Northwestern University, September 15, 2009. "A Conversation with Justice Ruth Bader Ginsburg." C-SPAN Video Library.
62. Urofksy, 1985, 320.
63. See Roots (2005, 30) discussing the right to drive; see also Manheim, 2005 (noting that due to constitutional right to travel questions and strong protests, drivers were initially neither required to get license plates containing numbers for automobiles nor to obtain licenses to drive them). See also www.lawfulpath.com/ref/DLbrief.shtml.
64. *Lawson* (1981) 1367–1368. See also Machlin (1990).
65. They are embedded in Walt Whitman's writings, especially in his "Song of the Open Road." They are reflected, too, in the spirit of Vachel Lindsay's "I Want to Go Wandering," and by Henry D. Thoreau. *Lawson v. Kolender*, 658 F.2d 1362, 1368 (1981) from *Papachristou v. City of Jacksonville*, 405 U.S. 156, 164 (1972).
66. *Ibid.*
67. *Buck v. Kuykendall*, 267 U.S. 307 (1925).
68. See, e.g., *Boyd v. United States*, 116 U.S. 622–623 (1886) (recognizing that a search and seizure was equivalent to a compulsory production of a man's private papers and was unreasonable within the meaning of the Fourth Amendment).
69. See, e.g., *Griswold v. Connecticut*, 381 U.S. 479 (1964) Sobel et al, 2013.

70. Nowak and Rotunda, 1983, 734–735 ("the oldest constitutional right to privacy is that protected by the Fourth Amendment's restriction on governmental searches and seizures"); see generally Sobel, Horwitz, and Jenkins, 2013.

71. *Meyer v. Nebraska*, 262 U.S. 402–403 (1923) (using the right to privacy to protect the freedom of schools to teach subjects in languages other than English); see *Pierce v. Society of Sisters*, 282 U.S. 534–535 (1925) (using the right to privacy to protect parents' decision to have their children attend private schools); see, e.g., *Lawrence v. Texas*, 539 U.S. 558 (2003); see, e.g., *Village of Belle Terre v. Boraas*, 416 U.S. 1 (1974) (to protect the intimate and family lives of citizens).

72. *Griswold*, 410 U.S. 483; see *Roe v. Wade*, 153 (1973); see also *Planned Parenthood v. Casey*, 505 U.S. 851 (1982) (upholding the bodily autonomy of individuals); see also Oral Argument Transcript at 43, *National Federation of Independent Business. v. Sebelius*, 132 U.S. 2566 (March 27, 2012) (referencing "means of travel").

73. See *Roe v. Wade*, 410 U.S. 113 (1973) (Douglas, J., concurring). *Doe v. Bolton*, 410 U.S. 209, 1973 (Douglas, J., concurring).

74. *Kent v. Dulles*, 357 U.S. 116, 125–126 (1958); *Shapiro v. Thompson*, 394 U.S. 629 (1969). *Kent* and *Shapiro* established that the right to travel must be free from government interference, thus associating the right to privacy with the exercise of the right to travel. *Kent*, 125–126; *Shapiro*, at 629.

75. *Kolender v. Lawson*, 461, 353–354 (1983), and *Hiibel* 542 U.S. 177 (2004), See also Chapter 3, note 30, for dissent dicta about the right not to be identified.

76. *Kolender*, 353–354.

77. *Kolender*, 353. See note 82 on *Lawson* defining, "Credible and reliable" as "reasonable assurance"; it is "authentic" "for later getting in touch with the person." It gives as an example "that a jogger, who was not carrying identification, could ... be required to answer a series of questions concerning the route that he followed to arrive at the place where the officers detained him," by "simply by reciting his name and address."

78. *Lawson*, 1362 (1981).

79. *Lawson*, 1367. See also Machlin (1990).

80. *Lawson*, 1367–1368.

81. *Kolender*, 353–354.

82. *Hiibel*, 185 (2004). For *Hiibel* as opposed to *Kolender* to apply, a state must have a stop-and-identify law, and there must be reasonable suspicion of a crime. See also Machlin (1990) on the failings of reasonable suspicion as a substitute for probable cause.

83. *Hiibel*, at 177. See also *Delaware v. Prouse* 440 U.S. 648 (1979) where the Court held that "citizens were not shorn of their fourth amendment right of

liberty merely because they 'stepped from the sidewalk to their automobile'"
(Machlin, 1990, 1263).
84. *Hiibel*, 185.
85. *Gomez v. Turner*, 672 F.2d 134, 143 n.18 (D.C. Cir. 1982).
86. See *John Doe No. 1 v. Ga. Dep't of Pub. Safety*, 147 F. Supp. 1369, 1375 (2001).
87. See generally *Monarch Travel Service, Inc. v. Association Cultural Clubs, Inc.*, 44 F. 2d. 552 (1972).
88. The court only mentioned that limitations on travel derived from *lack of personal wealth*. *Ibid.*, 554; see generally *Harris v. McRae*, 448 U.S. 297 (1980) (establishing a similar economic argument as *Monarch* that the government does not have to allocate funds or resources to facilitate the exercise of certain rights). See *Gilmore* (2006).
89. *Miller v. Reed*, 176 F.3d. 1204 (1999).
90. *Ibid.*, 1205.
91. *Ibid.*, 1206. Miller could still use his personal vehicle, but could not legally drive it, since he had no license (indicating the required skills to do so). He could, however, have someone else drive his vehicle for him. Miller could also ride public transit or other modes of transportation. *Ibid.*; see Roots, 245 (2005) (discussing the right to drive); and Manheim, 2005 (noting that due to constitutional right to travel and strong protests, drivers were initially neither required to get license plates containing numbers for automobiles nor to obtain licenses to drive them).
92. See *Shapiro v. Thompson*, 394 U.S. 618, 638 (1969).
93. See 49 U.S.C. § 40101, § 40103.
94. *Beckman v. Saratoga & Schenectady R.R., Co.*, 3 Paige 45, 75 (1831).
95. Some cities within Alaska, for instance, the capital Juneau, are only accessible by air or sea, air being the only timely mode. Intrastate travel in some states is more convenient by air for travel between cities within a state separated by great distances and/or natural barriers, e.g., California, Florida, Illinois, New York, and Texas.
96. *United States v. Kroll*, 481 F.2d, 884, 886 (1973).
97. *United States v. Alvarado*, 495 F.2d 795, 806 (1974). However, in *Town of Southold v. Town of East Hampton*, the Second Circuit stated that travelers do not have "a constitutional right to the most convenient way of travel" and that minor restrictions do not abridge the right to travel. 54 (2007) (referencing *City of Houston v. F.A.A.*, 674 F.2d. 1184, 1198 (1982)). This decision conflicts with *Kroll* and *Alvarado*, and with the right of citizens to enjoy the benefits and access to all public transportation modes.
98. See *Latif v. Holder*, No. 3:10-cv-750, 2013 WL 4592515, at p. 8 (D. Or. August. 28, 2013) (noting that flight is often the only feasible form of international travel); *Ibrahim v. Department of Homeland Security*, 2012, p. 7.

99. *Mohamed v. Holder*, 955 F.2d 520, 2014, 12–13. See also *Latif v. Holder* (No. 3:10-cv-750, 2013) (noting that flight is often the only feasible form of international travel) and *Ibrahim v. Dept. of Homeland Security*, 2012, at 7.

100. Papers, Please (2006). August 16, 2006 and *Gilmore v. Gonzales* (2006).

101. For example, Common Carrier passenger ship service does not exist between the continental United States and Puerto Rico. See *Tourist Information*, Welcome to Puerto Rico, www.topuertorico.org/tinfo.shtml (last accessed May 26, 2014). The Passenger Vessel Services Act of 1886 established that passenger transport within the United States could only be carried out on a US registered vessel. This would make any common-carrier scheduled ship passenger service expensive, unprofitable, and therefore nonexistent (46 App. U.S.C. §289 (2006)). For Puerto Rico, see the section pertaining to the transportation of passengers between Puerto Rico and other US ports; foreign-flag vessels; unavailability of US flag service (46 App. U.S.C. § 289c (2006)). This section authorizes passenger service between the contiguous United States and Puerto Rico under certain conditions. This allows cruise ship services to stop in Puerto Rico when traveling directly between US territories. *Ibid*. But this does not constitute common carrier passenger ship service between the contiguous United States and Puerto Rico. *Ibid*. Hence, cruise ships do not provide service between noncontiguous parts of the United States, since their business purpose and schedule are not intended for point-to-point passenger and freight transportation. *Ibid*.

102. *Mohamed*, 2014, 6.

103. Air travel has allowed Congress to remain in session more days throughout the year and for members to return home for every recess and even weekly. Jillson, (2009), 234.

104. The "single mode doctrine" also conflicts with federal law requiring that modes of transportation be accessible. The federal government mandates that most public buildings, including airports and train stations, be accessible to people with disabilities. See 49 U.S.C. § 40101 (2006) (addressing handicap accessibility); *ibid.*, at § 41705 (addressing discrimination laws); see also *ibid.*, at § 4151–4157. Similarly, federal law ensures that citizens living in remote areas are entitled to subsidized scheduled air service. A regular, subsidized minimum air service is maintained to many small communities in the United States. Papers, Please!, "Mocek" (last accessed May 25, 2014).

105. While the focus here is on domestic travel, the citizenship rights to travel encompass the ability of citizens to leave the United States and not to be deported or forced into exile. In short, it is a right against coerced travel or immobility regarding any part of the United States. As the right to remain silent is part of freedom of speech, the right not to be coerced to move (or to be kept within the United States) is part of the right to travel. See Chapters 2 and 5, note 4 on American citizen international travel rights.

106. Schneier, 2008. See also www.tsa.gov/press/happenings/enhance_id_require
     ments.shtm, November 2015 (no longer on the TSA site).
107. Schneier, 2008 (emphasis added). Like prohibition against refusing to
     provide voter identification because of principled opposition to require-
     ments to produce government ID to vote (and proposing it as a "reasonable
     impediment" to getting an ID) *South Carolina v. Holder*, fn 5. p. 10, holds
     that "statements simply denigrating the law – such as, 'I don't want to' –
     need not be accepted." Penalizing travelers who assert their right to travel
     without identification violates the free speech and travel rights of American
     citizens and others. (See Solove, 2008, on how the TSA rule prevents
     people with conscientious objections to presenting identification from
     flying.)
108. See also *United States v. Graham*, 846 F.Supp. 384 (2012) on the privacy
     rights in locational mobility. See also note 145. The Obama administration
     proposed connecting placement on the No-Fly List with the background
     checks for buying guns. House Speaker Paul Ryan (R-Wis.) criticized the
     idea as a "halfhearted attempt to defend and distract from a failing policy."
     Ryan said government officials put people on terrorism watch lists without
     any due legal process, so denying those listed the right to bear arms would
     violate their rights. He said that if someone is suspected of plotting an
     attack, law enforcement officials should arrest him. See Bacon, 2015. See
     also note 38 in Chapter 2 here on militia and bearing arms.
109. The following section is based on the description and analysis in Papers
     Please (2015).
110. Because date of birth and gender are personal data not needed unless there
     is the rare occurrence of a name's match, the airlines and privacy advocated
     propose that birthdate and gender not be routinely collected. They were
     ignored in the Regulation comments and in a petition afterwards. See
     Cyber Privacy Project et al., Petition to the TSA, November 1, 2010.
111. TSA, "Identification," and FAQs, 2015. "Alternate Acceptable" forms of
     identification include "US Passport" to "travel domestically." The idea
     that a passport, meant for international travel has to be used in order to
     "travel domestically," inverts the purpose of a broad union, where citizens
     may among their privileges and immunities travel without passports. See
     Justice Ginsburg's statement that "[t]here is a right to travel ... We have had
     a common market in that respect from the very beginning. You can go from
     one state to another without any passport." See note 61. See Storm, 2014.
112. TSA, "Frequently Asked Questions," visited February 9, 2016. www.tsa
     .gov/travel/frequently-asked-questions#realid. In addition, if you "Forgot
     Your ID?" "In the event you arrive at the airport without valid identifica-
     tion, because it is lost or at home, you may still be allowed to fly. The TSA
     officer may ask you to complete a form to include your name and current
     address, and may ask additional questions to confirm your identity. If your

identity is confirmed, you will be allowed to enter the screening checkpoint. You may be subject to additional screening. You will not be allowed to fly if your identity cannot be confirmed, you chose to not provide proper identification or you decline to cooperate with the identity verification process" (TSA, "Identification"). See also notes 127 and 129.

113. See articles on TSA mass searches at train and bus stations, and Amtrak and bus ID requirements. Schneier, 2008, Quraishi, 2011, Patterson, 2012, Amtrak, "Passenger Identification," 2015.

114. Southwest Airline's motto used to be "You are free to move around the country." JetBlue has recently advertised in subways its "Flights for Your Rights."

115. Houseman, 1979, 86.

116. See Sobel (2005a), on licenses and passes to travel. Especially, since a Hungarian soldier asked for my papers on a train during the 1980s before the end of the Communist government, travel credentials have seemed a detrimental idea.

117. For background on subway bag searches, see Jafarzadeh and Timmins, 2011; Maya, 2014; Briscoe and Meisner, 2014; Baker, 2007.

118. Sobel, 2005a. A coalition of conservatives and liberals opposed similar proposals. *The New York Times* (May 5, 2005), and *Wall Street Journal* (October 10, 2006), editorialized against the REAL ID bill as "sneaky business" and "irresponsibility."

119. *United States v. Davis*, 482 F.2d. 913 (1973); see also *United States v. Kroll*, 485 F.2d. 886 (1973).

120. The travel right also includes the right to movement on common carriers. "A carrier becomes a common carrier when it 'holds itself out' to the public, or to a segment of the public, as willing to furnish transportation within the limits of its facilities to any person who wants it." See Torres (2012) and Brennan (1986). US government exercises national jurisdiction over its territory and "in-flight" aircraft, even outside national airspace. Thus, travel conducted between contiguous and noncontiguous United States by air remains within national jurisdiction. And regulation must follow US federal law, rules, and Constitution, and specific rights and privileges of citizenship. Accordingly, the expansiveness of the jurisdiction empowers citizens to exercise broadly their right to travel. This is applicable when travel adheres to the US Code for the mode of transportation, including on common carriers by ground or water.

121. *Shapiro v. Thompson*, 630–631 (1969) (overruled in parts unrelated to the right to travel by *Edema v. Jordan*, 415 U.S. 651 (1974); see also *Edema v. Jordan*).

122. *United States v. Guest*, 383 U.S. 745, 757 (1966).

123. *Gilmore v. Gonzales*, 435 F.3d 1125, 1136–1137(9th Cir. 2006).

124. *Gilmore*, 1155.

125. *Gilmore*, Section III on "The Right to Travel."

126. See *State of New Mexico v. Phillip Mocek* (2011), papersplease.org, www
     .papersplease.org/wp/mocek/ (last accessed May 25, 2014); see also *Mocek v.
     City of Albuquerque*, 2013 WL 312881 (D.N.M. January 14, 2013).
127. Mocek transcript, January 14, 2013, at 10:15.
128. See Update to the U.N. Human Rights Committee (2014), available at
     http://papersplease.org/wp/wp-content/uploads/2014/02/idp-iccpr-update-
     travel.pdf (Identity project stating to the U.N. Human Rights Committee
     that the United States violates the right to travel). TSA is required by federal
     law (49 USC § 40101) to consider this right when it issues regulations. *State
     of New Mexico v. Phillip Mocek*, papersplease.org (last accessed May 25,
     2014), PP. See *Green v. TSA* (2005), *Bey v. TSA* (2013), and *Bey v. DHS-
     TSA (2015)* for more recent challenges to the air identification requirement.
129. The TSA has variously indicated and removed alternatives to official gov-
     ernment ID in order to travel. Under "Forgot Your ID?" it noted, "In the
     event you arrive at the airport without proper ID, because it is lost or at home,
     you may still be allowed to fly. TSA officers will request you present two
     other forms of ID bearing your name. One of the items must bear your name
     and other identifying information such as photo, address, phone number,
     social security number. There is no standard list of what alternative forms of
     ID are acceptable. Examples include: temporary paper driver's licenses,
     non-driver IDs, social security cards, birth certificates, marriage licenses,
     business cards and credit cards. You may also be asked to provide additional
     information. TSA has other ways to confirm your identity, like using publicly
     available databases, so you can reach your flight. If your identity cannot be
     verified, you will not be allowed to enter the screening checkpoint." www.tsa
     .gov/travel/security-screening identification (last accessed November 25,
     2015). See also note 112.
130. ACLU, 2014.
131. See Sobel and Torres, 2013, and Sobel, 2014, on the privacy intrusions
     of nude body scanners and intrusive searches. Alternative approaches
     in technologies such as explosive detections in swabbing procedures,
     puffer machines, and metal detectors make the current intrusions
     unnecessary.
132. See *Latif v. Holder*, No. 3:10-cv-750, 2013 WL 4592515, p. 8 (D. Or.
     August 28, 2013) (noting that flight is often the only feasible form of inter-
     national travel); *Ibrahim v. Department of Homeland Security*, 2012, at p. 7.
133. *Mohamed v. Holder*, 2014, 528.
134. *Mohamed v. Holder*, 2014, 528.
135. *Mohamed*, 537.
136. *Mohamed v. Holder* (1:11-cv-50, AJT/MSN), July 16, 2015.
137. Because inclusion on the No-Fly List harms liberty interests in travel and
     reputation, due process requires the government to provide them an

explanation and a hearing to correct the mistakes that led to their inclusion. See ACLU, 2015.

138. *Corbett v. U.S.* Motion (May 27, 2011) held that TSA procedures are "the most radical, expansive, intrusive and invasive administrative search that the federal government has ever attempted to impose on the general public absent any sort of suspicion whatsoever" (4). It complains that the procedure "constituted sexual assault [by the government of the United States], on a scale of ... tens of thousands of individuals per day" (1, 9). It is also questionable how effective the most intrusive security procedures are since the GAO concluded that the nude scanners would likely not have caught the Detroit terrorist (GAO Report, 2005). Even the non-x-ray scanners are objectionable for the submissive posture they require of all travelers to take and the likelihood of missing some concealed objects.

139. Corbett's Complaint for Violation of the Fourth Amendment notes that "The TSA has many other effective and less invasive options available to it, including ... metal detectors (both freestanding and hand wands), standard pat downs, explosive trace detection (both via swabs and via 'puffer machines'), explosive sniffing dogs, behavior analysis, traveler databases (including the no-fly list), intelligence gathering and others" (No. 23). In short, there are constitutional technological alternatives to unconstitutional intrusions.

140. See *Frank vs. State of MD*, 359 U.S. 360, 365, 1959; compare, e.g., *FTC v. Am. Tobacco Co.*, 264 U.S. 298 (1924); *Boyd v. United States*, 616 (1886); *I. C.C. v. Brinson*, 447 (1894); *Tropicana v. United States*, 789 F.Supp. 1154 (1992).

141. *U.S. v. Graham*, 846 F, Supp 384 (2012).

142. At the same time, a dozen states are offering driver's licenses without Social Security numbers to undocumented immigrations.

143. *Jensen v. Quaring*, 1985. See also *Beach v. Oklahoma* (114, 126) (2016) for a case against requiring digital photographs on licenses as a violation of religious freedom.

144. See Martin Anderson, 1988, and Analisse Anderson, 1986. The Mark of the Beast biblical reference from *Revelation* 13: 16–18 was responding to Martin Anderson's comment at the cabinet meeting that "All we have to do is tattoo an identification number on the inside of everybody's arm." To this Reagan, recognizing the Biblical Reference to Revelation, joked that "maybe we should just brand all the babies," and, as Martin Anderson noted, "that was the end of the national identification card for 1981" (M. Anderson, 1988, 276). See also Lerner (2013, 2015) on the religious significance of biometrics.

145. Because sophisticated and pervasive national identification systems and movement controls from internal passports have not stopped terrorism in Russia or China, or even recently in France and Germany, other countries'

experiences with ID systems should warn those here citing anti-terrorism as a justification for imposing a foreign-style national identification schemes like REAL ID for air travel on the U.S. that it will not make us safer, only less free. The meaning and lesson for America is to dismantle and repeal E-Verify and REAL ID before they ultimately undermines US citizenship and its rights.

6. THREATS TO CITIZENSHIP RIGHTS IN IDENTIFICATION REGIMES

1. The "ideal republican government" would be constructed through what Madison called "filtration." "Ordinary voters would elect local representation, who would elect the next tier of representatives and so on up the political ladder in a process of refinement that left the leaders at the top connected only distantly with the original electorate and therefore free to make decisions that might be unpopular. A republic under this filtration scheme was a political framework with a democratic base and a hierarchical superstructure" (86).
2. Twight (2002, 185) (quoting Richard Sobel). See also Sobel (1998).
3. Requiring proof of citizenship to receive social welfare benefits such as Medicaid or Social Security for citizens also removes the presumptions of citizenship, (see *Bell v. Leavitt*, 2007).
4. As if they did not have the right in the first place, citizens cease to have a right if they are required first to provide identification, and can only then proceed once the interfering identification demand is met. This prior restraint on exercising a basic occupational right of citizens constructively severs citizenship from taking employment. These disenfranchising transformations instantly turn citizens into stateless persons without rights. As *Elrod* noted, even a momentary suspension of rights is irredeemable harm. "The deprivation of a constitutional right, even for a brief period of time, amounts to an irreparable injury." See *Elrod v. Burns* (1976) (plurality opinion). ("The loss of First Amendment freedom, for even minimal periods of time, unquestionably constitutes irreparable injury.") *North Carolina NAACP v. McCrory*, 2015.
5. See, e.g., Gates, 1998, xx–xxi, 207–208.
6. Sobel, 2002a.
7. See Stolberg, 1998, 23 (quoting Richard Sobel); see also 142 *Congressional Record*, §3328–04 (1996) (statement of Sen. Abraham noting that IIRIRA and a pilot program for checking work eligibility against a national databank set "in place the infrastructure necessary for a mandatory national system and establishes the principle that companies should gain Government approval before hiring any employee").

8. See also how the privileges and immunities clause of the US Constitution protects rights that "belong … to the citizens of all free governments" (Shankman and Pilon, 1998, 8).

9. In this sense, the individual becomes property of the state. The card and associated records are declared government property. "Forcing people into carrying a national ID card tells them effectively: 'You belong to the state. You only exist when the government says you do.' It is utterly antithetical to the founding principles of the American republic" (*Santa Ana Register* editorial, July 14, 1994). Many private and public identification cards say they are "property of" the corporation or governmental unit, essentially arrogating to the entity the identities and rights of the persons, including citizens. This includes government identification cards saying "Property of the U.S. Government," making personal identity and rights government property.

10. See discussion of Chinese *hukou* and Russian *propiska* household registration systems in Chapter 7.

11. See *League of Women Voters of Wisconsin v. Walker* (2014); *Frank v. Walker* (2014), Posner, "On Suggestion of Rehearing En Banc," 2014, 19, 21.

12. See US Const., Art. IV, § 2 on "the citizens of each state shall be entitled to all privileges and immunities of citizens in the several states." See also US Constitution Fourteenth Amendment, § 2, that "[n]o State shall make or enforce any law which shall abridge the privileges or immunities of the citizens of the United States."

13. In a study conducted in 1978–1979, 72 percent of the public felt the police should not have the right to stop people on the street to demand identification if the person was not doing anything illegal. See Harris and Westin (1981, 70).

14. See Sobel, 2001, and Chapter 6 here, for a critique of the idea of national identification as constitutionally infirm, especially under Amendments III–V, XIII–XV. See generally Amar, 1999.

15. See 45 C.F.R. § 164.512 (2001).

16. See The Uniting and Strengthening America by providing Appropriate Tools Required to Intercept and Obstruct Terrorism (USA PATRIOT Act) Act of 2001, Pub. L. No. 107–156, 115 Stat. 272 (2001) [USA PATRIOT Act]; see also Amy Pagnozzi, "Uncloaking a Fleecing of Rights", *Hartford Courant*, January 15, 2002, BI.

17. *Olmstead v. United States*, 478 (1928) (Brandeis, J., dissenting) (warning about beneficent government actions).

18. See Warren and Brandeis (1890); see also R. E. Smith, 1997.

19. R. E. Smith, 1997, 58; see also *United States v. White*, 790 (1971) (Harlan, J., dissenting) ("[A]n ordinary citizen … may carry on his private discourse freely, openly, and spontaneously without measuring his every word.").

20. See Suro (1999, A2) (on Chief Justice Rehnquist's concerns about expansion of state responsibilities into the federal realm); see also Rehnquist (1999), available at www.uscourts.gov/ttb/jan99ttb/january1999.html ("The trend to

federalize crimes that traditionally have been handled by the state courts...
threatens to change entirely the nature of our federal system.").

21. See Department of Homeland Security (2015), Meyers (2014), National
    Center of State Legislatures (2016).

22. Section 12(a) of the Illinois Right to Privacy in the Workplace Act prohibited
    Illinois employers from using E-Verify to verify the work authorization of
    employees. The US Department of Homeland Security sued to prevent the
    law from taking effect as scheduled on January 1, 2008. On March 12, 2009, the
    US District Court for the Central District of Illinois ruled the Illinois law invalid
    under the Supremacy Clause to the US Constitution because it conflicts with
    the federal Illegal Immigration Reform and Immigrant Responsibility Act
    (IIRIRA). *United States v. Illinois* (No. 07–3261, C.D. Ill., 2009). As a rule,
    E-Verify is not required in Illinois. In fact, Illinois is the only state that has tried
    to block the use of E-Verify by private employers. Concerned about inaccura-
    cies in the E-Verify data kept by the federal government as well as ongoing
    privacy implications for workers, the Illinois legislature enacted a law in 2007
    that would have prohibited private employers from using E-Verify until the
    federal government made specific improvements to the system. While the
    provision of the Illinois law prohibiting employers from using E-Verify was
    struck down, the rest of the statute survived. An amended version of the law was
    enacted in August 2009, and went into effect on January 1, 2010 [820ILC255/
    1]. Under the new law, which amends the Illinois Right to Privacy in the
    Workplace Act, Illinois employers are required to sign a sworn attestation either
    upon initial enrollment in E-Verify or by January 31, 2010, if they are already
    enrolled in the program, Alexandra (2008). "Notice for Illinois Employers
    about E-Verify." United States Department of Homeland Security. October
    6, 2008. "E-Verify again eligibility verification option for Illinois employers."
    Retrieved December 26, 2009. "New Illinois E-Verify Law Takes Effect on
    January 1, 2010: Special Illinois Procedures Required." Retrieved July 7, 2012.

23. For examples of how a system like employment verification could expand well
    beyond its initial mission, see Stravato, 2013. See also the expansion of the
    New Hires database to include parents owing child support. See Cochrane
    (2013) on how the "monster lurking" in the CIR bill would consist in system
    of universal E-Verification magnifying government intrusion.

24. See Hawkins (2001, 56); Banisar, 2001, 1; and Fried, 2000, 1 for reports on
    the failings of new technologies such as biometrics.

25. See Lowry, 2002, 32; Armstrong and Pereira, 2001, 1.

26. A national identification card would not solve problems of terrorism (or illegal
    immigration). First-time or unknown terrorists can get false IDs or travel on
    foreign passports that do not tie into domestic databanks because, as Schneier
    notes, there is no "preexisting database of bad guys" (2001, 284–285). For
    instance, the 9/11 terrorists entered on foreign passports, and using passports,
    for instance, to fly would be unaffected by a US national identification system.

Relatively few terrorists are on intelligence watch lists, and many of the names that appear there are approximated or misspelled (Schneier, 285). It does not follow that 325 million American citizens should have to carry identity cards in order to try to find a few terrorists or undocumented immigrants.

27. For a discussion of Americans' preferences in fighting terrorism, see Sobel et al., 1999 and Sobel, 2001, 1. See R. E. Smith, 2001. See also Pickel, 2002, 6A. The implementation of better foreign policy, developing international coalitions, improving the collection of external intelligence, and undermining of terror abroad to remove the funding, bases, and perpetrators of terrorism develop better national and international security.

28. Most perpetrators with destructive devices can forge documents or choose not to travel on a plane they have put in jeopardy. The few choosing to martyr themselves are better prevented through physical protections like metal detectors, reinforced cockpit doors, air marshals, trained crews, baggage prescreening, inflight security procedures, and an alert flying public that can protect against hijacking without treating citizens as suspects or denying them the right to travel. Integrating watch lists for law enforcement at border crossings or abroad would do a better job at keeping people out of the country than trying to keep them off airplanes through facial recognition or identification technologies. Bag matching and complete baggage screening increase air safety without undermining individual rights. See Sobel, 2002a, and R.E. Smith, 2001, 5. See also Pickel, 2002, 6A; Sobel and R.E. Smith, 2010, and Sobel 2010a.

29. For instance, where courts held unconstitutional attempts by local communities to require service workers to carry identification cards, see *Wallace v. Palm Beach* (1985) and *Service Machine & Shipbuilding Corp. v. Edwards* (1980). The pattern to substitute driver's license numbers for Social Security Numbers was first recognized around 2003 when trying to use an American Express Card in American Express Office to get foreign currency for travel and the employee's refusing to provide money without a Driver's License number.

30. Mark Lerner, Personal Communication, February 18, 2016.

31. An amusing example of ID creep appeared in a VISA commercial in 1997, where everyone greets former Senator and 1996 presidential candidate Bob Dole (R-KA) by name in his Kansas hometown until he wanted to pay for lunch with a check, and then they wanted to "see some ID." www.youtube.com/watch?v=6JScNmad-Vg

7. OTHER COUNTRIES' SYSTEMS CONSTITUTE WARNINGS

1. In relationship to citizenship in the United States, other countries may have stronger rights and naturalization rules.

2. See note 45 on how the derivative Rwandan identification régime abetted genocide by permitting discrimination between Hutus and Tutsis.

3. See "Controle et verification d'identite pour toute information." vosdroits. service-public.fr/arbo/210109-nxpap110.html.

4. "Elections are held regularly, and government commissioned public opinion polls are taken frequently, but it is a common assumption that French public opinion has little effect on French foreign policy." Howard and Howard, in Sobel and Shiraev, 2003, 107. This might be summarized as "Au dessus de tout il y a la raison de l'Etat': Above all, the State is right."

5. Speech to the members of the Council of State, 28 January 1960, quoted by Tricot, 1972. DeGaulle is also reputed to have said, "La France ne se trompe jamais. Ce sont les Francais qui se trompent": "France is never mistaken. It is the French who are mistaken."

6. "A National ID Card?", 1986, Recent experiences with terrorism have led to proposed constitutional changes permitting the state to remove citizenship from dual citizens convicted of terrorists acts (Meichtry and Bisserbe, 2015; Horobin, 2016, 4). See also, "A National Identity Card?", 1990; and "A Real Bad ID," 2006.

7. Agar, 2001, 116.

8. *Ibid.*

9. See R.E. Smith (2002, 6) on the British High Court decision against national IDs.

10. Joint Committee on Human Rights of the House of Lords and House of Commons January 26, 2005, found the identification bill violated key provisions of the European Convention on Human Rights (ECHR). It conflicts with "compatibility of provisions of the Bill with the right to respect of private life under Article 8 of the European Convention on Human Rights (ECHR) and the right to non-discrimination in the protection of the Convention rights under Article 14 ECHR" (3). Its requirement for registration and "designated documents" would "render registration and identification cards compulsory for people who hold these documents, with the potential for arbitrary and disproportionate interference with Article 8, and for discrimination against Article 14" (2).

11. Privacy International (2004) finds "Almost no empirical research has been undertaken to clearly establish how identity tokens can be used as a means of preventing terrorism" (1). The PI report demonstrates (6) the lack of connection between national identification cards and terrorism prevention: "Of the 25 countries that have been most adversely affected by terrorism since 1986, eighty percent have national identity cards, one third of which incorporate biometrics. This research was unable to uncover any instance where the presence of an identity card system in those countries was seen as a significant deterrent to terrorist activity" (2).

12. *Willcock v. Muckle*, 49 LGR 584 (1951).

13. *Willcock*, 49 LGR 584.

14. A May 2004 YouGov poll for Privacy International found one in six Britons would participate in a civil disobedience against the national identification plan, and 6 percent would go to prison rather than register for the card (Privacy International, "A Nation Divided").

15. Sobel, "Review," 2005b. Whitehead, July 1, 2009.

16. Requiring the carrying of national IDs should be limited to terrorists and politicians who support governmental identification systems. If needed, different IDs can be tailored for limited and specific purposes. See chapter below on the impossibilities of democratic IDs.

17. The alleged justifications in fraud and terrorism prevention in the United Kingdom (or US) are unproven (see note 11 here). That a card was justified as "timely," since British passports began containing biometric data to meet the "International Civil Aviation Organization," (ICAO) requires it, places the mandate of an unaccountable quasi-private organization over British citizens. Privacy International (2004) and the ACLU opposed this biometric passport plan as a widespread invasion of private information by "capturing" and disseminating intimate personal characteristics and biometric "data" internationally for unproven "security" purposes.

18. For discussion of opposition to the Australia card, see Privacy International, 1987, and Johnston, 2006.

19. Privacy International website www.pi.org, in R.E. Smith, 2002, 41.

20. In 2001, Malaysia, of which Singapore was a part until the middle 1960s, when both became independent of Britain, which had imposed an earlier identification system, introduced in 2001 the "Mykad," "which electronically wraps identity, digital thumbprints and personal details into a compulsory piece of plastic the size of a credit card." Mykad is "basically a microcomputer. The key features are an intelligent circuit chip, biometrics and encryption technology. It uses two biometric measures of individuals' physical characteristics to authenticate identity, the face and fingerprints. Apart from the name and address of the cardholder, all other data can only be accessed through a card reader available only to enforcement officers. Every Malaysian citizen over the age of 12 carried a paper identity card containing their thumbprints long before the smart card existed" (Ng, 2001).

21. Federal Research Division, 1989.

22. *Ibid.*, 177, 185, 197.

23. *Ibid.*, 197, 262, xvi, xxiii.

24. "Keeping records of speakers," *The Straits Times*, May 9, 2000.

25. "Patients' database planned," *The Straits Times*, August 17, 1999.

26. Freedom House website, www.freedomhouse.org/ratings/index.htm, 2002 rated Singapore at 5.5, at the dividing point between "partly free" and "not free."

27. Singapore Immigration and Checkpoint Authority, www.sir.gov.sg/citi zen_sc/icregn-01.html. http://www.ica.gov.sg/.
28. Singaporeans also may carry an Immigration Automated Clearance System (IACS) Access Card for checkpoints by harnessing biometrics and smart card technologies. The Access Card is a smart card which stores the holder's fingerprint data. The IACS is available at the International Airport and the bus passenger checkpoints. At the automated lanes, card holders insert their Access Card into a card reader and place their right thumb on the fingerprint scanner for verification. The automated gate opens for the holder to leave when the system authenticates the fingerprint.
29. A similar system could locate all Americans in a metropolitan area, and could charge a fee to individual drivers for the service.
30. Cole, 2002, 163.
31. Fingerprint identification allowed law enforcement officials to ignore the reality of human variation: that the "races" were arbitrary categories that masked both the enormous breadth of interracial variation and the existence of individuals who blurred racial boundaries. Instead, the widespread adoption of the fingerprint system allowed the mythical tripartite categorization of all people into "black," "white," and "yellow" to persist. This crude categorization has, of course, had profound consequences in the exigencies of policing in the United States" (Cole, 2002, 163).
32. 22 U.S.C. § 211a (2001).
33. See Cole, 2002, 147; 164.
34. Restrictions on passports are more familiar to Americans than travel-related restrictions on driver's licenses which are more likely in the future.
35. See *Kent v. Dulles*, 357 U.S. 116 (1958) (holding that the Fifth Amendment prohibits the Secretary of State from denying passports to individuals because of their alleged Communist beliefs and associations and their refusal to file affidavits concerning present or past membership in the Communist Party); see also *Aptheker v. Secretary of State* 378 U.S. 500 (1964) (holding Section 6 of the Subversive Activities Control Act of 1950 unconstitutional on its face because it "too broadly and indiscriminately restricts the right to travel and thereby abridges the liberty guaranteed by the Fifth Amendment"); *Saenz v. Roe* 526 U.S. 489 (1999) (holding that California's residency requirement for receiving welfare benefits violated the right to travel under the privileges and immunities clause).
36. See *Zemel v. Rusk*, 381 U.S. 1, 13 (1965) (holding that the Passport Act of 1926 allows the Secretary of State to deny an individual a passport for travel to Cuba "not because of any characteristic peculiar to appellant, but rather because of foreign policy considerations affecting all citizens").
37. See Committee on Foreign Affairs (1966). But see *Haig v. Agee*, 453 U.S. 280 (1981) (upholding the denial of a passport when travel is a threat to national security).

38. See also Sobel, 2002a, 343–349, and PrivacyActivism et al. (2003) *Hiibel* Amicus brief on the historical abuses through identification systems and documents.

39. Even before the censuses, Germany had collected health records that ultimately aided the process of targeting Jews. See Twight (2002).

40. Hilberg, 1985; Sobel, 2002a, note 155, 119.

41. See Black, 2001, 201 (quoting Jews in Cracow Move to Ghettos, 1940, 3); see also Sobel, 2002a, note 77, for the origins of Black's awareness of IBM technology's role in the Holocaust. But see Gentry (1991) on how former FBI director J. Edgar Hoover opposed the relocation of Japanese-Americans when he felt the "most likely spies had already been arrested" by the FBI soon after Pearl Harbor.

42. See also IBM (2001) ("It has been known for decades that the Nazis used Hollerith equipment and that IBM's German subsidiary during the 1930s – Deutsche Hollerith Maschinen GmbH (Dehomag) – supplied Hollerith equipment").

43. See also Cole (2002, 5, 250) ("In a sense, the use of punch cards to represent individuals brought identification full circle, since the problem of personal identification had stimulated the development of the punch card").

44. See also Immigration and Refugee Board of Canada, 1998.

45. Shortly after these atrocities were carried out, partially though the Hutus' ability to identify the Tutsis through identification cards, the United States was implementing the Illegal Immigration Reform and Immigrant Responsibility Act (IIRIRA) in 1996, and the FAA was requiring identification in order to fly and implement the CAPPS (1995) passenger screening system. See IIRIRA (1996) 10; Federal Aviation Reauthorization Act of 1996, Pub. L. No. 104–264, § 307, 10 Stat. 3213 (1996).

46. President Clinton's speech to Genocide Survivors, Assistance Workers, and US and Rwandan government officials at Kigali Airport in Rwanda in March 25, 1998 (Clinton, 1998).

47. U.S. Const. Art. I, § 2, el. 3.

48. 44 U.S.C. § 2108(b) (1994). See 36 C.F.R. § 1256A(a)(3) (2001) ("NARA will not grant access to restricted census and survey records of the Bureau of the Census less than 72 years old containing data identifying individuals enumerated in population censuses in accordance with 44 U.S.C. § 2108 (b).").

49. 13 U.S.C. § 214 (1994).

50. 13 U.S.C. § 9 (1994).

51. See Toland (1982) and Reeves (2015) about the *Infamy* of the Japanese American Internment in the United States during World War II.

52. See Toland (1982) at 285. See *Korematsu v. United States*, 320 U.S. 214 (1944); see also *Hirabayashi v. United States*, 320 U.S. 81 (1943). *Korematsu*, at 233.

53. *Korematsu* 214; *Hirabayashi* 81. But see *Ex Parte Mitsuye Endo*, 328 U.S. 283 (1944), where a loyal citizen, not charged with any offense, was entitled to be released from confinement under a writ of habeas corpus. Rehnquist (2000) called *Endo* "a minor victory for civil liberties." See Bannnai (2015, 42), that "as an American citizen, he had a constitutional right to remain free [and] … did not have to invoke his constitutional rights to be able to exercise them."

54. See Rehnquist (1998, 221). *Korematsu*, 233. See Gross (2015), on how during the Depression, more than a million people of Mexican descent were sent ("repatriated") to Mexico; an estimated 60 percent American citizens, many of whom had never lived in Mexico.

55. Similar restrictions for the Japanese (Proclamation 2525) were applied initially to German (Proclamation 2526) and Italian (Proclamation 2527) enemy aliens (citizens of countries at war with the United States) at the start of World War II. But they were removed under political pressures in part because the Italians and Germans (including those of ethnic descent) were the largest immigrant groups in the United States at the time. In the 1940 census, there were about 5,236,613 (4,949,780) Germans (foreign born, foreign or mixed parentage, or descended from Germans) and about 4,594,780 (3,766,820) of Italian descent in the United States (*World Almanac*, 1949, 202–203). Though initially Italian and German immigrants were defined as enemy aliens, including those concentrated on the west coast like Joe DiMaggio's parents, and some were arrested or interned (11,507 ethnic Germans ("Internments of German Americans," 2016) and 1,521 Italian aliens) ("Internment of Italian Americans," 2016), for the millions of citizens and nationals of Italian and German descent, the restrictions were Moved; for Italians by Columbus Day 1942. In 1940, there were 126,947 Japanese, 321,080 (of about 1,237,772 foreign born) Germans, and 703,445 (of about 1,627,508 foreign born) Italians (Italian citizens) registered with the US government (*Statistical Abstract* for 1941; *World Almanac*, 1949). Before the War, only about half of those immigrants of Italian or German descent in the United States were naturalized citizens. National Archives, 2015; Texas Historical Commission, 2015. In 1940, roughly one-third of all foreign born living in the United States were not citizens according to the US Census (*Statistical Abstract*, 1941).

BIBLIOGRAPHY

BOOKS AND ARTICLES

Agar, Jon, "Modern Horrors: British Identity and Identity Cards," in Jane Caplan and John Torpey, eds., *Documenting Individual Identity: The Development of State Practices in the Modern World*, Princeton, 2001, pp. 101–123.

Aguila, Sissi, "Kwame Appiah Discusses 'World Citizenship' at FIU," April 23, 2010. news.fiu.edu.

Amar, Akhil, *America's Constitution: A Biography*, Random House, 2006.

Amar, Akhil, *America's Unwritten Constitution (The Precedents and Principles We Live by)*, Basic Books, 2012.

Amar, Akhil, *The Bill of Rights: Creation and Reconstruction*, Yale, 1999.

Amtrak, 2015 "Passenger Identification," www.amtrak.com/servlet/Content Server?pagename=am/AM_Snippet_C/IBLegacy&ibsref=PassengerID.

"A National Identity Card?," *The Wall Street Journal*, September 2, 1986.

"A Nation Divided: Views of the British Public on the Government's Proposed National Identity Card," UK public survey commissioned by Privacy International, www.privacyinternational.org/issues/idcard/uk/idpollanalysis.pdf, May 2004.

"A National Identity Card?", *Wall Street Journal*, April 3, 1990, p. A20.

Anderson, Annalise, *Illegal Aliens and Employers: Sanctions Solving the Wrong Problem*, Hoover Institution Press, April 1986.

Anderson, Martin, "Mark of the Beast," in *Revolution: The Reagan Legacy*, Hoover Institution Press, 1990.

Anton, Annie, "National Identification Cards," Information Policy Report for PUBP 8100, Georgia Tech, December 17, 1996.

"An Unrealistic 'Real ID': *New York Times*, May 4, 2005.

Appiah, Kwame Anthony, *Cosmopolitanism: Ethics in a World of Strangers*, Norton, 2006.

Appiah, Kwame Anthony, *"Citizen of the World,"* Chicago Humanities Festival, November 1, 2014 (including personal communications).

Appiah, Kwame Anthony, "Kindness of Strangers," in Appiah, 2006.

Armstrong, David and Joseph Pereira, "Flight Risks: Nation's Airlines Adopt Aggressive Measures for Passenger Profiling," *The Wall Street Journal*, October 23, 2001, p. 1.

Aron, Raymond, *An Essay on Freedom*, NY World, 1970.

Asahina, Robert, *Just Americans: How Japanese-Americans Won a War at Home and Abroad*, Gotham, 2006.

Bacon, John, "Conn. to Ban Gun Sales to 'No Fly' Listers," *USA Today*, December 10, 2015. www.usatoday.com/story/news/nation/2015/12/10/connecticut-ban-gun-sales-no-fly-listers/77102094/.

Baker, Al, "Subway Searches Go on Quietly, Just How Police Like Them," *The New York Times*, July 6, 2007. www.nytimes.com/2007/07/06/nyregion/06bags.html?_r=0.

Baker, S. A. "Comment: A Strict Scrutiny of the Right to Travel," *UCLA Law Review*, 22 (1975), pp. 1129–1160.

Banisar, David, "A Review of New Surveillance Technologies," *Privacy Journal*, November (2001), p. 1.

Bannai, Lorraine K. Enduring Conviction, Fred Korematsu and His Quest for Justice, University of Washington Press, 2015.

Barnett, Randy, *Restoring the Lost Constitution*, Princeton, 2004.

Barreto, Matt et al., "The Disproportionate Impact of Photo Identification Requirements on the Indiana Electorate," paper presented at the American Political Science Association Meeting, Boston, September 2008.

Baruch, Bernard M., *My Story: The Public Years*, Holt, 1960.

Bates, Edward, "Citizenship of Children Born in the United States of Alien Parents," Opinion of Attorney General Bates on Citizenship, US Government Printing Office, 1862.

Baubock, Rainer. "Recombinant Citizenship." Institute for Advanced Studies, Vienna 67 (1999): 2–10. Print. www.ihs.ac.at/publications/pol/pw_67.pdf.

Bellamy, Richard, *Citizenship: A Very Short Introduction*, Oxford University Press, 2008.

Bellow, Saul, *The Adventures of Augie March*, Penguin Classics, 1953, 2006.

Bendery, Jennifer, "Obama Has No Authority for Drone Strikes against Americans on U.S. Soil, White House Says," *Huffington Post*, March 7, 2013. www.huffingtonpost.com/2013/03/07/obama-drone-strikes_n_2830174.html.

Benhabib, Seyla, "Borders, Boundaries, and Citizenship," *PSonline*, 38:4 (October 2005), pp. 673–677.

Benhabib, Seyla, *Dignity in Adversity, Human Rights in Troubled Times*, Polity Press, 2011.

Benhabib, Seyla, *The Rights of Others, Aliens, Residents and Citizens*, Cambridge University Press, 2004.

Benhabib, Seyla, *Transformation of Citizenship: Dilemmas of the Nation State in the Era of Globalization*, Spinoza Lectures, Koninklijke Van Gorcum, 2001.

Berman, Ari, *Give us the Ballot: The Modern Struggle for Voting Rights in America*, Farrar, Straus and Giroux, 2015a.

Berman, Ari, "Inside John Roberts' Decades-Long Crusade against the Voting Rights Act," Political.com, August 10, 2015b. www.politico.com/magazine/story/2015/08/john-roberts-voting-rights-act-121222#ixzz41b228KXH.

Bhandari, Esha, "Yes, the U.S. Wrongfully Deports Its Own Citizens," ACLU Speech, Privacy and Technology Project, April 25, 2013. www.aclu.org/blog/speakeasy/yes-us-wrongfully-deports-its-own-citizens.

Bickel, Alexander M., "Citizenship in the American Constitution," *Arizona Law Review*, 15 (1973), pp. 369–387.

Black, Edwin, *IBM and The Holocaust: The Strategic Alliance between Nazi Germany and America's Most Powerful Corporation*, Crown Books, 2001.

Black, Henry Campbell, *Black's Law Dictionary*, Abridged Sixth Edition, West, 1991.

Blackstone, William, "Of the Absolute Rights of Individuals," *Commentaries on the Laws of England (1765–1769)*. Book 1, Chapter 125, 1769.

Blomberg, Jeffrey, A., "Protecting the Right Not to Vote from Voter Purge Statutes," *Fordham Law Review*, 64:3 (1995), pp. 1015–1050. ir.lawnet.fordham.edu/cgi/viewcontent.cgi?article=3223&context=flr.

Bobbitt, Philip, *Constitutional Fate: Theory of the Constitution*, Oxford University Press, 1982.

Bosniak, Linda, *The Citizen and the Alien: Dilemmas of Contemporary Membership*, Princeton University Press, 2006.

Bosniak, Linda, "Citizenship Denationalized," *Indiana Journal of Global Legal Studies*, 7:2 (2000), pp. 447–509.

Bosniak, Linda, "The Citizenship of Aliens," *Social Text*, 16:3 (Autumn 1998), pp. 29–35.

Bosniak, Linda, "Constitutional Citizenship through the Prism of Alienage," *Ohio State Law Journal*, 63:5 (2002), pp. 1285–1326.

Bosniak, Linda, "Membership, Equality, and the Difference that Alienage Makes," *New York University Law Review*, 69:6 (1994), pp. 1047–1059.

Bosniak, Linda, "Universal Citizenship and the Problem of Alienage," *Northwestern University Law Review*, 94 (2000), pp. 963–982.

Branca-Santos, Paula, "Injustice Ignored: The Internment of Italian-Americans during World War II," *Pace International Law Review*, 13:1 (Spring 2001), pp. 151–182.

Brennan, William T., "Private Carriage versus Common Carriage of Persons or Property," *Federal Aviation Administration*, April 24, 1986. www.faa.g ov/documentLibrary/media/Advisory_Circular/AC%20120-12A.pdf.

Breyer, Stephen, *Active Liberty: Interpreting Our Democratic Constitution*, Harvard, 2005.

Breyer, Stephen, *The Court and the World: American Law and the New Global Realities*, Knopf, 2015.

Brill, Steven, "The Biggest Hole in the Net: ONE DAY SOON, America May Be Rocked by a Suicide Bomber. We Have No System to Deal with That Eventuality. Why the Debate over a National ID Card Is Long Overdue," *Newsweek*, December 30, 2002, p. 48.

Briscoe, Tony and Jason Meisner, "Chicago Police to Check CTA Riders' Bags for Explosives," *Chicago Tribune*, October 24, 2014, www.chicagotri bune.com/news/ct-cta-safety-explosives-check-met-20141024-story.html.

Brubaker, Roger, *Citizenship, and Nationhood in France and Germany*, Harvard University Press, 1998.

Brzezinski, Mathew, "Fortress America," *The New York Times Magazine*, February 23, 2003. www.nytimes.com/2003/02/23/magazine/fortress-america.html.

Caplan, Jane and John Torpey, *Documenting Individual Identity: The Development of State Practices in the Modern World*, Princeton, 2001.

Caplan, Lincoln, "Rhetoric and Law, the Double Life of Richard Posner, America's Most Contentious Legal Reformer," *Harvard Magazine*, December 2015.

Caro, Mark, "CSO's Citizen Musician Seeks Right Note," *Chicago Tribune*, March 4, 2013. http://articles.chicagotribune.com/2013-03-04/entertainment/chi-cso-citizen-musician-20130301_1_citizen-musi cian-cso-riccardo-muti.

Chafee, Zacharia, *Three Human Rights in the Constitution of 1787*, University of Kansas, 1956.

Chafee, Zacharia, "Comment: A Strict Scrutiny of the Right to Travel," *UCLA Law Review*, 22 (1975), pp. 171–181.

Chapman, Steve, "Why Citizenship Should Remain a Birthright: Unauthorized Immigrants Came Here in Search of Jobs and Family

Unification, Not the Nearest Maternity Ward," *Chicago Tribune*, August 22, 2015, p. 17.

Choudhury, Nusrat, "Victory! Federal Court Recognizes Constitutional Rights of Americans on the No-Fly List," ACLU Racial Justice Program, 2015. www.aclu.org/blog/victory-federal-court-recognizes-constitutional-rights-americans-no-fly-list.

Citizen Attestation Employment Pilot Program, April 6, 1999. www.gpo.gov/fdsys/granule/FR-1999-04-06/99-8354.

Clinton, William J., "Remarks by the President to Genocide Survivors, Assistance Workers, and U.S. and Rwandan Government Officials at Kigali Airport, Rwanda," Office of the Press Secretary, The White House, March 25, 1998. http://clinton6.nara.gov/1998/03/1998-03-25-remarks-to-survivors-rwanda.html.

Cochrane, John, "Think Government Is Intrusive Now? Wait Until E-Verify Kicks In," *The Wall Street Journal*, August 1, 2013.

Cole, David, "Are Foreign Nationals Entitled to the Same Constitutional Rights as Citizens?," *Georgetown Law Journal, Thomas Jefferson Law Review*, 2003, pp. 367–388. http://scholarship.law.georgetown.edu/cgi/viewcontent.cgi?article=1302&context=facpub.

Cole, Simon, *Suspect Identities: A History of Fingerprinting and Criminal Identification*, Harvard University Press, 2002.

Committee on Foreign Affairs, Subcommittee on State Department Organization and Foreign Operations, *Passports and The Right to Travel: A Study of Administrative Control of the Citizen*, Library of Congress, 1966 (on file with the Harvard Law School Library).

Committee on Immigration and Naturalization, "Citizenship and Naturalization of Married Women," Report No. 2693, February 16, 1931.

Connolly, William, *Identity/Difference: Democratic Negotiations of Political Paradox*, Cornell University Press, 1991.

Constitutional Accountability Center, "Celebrating the 17th Amendment and the Constitution's Progressive Arc," April 8, 2011. http://theusconstitution.org/text-history/2913.

"Controle et verification d'identite pour toute information." www.service-public.fr/particuliers/vosdroits/F1036.

Cooke, Frederick H., "The Right to Engage in Interstate and Foreign Commerce as an Individual or as a Corporation," *Michigan Law Review*, 8:6 (April 1910), pp. 458–467.

Crews, Clyde Wayne, "Human Bar Code, Monitoring Biometric Technologies in a Free Society," Cato Institute Policy Analysis No.

452, September 17, 2002. www.cato.org/publications/policy-analysis/
human-bar-code-monitoring-biometric-technologies-free-society.

C-SPAN, "A Conversation with Justice Ruth Bader Ginsburg." C-SPAN
Video Library, September 15, 2009. www.c-spanvideo.org/program/
288900-1.

Dellinger, Walter, "Legislation Denying Citizenship at Birth to Certain
Children Born in the United States," Statement before the
Subcommittees on Immigration and Claims and on the Constitution,
House Committee on the Judiciary, December 13, 1995.

d'Entreves, Maurizio Passerin, "Hannah Arendt," *Stanford Encyclopedia
of Philosophy*, ed. by Edward N. Zalta, CSLI, Stanford University,
2006.

Department of Homeland Security, "Current Status of States and
Territories" [of REAL ID], December 31, 2015. www.dhs.gov/cur
rent-status-states-territories.

Dillin, John, "Repeal Employer Sanctions, Senators Say," *Christian
Science Monitor*, June 29, 1990

Douglas, Joshua A., "Is the Right to Vote Really Fundamental?," *Cornell
Journal of Law and Public Policy*, 18 (2008), pp. 143–201.

Drew, Christopher, "Lower Voter Turnout Is Seen in States That Require
ID," *The New York Times*, February 21, 2007.

Eggen, Dan, "Criticism of Voting Law Was Overruled, Justice Department
Backed Georgia Measure Despite Fears of Discrimination," *The
Washington Post*, November 17, 2005, p. A1.

Eisgruber, Christopher, "Birthright Citizenship and the Constitution,"
NYU Law Review, 72:1 (1997), pp. 54–96.

Eisgruber, Christopher, "The Fourteenth Amendment's Constitution,"
Southern California Law Review, 69:47 (1995), pp. 47–103.

Electronic Privacy Information Center, "EPIC Files Lawsuit Against FBI
to Obtain Documents about Massive Biometric Identification
Database," April 10, 2013. Epic.org.

Electronic Privacy Information Center, "EPIC Sues FBI to Obtain Details
of Massive Biometric Database," Epic.org, April 8, 2013. https://epic
.org/2013/04/epic-sues-fbi-to-obtain-detail.html.

Electronic Privacy Information Center, "Secure Flight," Epic.org,
October 10, 2013. https://epic.org/privacy/airtravel/secureflight.html.

Electronic Privacy Information Center, "Your Papers Please, From the
State Driver's License to a National Identification System," Policy
Report 1, February 2002, https://epic.org/reports/yourpapersplease.pdf.

Elkins, Caroline, *Imperial Reckoning: The Untold Story of Britain's Gulag in Kenya*, Holt, 2005.

Ellis, Joseph J., *The Quartet: Orchestrating the Second American Revolution, 1783–1789*, Knopf, 2015.

Erler, Edward, "Birthright Citizenship and Dual Citizenship: Harbingers of Administrative Tyranny," *Imprimis*, 37:7 (2008). http://imprimis.hillsdale.edu/birthright-citizenship-and-dual-citizenship-harbingers-of-administrative-tyranny/.

Etzioni, Amitai, *The Limits of Privacy*, Basic, 1999.

Farber, Daniel A., "National Security, the Right to Travel, and the Court," *Supreme Court Review*, 1981, pp. 263–287.

Federal Register, "Privacy Act of 1974; Department of Homeland Security Transportation Security Administration-DHS/TSA-019 Secure Flight Records System of Records," January 5, 2015.

Federal Research Division, *Singapore: A Country Study*. Library of Congress (Area Handbook Series), 1989.

Fehrenbacher, Don E., *The Dred Scott Case, Its Significance in American Law and Politics*, Oxford, 2001.

Filipov, David, "In Moscow, They're Alien in Own Nation," *The Boston Globe*, October 26, 1997.

Foley, Elizabeth P., *Liberty for All: Reclaiming Individual Privacy in a New Era of Public Morality*, Yale, 2006.

Foner, Eric, *Reconstruction: America's Unfinished Revolution, 1863–1877*, HarperCollins, 1988.

Fossen, Thomas, "Agonistic Critique of Liberalism: Perfection and Emancipation," *Contemporary Political Theory*, 7 (2008), pp. 376–394.

Fried, John, "Biometrics: Ready For Primetime?," *Privacy Journal*, June 2000.

Friedman, Milton and Rose, *Capitalism and Freedom (Fortieth Anniversary Edition)*, University of Chicago Press, Originally 1962, 2002.

Friedman, Milton and Rose, *Free to Choose*, Harcourt, 1980.

"Fundamental Rights," The Constitutional Society, 2015, www.constitution.org/cons/india/p03.html.

"Fundamental Rights," Legal Information Institute, Cornell University Law School, 2015. www.law.cornell.edu/wex/fundamental_right.

"Fundamental Rights," Wikipedia, 2015. https://en.wikipedia.org/wiki/Fundamental_rights.

Garcelon, Marc, "Colonizing the Subject: The Genealogy and Legacy of the Soviet Internal Passport," in Jane Caplan and John Torpey, eds.,

Documenting Individual Identity, The Development of State Practices in the Modern World, Princeton, 2001, pp. 83–100.

Gates, Henry Louis Jr., *Thirteen Ways of Looking at a Black Man*, Vintage Books, 1998.

Gentry, Curt, *J. Edgar Hoover: Man of Secrets*, W.W Norton, 1991.

Gessen, Masha, "Passport for Life," *The New York Times*, January 16, 2012.

Glover, Robert W., "Radically Rethinking Citizenship: Disaggregation, Agonistic Pluralism and the Politics of Immigration in the U.S.," *Political Studies*, 59:2 (June 2011), pp. 209–229.

Gordon, Charles, "Who Can Be President of the United States? The Unresolved Enigma," *Maryland Law Review*, 28:1 (Winter 1968), pp. 1–32.

Governmental Accountability Office, "Issues Related to State Voter Identification Laws," GAO-14–634, Published: September 19, 2014. Publicly Released: October 8, 2014. www.gao.gov/products/GAO-14-634 [Reissued on February 27, 2015].

Governmental Accountability Office, "Secure Flight: Additional Actions Needed to Determine Program Effectiveness and Strengthen Privacy Oversight Mechanisms," GAO-14-796 T, Washington, DC Published: September 18, 2014. Publicly Released: September 18, 2014.

Governmental Accountability Office, "Secure Flight: TSA Should Take Additional Steps to Determine Program Effectiveness," GAO-14–531, Washington, DC Published: September 9, 2014. Publicly Released: September 18, 2014.

Governmental Accountability Office, "Secure Flight: TSA Could Take Additional Steps to Strengthen Privacy Oversight Mechanisms," GAO-14–647, Washington, DC Published: September 9, 2014. Publicly Released: September 18, 2014.

Green, Frederick, "Corporations as Persons, Citizens, and Possessors of Liberty," *University of Pennsylvania Law Review*, 94 (1947), pp. 202–237.

Greenleaf, Graham and Kyung Hee, "India's National ID system: Danger Grows in a Privacy Vacuum," *Computer Law & Security Review*, 26:4 (July 2010). www2.austlii.edu.au/~graham/publications/2010/India_ID_system0710.pdf.

Gross, Terry, Author Interviews, Francisco Balderrama, "America's Forgotten History of Mexican-American 'Repatriation,'" *NPR*, Fresh Air, September 10, 2015.

Gwin, Peter, "Proof: Revisiting the Rwandan Genocide: Hutu or Tutsi?" National Geographic Online. April 5, 2014 http://proof.nationalgeo graphic.com/2014/04/05/revisiting-the-rwandan-genocide-hutu-or-tutsi/

Hale, Edward Everett, *The Man without a Country*, Little Brown, 1888.

Handeyside, Hugh, "Federal Courts Deal Setbacks to No-Fly List," ACLU National Security Project, January 24, 2014. www.aclu.org/blog/federal-courts-deal-setbacks-no-fly-list.

Harper, Jim. "US to Share Biometric Data with Foreign Countries," CATO, August 26, 2009. www.cato.org/blog/us-share-biometric-data-foreign-countries.

Louis Harris & Associates and Alan F. Westin, "The Dimensions of Privacy," *Sentry Insurance*, 70, 1981.

Hawkins, Dana et al., "Tech vs. Terrorists: New Scanners Might Foil Some Plots, but Every Fix has its Flaws," *U.S. News & World Report*, 131:14 (October 2001), p. 56.

Higginbotham, A. Leon, Jr., *In the Matter of Color, Race and the American Legal Process: The Colonial Period*, Oxford, 1978.

Hilberg, Raul, *The Destruction of The European Jews*, Holmes & Meier, 1985.

Hingley, Ronald, *The Russian Secret Police: Muscovite, Imperial Russian, and Soviet Political Security Operations*, Simon and Schuster, 1971.

Ho, James, "Defining American: Birthright Citizenship and the Original Understanding of the Fourteenth Amendment," *The Green Bag*, 9:4 (Summer 2006), pp. 359–368.

Holstege, Sean, "Case Centers on Secret ID Directive," *Inside Bay Area*, December 9, 2005.

Honig, Bonnie, *Democracy and the Foreigner*, Princeton, 2001.

Honig, Bonnie, "Immigrant America? How Foreignness 'Solves' Democracy's Problems," *Social Text*, 16:3 (Fall 1998), pp. 1–27.

Horobin, William, "Security Laws Spur Divide in French Parliament," *Wall Street Journal*, February 10, 2016, p. 4.

Hosie, Duncan, "Chief Justice Roberts' Bait and Switch," *Huffington Post*, September 12, 2014. www.huffingtonpost.com/duncan-hosie/chief-justice-roberts-bai_b_5793194.html.

Houseman, Gerald L., *The Right of Mobility*, Kennikat Press, 1979.

Howard, Marc Morjé and Lise Morjé Howard, "*Raison d'etat or Raison populaire?*, The Influence of Public Opinion on France's Bosnia Policy," in Sobel and Shiraev, 2003.

Hurd, John C., *The Law of Freedom and Bondage in the United States*, Little Brown, 1858.

"Hukou System," Wikipedia, 2015. https://en.wikipedia.org/wiki/Hukou_system.

IBM, Statement on Nazi-era Book and Lawsuit, February 14, 2001. http://ib
  m.com/Press/pmews.nsf/jard E761868F46444 B06852569F20064F555.
"Identity Cards in the UK-a lesson from history." The Report of The Joint
  Committee on Human Rights of the House of Lords and House of
  Commons on the Identity Cards Bill (5th Report of Session 2004–2005),
  January 26, 2005. www.statewatch.org/news/2003/jul/26ukid.htm.
Immigration and Refugee Board of Canada, "Russia: The Propiska (regis-
  tration) system and internal passports," May 1, 1998.
"Internment of German Americans," Wikipedia, 2016. https://en.wikipe
  dia.org/wiki/Internment_of_German_Americans.
"Internment of Italian Americans," Wikipedia, 2016. https://en.wikipedia
  .org/wiki/Internment_of_Italian_Americans.
Isikoff, Michael, "GAO Says 1986 Law Led to Hiring Discrimination
  Against Hispanics, Ethnics," Washington Post, March 30, 1990, A11.
Jafarzadeh, Sabra and Megan Timmins, "Metro Bag Searches:
  Inconvenient or Unconstitutional?," American Bar Foundation, April
  2011. www.americanbar.org/publications/law_practice_today_home/
  law_practice_today_archive/april11/metro_bag_searches.html.
James, Deborah S., "Voter Registration: A Restriction on the Fundamental
  Right to Vote," The Yale Law Journal, 96:7 (June 1987), pp. 1615–1640.
Jefferson, Thomas, "Argument in the Case of Howell v. Netherland," The
  Writings of Thomas Jefferson (1892).
"Jews in Crakow Move to Ghettos: 80,000 Being Forced Into Areas Under
  Strict Nazi Regime of Governor Frank," The New York Times, March 16,
  1940, p. 3.
Jillson, Cal, American Government: Political Development and Institutional
  Change (5th edition), Routledge, 2009.
Johnston, Anna, "Why 'Australia Card Mark II' Is Still a Dumb Idea,"
  Australian Policy Online, January 27, 2006. http://apo.org.au/commentary/
  why-australia-card-mark-ii-still-dumb-idea.
Joint Committee on Human Rights – Fifth Report, 2008. www.publications
  .parliament.uk/pa/jt200708/jtselect/jtrights/37/3702.htm.
Jones, Emma and John Gaventa, Concepts of Citizenship: A Review, 3–4
  (2002).
Kahn, Ronald, The Supreme Court and Constitutional Theory, 1953–1993,
  University Press of Kansas, 1994.
Karlan, Pamela, "Forum," in Glenn Loury, ed., Race, Incarceration and
  American Values, Boston Review Press, 2008.
Karst, Kenneth, Belonging to America: Equal Citizenship and the
  Constitution, Yale University Press, 1991.

Katayal, Neal and Paul Clement, "On the Meaning of 'Natural Born Citizen'," *Harvard Law Review Forum*, March 11, 2015.

"Keeping Record of Speakers," *The Straits Times*, May 9, 2000, p. 39.

Keyssar, Alexander, *The Right to Vote, A Contested History of Democracy in the United States*, Basic Books, 2000.

Khalek, Rania, "Why Are American Citizens Getting Locked Up and Even Deported By Immigration Authorities?," *AlterNet*, December 28, 2011. www.alternet.org/story/153499/why_are_american_citizens_get ting_locked_up_and_even_deported_by_immigration_authorities.

Klinghoffer, Arthur Jay and Judith Apter Klinghoffer, *International Citizens' Tribunal: Mobilizing Public Opinion to Advance Human Rights*, New York: Palgrave, 2002.

Knight, Amy, *The KGB: Police and Politics in the Soviet Union*, Unwin Hyman, 1990.

Kreimer, Seth, "The Law of Choice and Choice of Law: Abortion, the Right to Travel, and Extraterritorial Regulation in American Federalism," University of Pennsylvania Law School Faculty Legal Scholarship Paper, 1336 (1992). http://scholarship.law.upenn.edu/faculty_scholarship/1336.

Kymlicka, Will and Wayne Norman, "Return of the Citizen: A Survey of Recent Work on Citizenship Theory," *Ethics*, 104:2 (January 1994), pp. 352–381.

Laney, Garrine, "The Voting Rights Act of 1965, As Amended: Its History and Current Issues," *Congressional Research Service*, June 12, 2008, pp. 1–55.

Lerner, Mark, "Biometrics and Biblical Prophecy," ConstitutionalAlliance .org, 2015.

Lerner, Mark, "Christians and non-Christians are being enrolled into a global system of identification and financial control," *Constitutional Alliance*, June 3, 2013. http://constitutionalalliance.org/articles/chris tians-and-non-christians-are-being-enrolled-global-system-identifica tion-and-financial.

Lewis, Sinclair, *It Can't Happen Here*, New American Library, [1935], 2005.

Liptak, Adam, "Assets not Linked to Crimes Can't be Frozen, Justices Rule," The *New York Times*, March 31, 2016, p. A17.

Longman, Timothy, "Identity Cards, Ethnic Self-Perception, and Genocide in Rwanda," in Jane Caplan and John Torpey, eds., *Documenting Individual Identity: The Development of State Practices in the Modern World*, Princeton, 2001, pp. 345–358.

Lowry, Richard, "Profiles in Cowardice: How to Deal with the Terrorist Threat – and How Not To," *National Review*, January 28, 2002. www .nationalreview.com/article/270777/profiles-cowardice-rich-lowry.

Ma, Yo-Yo, "Art for Life's Sake: A Roadmap from One Citizen Musician," Nancy Hanks Lecture on Arts and Public Policy, Kennedy Center, April 8, 2013. www.americansforthearts.org/sites/default/files/ pdf/events/2013/hanks/Art_for_Lifes_Sake_Hanks_2013.pdf.

Machlin, Tracey, "Decline of the Right to Locomotion: The Fourth Amendment on the Streets," *Cornell Law Review*, 75:6 (September 1990), pp. 1258–1337. http://scholarship.law.cornell.edu/cgi/viewcon tent.cgi?article=3471&context=clr.

Madsen, Wayne, *Handbook of Personal Data Protection*, Palgrave Macmillan, 1992.

Magnette, Paul, *Citizenship: The History of an Idea*, European Consortium on Political Research Press, 2005.

Manheim, Karl, "The Right to Travel," *Constitutional Law II Blog*, 2005. http://classes.lls.edu/archive/manheimk/conlaw2-manheim-s05/charts/tra vel.pdf.

Marshall, T. H., *Citizenship and Social Class*, Cambridge University Press, 1950.

Marshall, T. H., *Class, Citizenship and Social Development*, Doubleday, 1965.

Maya, "Police Conduct Warrantless Bag Searches at Transit Checkpoints," *The Bay State Examiner*, April 6, 2014. www.baystateexaminer.com/arti cles/police-conduct-warrantless-bag-searches-at-transit-checkpoints.

Mayer-Schoenberger, Viktor, "Perspectives on Privacy and Security," Presentation to Conference on Building Effective E-Government, John F. Kennedy School of Government, Cambridge, MA, January 25, 2002.

Maynard, Christopher S., "Nine Headed Caesar: The Supreme Court's Thumbs-Up Approach to the Right to Travel", 51 *Case Western Reserve Law Review*, 297–352 (2000)

McPherson, James M., *The War that Forged a Nation: Why the Civil War Still Matters*, Oxford University Press, 2015.

Meichtry, Stacy and Noemie Bisserbe, "France Proposes Constitution Change after Terror Attacks," *The Wall Street Journal*, December 23, 2015, p. 1. www.wsj.com/articles/france-moves-to-shield-emergency-measures-from-legal-challenge-1450873849.

Meyers, Jessica, "Mass. IDs at Odds with Federal Law," *Boston Globe*, August 26, 2014. www.bostonglobe.com/news/nation/2014/08/25/mas

sachusetts-licenses-rejected-parts-washington/iQl5H871MxTHAqpn
N1Rj7N/story.html.

Miller, John J. and Stephen Moore, "A National ID System: Big Brother's
Solution for Illegal Immigration," Cato Institute Policy Analysis No.
237, September 7, 1995. www.cato.org/publications/policy-analysis/
national-id-system-big-brothers-solution-illegal-immigration.

Mineo, Liz, "Legal Scholars debate Cruz's Eligibility to serve as
President," *Harvard Law Today*, today.harvard.edu, February 8, 2016.

Minnite, Lorraine, *The Myth of Voter Fraud*, Cornell University Press, 2010.

Moore, Stephen, "National Identification System," Testimony to Congress,
House Committee on the Judiciary, May 13, 1997. www.cato.org/publica
tions/congressional-testimony/national-identification-system.

Motomura, Hiroshi, "Americans in Waiting: The Lost Story of
Immigration and Citizenship in the United States," University of
North Carolina Legal Studies Research Paper 927229, Oxford
University Press, 2006.

Mouffe, Chantal, *On the Political (Thinking in Action)*, Routledge, 2005.

Mouffe, Chantal, *The Return of the Political*, Verso, 1993.

National Archives, "Brief Overview of the World War II Enemy Alien
Control Program." www.archives.gov/research/immigration/enemy-
aliens-overview.html.

National Center of State Legislatures, "Real ID Enforcement Update,"
January 21, 2016.

"National Identification: Protecting Privacy and Ensuring Data Security,"
Panel 5, "National Identification Conference," "21st Century
Identification Systems, Data, Politics, Protection," Harvard School of
Public Health, November 2015. https://wordpress.sph.harvard.edu/nidc/
panel5/.

National Research Council, *IDs – Not That Easy: Questions About
Nationwide Identity Systems*, Washington DC: National Academy
Press, 2002.

Nelson, Shellie, "Illinois Voters Pass Tougher Crime Victims' Rights and
Anti-Discrimination Laws," November 5, 2014. http://wqad.com/2014/
11/05/illinois-voters-pass-tougher-crime-victims-rights-and-anti-discri
mination-laws/.

Ng, Eileen, "'Smart' Identity Cards Could Be New Weapon in War on
Terrorism," *Agence France Presse/Canberra Times*, September 21, 2001.

Nickel, James, "Is There a Human Right to Employment?," *Philosophical
Forum*, 10:2 (1978), pp. 149–170.

Nicolosi, Ann Marie, "We Do Not Want Our Girls to Marry Foreigners: Gender, Race, and American Citizenship," *National Women's Studies Association Journal*, 13:3 (Autumn 2001), pp. 1–21.

"Ninth Amendment–Unenumerated Rights," 2015 Justia. http://law.jus tia.com/constitution/us/amendment-09.

Note, "Membership has its Privileges and Immunities. Congressional Powers to Define and Enforce the Rights of National Citizenship," 102 *Harvard Law Review* 1925–1931, n. 43, 1989, pp. 19–25.

Note, "The Right to Travel and Exclusionary Zoning," *Hastings Law Journal*, 26 (1975), pp. 849–854.

Nowak, John E. and Ronald D. Rotunda, *Constitutional Law* (fourth edition), West, 1983, 1991.

Nowak, John E. and Ronald D. Rotunda, *Constitutional Law* (seventh edition), West, 2007.

O'Harrow, Robert Jr. and Jon Krim, "National ID Card Gaining Support," *The Washington Post*, December 17, 2001, pp. A1, 18. www .washingtonpost.com/archive/politics/2001/12/17/national-id-card-gain ing-support/bd37ba6b-8812-4f5b-950f-f2ab2e343916/.

Omond, Roger, *The Apartheid Handbook: A Guide to South Africa's Everyday Racial Policies*, Penguin, 1986.

Ormes, Margaret, Mary Klein, Kathy Goodin, Healy Hamilton, and Kyle Copas. "NatureServe Citizen Science Strategy," Arlington, VA: NatureServe, 2014. www.natureserve.org/sites/default/files/publica tions/files/ns-citizensciencestrategy-final.pdf.

Page, Clarence, "Donald, Your Birthright Idea is Sounding like Racism," *Chicago Tribune*, August 21, 2015. www.chicagotribune.com/news/opi nion/page/ct-donald-trump-birthright-racism-perspec-0823-jm-20150821-column.html.

Pagnozzi, Amy, "Uncloaking a Fleecing of Rights," *Hartford Courant*, January 15, 2002. http://articles.courant.com/2002-01-15/news/ 0201150110_1_congress-checks-and-balances-green-party-members.

Papers, Please!, "Briefs on issues remaining after "no-fly" trial," December 17, 2013b.

Papers, Please!, "'CAPPS IV': TSA Expands Profiling of Domestic US Airline Passengers," January 10, 2015. http://papersplease.org/wp/ 2015/01/09/capps-iv-tsa-expands-profiling-of-domestic-us-airline-pas sengers/.

Papers, Please!, "GAO Audit Confirms TSA Shift to Pre-Crime Profiling of All Air Travelers," September 22, 2014. https://papersplease.org/wp/

2014/09/22/gao-audit-confirms-tsa-shift-to-pre-crime-profiling-of-all-air-travelers/.

Papers, Please!, "State of New Mexico v. Phillip Mocek," (last visited May 25, 2014). www.papersplease.org/wp/mocek/.

Papers, Please!, "How does the TSA decide if you are who you say you are?," June 9, 2016, https://papersplease.org/wp/2016/06/09/how-does-the-tsa-decide-if-you-are-who-you-say-you-are/Papers, Please!, "No-fly-trial," 2014.

Papers, Please!, "No Fly Trial, Day 4," December 5, 2013b.

Papers, Please!, "Want to Fly? Papers, Please," (last updated August 16, 2006). http://papersplease.org/gilmore/facts.html.

Parenti, Christian, *The Soft Cage: Surveillance in America from Slavery to the War on Terror*, Basic, 2004.

"Pass Laws," Wikipedia, en.wikipedia.org/wiki/Pass_laws, 2016.

"Passport System in the Soviet Union," Wikipedia, December 31, 2015. https://en.wikipedia.org/wiki/Passport_system_in_the_Soviet_Union.

"Patients' Database Planned," *The Straits Times*, August 17, 1999, p. 20.

Patterson, Thom, "TSA rail, subway spot-checks raise privacy issues," *CNN*, January 28, 2012. www.cnn.com/2012/01/28/travel/tsa-vipr-passenger-train-searches/index.html.

Paul, Ron, "If You Like the Surveillance State, You'll Love E-Verify," July 1, 2013. www.the-free-foundation.org/tst7-1-2013.html.

Paul, Ron, Statement of the Honorable Ron Paul before the House Subcommittee on Immigration and Border Security of the Committee of the Judiciary Hearing on the Legal Workforce Act, February 4, 2015. www.campaignforliberty.org/ron-paul-testimony-legal-workforce-act.

Pear, Robert, "Simpler Plan Being Sought in Congress to Identify All Eligible Workers," *The New York Times*, March 31, 1990, p. 1.

"Permanent Resident v. Citizen, What's the Difference?" Alllaw.com, 2016.

Pickel, Mary Lou, "War on Terrorism: Air Security: Impact Unknown for New Baggage Screening," *Atlanta Journal-Constitution*, January 17, 2002, p. 6A.

Pollmann, Christopher, "Capitalist Development, Personal Identity and Human Rights," Human Rights Program, Harvard Law School, February 14, 2001.

Powell, John A., "Symposium: The Needs of Members in a Legitimate Democratic State," *Santa Clara Law Review*, 44:4 (2004), pp. 969 – 997. http://digitalcommons.law.scu.edu/lawreview/vol44/iss4/2.

Powell, Lydia, "India's National ID: Entitlement to a Number-Will a new national ID actually fix any of India's problems?," *The Globalist,* January 13, 2014. www.theglobalist.com/indias-national-id-entitlement-number/.

"President Wilson's Letter to Senator Stone Announcing His Stand on Armed Liner Issue," *The New York Times,* February 25, 1916. http://qu ery.nytimes.com/mem/archive-free/pdf?res=9A00E7DC1F38E633A25 756C2A9649C946796D6CF.

Presser, Jacob, *The Destruction of the Dutch Jews,* Dutton, 1969.

Primus, Eva, "Disentangling Administrative Searches," *Columbia Law Review,* 111 (2011), pp. 254–262.

Privacy International, "Proposals for identity (ID) cards have provoked public outrage and political division in several countries. In this paper Simon Davies analyses the key elements of public opposition to ID Card schemes, and profiles the massive 1987 Australian campaign against a national ID card," 1987. http://wearcam.org/envirotech/simon_davie s_opposition_to_id_card_schemes.htm.

Privacy International, "Mistaken Identity: Exploring the Relationship between National Identity Cards & the Prevention of Terrorism," April 2004. www.privacyinternational.org/issues/idcard/uk/id-terror ism.pdf.

"Privacy Rights 'under assault': Ombudsman Says Canada Bowing to U. S. Pressure," *Calgary Herald,* January 30, 2003.

Quraishi, Jen, "Surprise! TSA Is Searching Your Car, Subway, Ferry, Bus, AND Plane," *Mother Jones,* June 20, 2011. www.motherjones .com/mojo/2011/06/tsa-swarms-8000-bus-stations-public-transit-sys tems-yearly.

Rawle, William, *A View of the Constitution of the United States of America,* Philadelphia: P.H. Nicklin, 1829.

Rawls, John, *Justice as Fairness: A Restatement,* edited by Erin Kelly, Harvard, 2001.

"Real Bad ID," *Wall Street Journal,* October 10, 2006.

"Reconsidering 'Birthright Citizenship' for Children of Illegal Aliens," *California Yankee,* December 12, 2005. http://cayankee.blogs.com/ cayankee/2005/12/reconsidering_b.html.

Reeves, Richard, *Infamy: The Shocking Story of the Japanese American Internment in World War II,* Holt, 2015.

Rehnquist, William H., "1998 Year-End Report of the Federal Judiciary," *Federal Sentencing Reporter,* 11:3 (November–December 1998), pp. 134–136. http://fsr.ucpress.edu/content/11/3/134.

Rehnquist, William H., *All the Laws but One: Civil Liberties in Wartime*, Vintage, 2000.

Ridge, Tom and Larry Bloom, *The Test of Our Times: America Under Siege … and How We Can Be Safe Again*, Thomas Dunne Books, 2009.

"Right to Employment," The Free Dictionary. 2015 legal-dictionary.the freedictionary.com/Fundamental+rights.

"Right to Work," Wikipedia, 2015. en.wikipedia.org/wiki/Right_to_work.

Roots, Roger I., "The Orphaned Right: The Right to Travel by Automobile, 1890–1950," *Oklahoma City University Law Review*, 30 (Summer 2005), p. 245. http://constitution.org/lrev/roots/orphaned_right.pdf.

Rosen, Jeffrey, "The Eroded Self," *The New York Times Magazine*, April 30, 2000, p. 46.

Rosen, Jeffrey, "Exclusion, Discrimination and the Making of Americans: America in Thick and Thin," *New Republic*, January 1989.

Ruwitch, John and Hui Li, "China Eyes Residence Permits to Replace Divisive Hukou System," *Reuters*, March 6, 2013. www.reuters.com/article/us-china-parliament-urbanisation-idUSBRE92509020130306.

Salyer, Lucy E., "Reconstructing American Citizenship: The Fenian Brotherhood and the Expatriation Act of 1868," paper Presented at the American Bar Foundation Seminar, February 2008.

Sassen, Saskia, "Citizenship Destabilized," *Liberal Education*, 89:2 (Spring 2003), pp. 14–21.

Sassen, Saskia, *Guests and Aliens*, New Press, 1999.

Scalia, Antonin and Byran A. Gardner, *Reading Law, The Interpretation of Legal Texts*, First Edition, West, 2012.

Schall, Jason, "The Consistency of Felon Disenfranchisement with Citizenship Theory," *Harvard Black Letter Law Journal*, 22 (2006), pp. 55–93.

Schuck, Peter, "Membership in the Liberal Polity: The Devaluation of American Citizenship," *Georgetown Immigration Law Review*, 3:1 (1989), pp. 37–161.

Schuck, Peter and Rogers Smith, *Citizenship without Consent: Illegal Aliens in the American Polity*, New Haven: Yale, 1985.

Schneier, Bruce. "National ID Cards," *Crypto-Gram Newsletter*, December 15.

Schneier, Bruce, "New TSA Requirements," June 11, 2008. www.schneier.com/blog/archives/2008/06/new_tsa_id_requ.html.

Schneier, Bruce, *Secrets and Lies: Digital Security in a Networked World*, Wiley, 2000.

Schroeder, Duane W., "The Right to Travel: In Search of a Constitutional Source," *Nebraska Law Review*, 55:1 (1975), pp. 117–132.

Seaman, Donna, "Trumped Again: Identity Cards," *The Economist*, February 5, 1994, p. 61.

Seltzer, William and Margo Anderson, "After Pearl Harbor: The Proper Role of Population Data Systems in Time of War," University of Wisconsin-Milwaukee, 2000 (Unpublished Paper), 1–55.

Shankman, Kimberly and Roger Pilon, "Reviving the Privileges or Immunities Clause to Redress the Balance Among States, Individuals, and The Federal Government," Cato Institute Policy Analysis No. 326, November 23, 1998, pp. 1–49.

Shestokas, David J., "Constitution's Ninth Amendment: Protecting Unenumerated Rights," August 22, 2014. www.shestokas.com/constitu tion-educational-series/constitutions-ninth-amendment-protecting-une numerated-rights/.

Shklar, Judith N., *American Citizenship: The Quest for Inclusion*, Harvard University Press, 1991.

Sidoti, Liz, "Law Team Rules McCain 'Natural Born,'" *Associated Press*, March 28, 2008.

Silverstein, Gordon, *Imbalance of Powers: Constitutional Interpretation and the Making of American Foreign Policy*, Oxford University Press, 1996.

Smith, Adam. *The Wealth of Nations* (Reprint Edition), Bantam, 2003.

Smith, Robert Ellis, "A National ID Card: A License to Live," *Privacy Journal*, 2002. www.privacyjournal.net/_center_a_national_id_card_a_ license_to_live__center__3079.htm.

Smith, Robert Ellis, "A National ID Card Violates American Traditions," *Privacy Journal*, March 1991, pp. 4–5.

Smith, Robert Ellis, *Ben Franklin's Website: Privacy and Curiosity from Plymouth Rock to the Internet*, Privacy Journal, 2000.

Smith, Robert Ellis, "False ID a Key Part of the Conspiracy," *Privacy Journal*, October 2001, p. 5.

Smith, Robert Ellis, "Remarks in Montreal, Canada on Privacy and Airline" Services: Requirement for Identification on Airlines" (September 23–26, 1997).

Smith, Robert Ellis, "The True Terror of Freedom Is in the Card," *The New York Times Magazine*, September 8, 1996, p. 58. www.nytimes.com/ 1996/09/29/magazine/l-the-true-terror-is-in-the-card-533068.html.

Smith, Robert Ellis and Richard Sobel, "Demands for Voter Identification Require a Constitutional Standard of Reasonable Suspicion of Illegal Activity," in Sobel 2009.

Smith, Rogers, *Civic Ideals: Conflicting Visions of Citizenship in U.S. History*, Yale University Press, 1997.

Sobel, Richard, "Anti-Terror Campaign Has Wide Support, Even at the Expense of Cherished Rights," *Chicago Tribune*, November 4, 2001, p. C1.

Sobel, Richard, "Citizenship as Foundation," *TriQuarterly*, Summer 2008. www.highbeam.com/doc/1G1-186314242.html.

Sobel, Richard, "The Degradation of Political Identity under a National Identification System," *Boston University Journal of Science and Technology Law*, Winter 2002a. www.bu.edu/law/journals-archive/sci tech/volume81/sobel.pdf.

Sobel, Richard, "The Demeaning of Identity and Personhood in National Identification Systems," *Journal of Law and Technology*, 15:2 (Spring 2002b). jolt.law.harvard.edu/articles/pdf/v15/15HarvJLTech319.pdf.

Sobel, Richard, *The High Cost of 'Free' Voter Identification Cards*, Charles Hamilton Houston Institute, Harvard Law School, June 2013, www .charleshamiltonhouston.org/wp-content/uploads/2013/06/Final-Executive-Summary-and-Tables-June-25-20131.pdf.

Sobel, Richard, "IRCA and Academe," Unpublished paper, University of Connecticut, 1986.

Sobel, Richard, "Immigration Policy: What's Driving Decisions?" Panel Discussion, Princeton University, May 27, 2016.

Sobel, Richard, "License to Spy: A National Driver's License – In Reality a National ID Card – Would Let the Government Track and Restrict All Our Movements," *The Boston Phoenix*, April 22, 2005. www.bostonphoe nix.com/boston/news_features/other_stories/documents/04621988.asp.

Sobel, Richard, "National and International Security," in John E. Rielly, ed., *Public Opinion and American Foreign Policy*, 1999, pp. 23–27.

Sobel, Richard, "National License a Danger to Basic Freedoms," *Cambridge Chronicle Online*, March 10, 2005, p. 14.

Sobel, Richard, "Not for Identification Purposes: National Identity numbers don't belong in an open society," Berkman Center Filter, August 12, 1998.

Sobel, Richard, "Opinion: New ID Rules Would Threaten Citizens' Rights," CNN.com, June 13, 2013a. www.cnn.com/2013/06/13/opi nion/sobel-id-immigration/.

Sobel, Richard, "The Politics of the White Collar Working Class: From Structure to Action," *Research in Micropolitics*, 4 (1994), pp. 225–242.

Sobel, Richard, "Preserving Citizen Rights for Present and Future Americans Under Immigration Reform," *Hoover Institution*,

November 11, 2013b. www.hoover.org/research/preserving-citizen-rights-present-and-future-americans-under-immigration-reform.

Sobel, Richard, Review of "Britain's Identity Crisis" by Erico Guizzo, for IEEE-Spectrum, December 2, 2005.

Sobel, Richard, Review of Klinghoffer, Arthur Jay and Judith Apter Klinghoffer, *International Citizens' Tribunal: Mobilizing Public Opinion to Advance Human Rights*, Palgrave, 2002, *Human Rights Review*, 7:4 (September 2006; pp. 119–121).

Sobel, Richard, "The Right to Travel and Privacy: Intersecting Fundamental Freedoms," *Journal of Information Technology and Privacy Law*, 30:4 (Summer 2014), pp. 639–666. repository.jmls.edu/jitpl/vol30/iss4/1/.

Sobel, Richard, "Voter ID Issues in Political Science and Politics," Guest editor, including "Editor's Introduction," *PS: Political Science & Politics*, 42:1 (January 2009). depot.northwestern.edu/jkh348/public_html/sobel2009.pdf.

Sobel, Richard, *The White Collar Working Class: From Structure to Politics*, Praeger, 1989.

Sobel, Richard, "Why a National ID is a Bad Idea," Unpublished Report March 15, 2003.

Sobel, Richard, "Why a National ID is a Bad Idea," Presentation at Harvard University, John F. Kennedy School of Government, November 8, 2001.

Sobel, Richard, Barry Horowitz and Gerald Jenkins, "The Fourth Amendment Beyond *Katz, Kyllo and Jones*: Reinstating Justifiable Reliance as a More Secure Constitutional Standard for Privacy," *The Boston University Public Interest Law Journal*, 22 (Winter 2013), pp. 1–17.

Sobel, Richard and Eric Shiraev, *International Public Opinion and the Bosnia Crisis*, Lexington, 2003.

Sobel, Richard and John Fennel, "Troubles with *Hiibel*: How the Court Inverted the Relationship between Citizens and State," *South Texas Law Review*, 48:3 (Spring 2007), pp. 613–643. law.bepress.com/cgi/viewcontent.cgi?article=8507&context=expresso.

Sobel, Richard and Ramon Torres, "The Right to Travel: A Fundamental Right of Citizenship," *Journal of Transportation Law, Logistics and Policy*, 80:1 (Spring 2013), pp. 13–47. dl.dropboxusercontent.com/u/3120352/Right%20to%20Travel.pdf.

Sobel, Richard and Robert Ellis Smith, "Voter ID Laws Discourage Participation, Particularly Among Minorities, and Trigger a

Constitutional Remedy in Lost Representation," *Political Science & Politics*, 42:1 (January 2009), pp. 107–110.

Sobel, Richard and Robert Ellis Smith, "We Can Protect Airplanes and Privacy Better," *Privacy Journal*, 36:3 (January 2010), pp. 1, 4.

Solove, Daniel, "The New TSA Identification Requirement," *Concurring Opinions*, June 12, 2008. http://concurringopinions.com/archives/2008/06/the_new_tsa_ide.html.

Sotomayor, Sonia, "Statehood and the Equal Footing Doctrine: The Case for Puerto Rican Seabed Rights," *Yale Law Journal*, 88:5 (April 1979), pp. 825–849.

Sparrow, Bartholomew, *The Insular Cases, and the Emergence of American Empire*, Kansas, 2006.

Speech to the members of the Council of State, January 28, 1960, quoted by Bernard Tricot in *Les Sentiers de la paix (The Paths of Peace)*, Plon, 1972.

Spencer, Shaun B., "Reasonable Expectations and the Erosion of Privacy," *San Diego Law Review*, 39:3 (Summer 2002a), pp. 843–915.

Spencer, Shaun B., "Security versus Privacy: Reframing the Debate," *Denver University Law Review*, 79:4 (2002b), pp. 519–585.

Spinner, Jeff, *The Boundaries of Citizenship: Race, Ethnicity and Nationality in the Liberal State*, Johns Hopkins University Press, 1995.

Stevens, Jacqueline, "Citizenship to Go," *The New York Times*, May 17, 2012. www.nytimes.com/2012/05/18/opinion/citizenship-to-go.html?_r=0.

Stevens, Jacqueline, *States without Nations: Citizenship for Mortals*, Columbia University Press, 2011a.

Stevens, Jacqueline, "U.S. Government Unlawfully Detaining and Deporting U.S. Citizens," *Virginia Journal of Social Policy and Law*, 18:3 (Spring 2011b), pp. 606–719.

Stevens, John Paul, *Six Amendments: How and Why We Should Change the Constitution*, Little Brown, 2014.

Stolberg, Sheryl Gay, "Health Identifier for All Americans Runs into Hurdles," *The New York Times*, July 20, 1998, pp. 1. www.nytimes.com/1998/07/20/us/health-identifier-for-all-americans-runs-into-hurdles.html?pagewanted=all.

Storm, Darlene, "Without REAL ID Driver's License, Will TSA Require Passport If Plane Never Leaves USA?," *ComputerWorld.com*, February 20, 2014. www.computerworld.com/article/2475946/security0/without-real-id-driver-s-license-will-tsa-require-passport-if-plane-never-leaves-usa-.html.

Strasser, Mark, "The Privilege of National Citizenship: On Saenz, Same-sex Couples and the Right to Travel," *Rutgers Law Review*, 52 (2000), pp. 553–588.

Stravato, Michael, "Security Check Now Starts Long Before You Fly," *The New York Times*, October 22, 2013. www.nytimes.com/2013/10/22/busi ness/security-check-now-starts-long-before-you-fly.html?hp&_r=0.

"Substantive Due Process – Fundamental Rights," National Paralegal College, 2015 http://nationalparalegal.edu/conLawCrimProc_Public/DueProcess/SubstantiveFundamentalRights.asp.

Suro, Roberto, "Rehnquist: Too Many Offenses are Becoming Federal Crimes," *The Washington Post*, January 1, 1999, p. A2.

Tambakaki, Paulina, "Global Community, Global Citizenship," *Culture Machine*, 8 (2006).

Taranovsky, Dmytro, "Fundamental Rights," MIT, May 7, 2003. http://web .mit.edu/dmytro/www/FundamentalRights.htm.

Tatelman, Todd B., "The REAL ID Act of 2005: Legal, Regulatory, and Implementation Issues," Congressional Research Service Report for Congress, April 1, 2008. www.fas.org/sgp/crs/misc/RL34430.pdf.

Texas Historical Commission, 2015. "Japanese, German, and Italian American & Enemy Alien Internment." www.thc.state.tx.us/preserve/projects-and-programs/military-history/texas-world-war-ii/japanese-german-and-italian.

Thompson, Dennis, *The Democratic Citizen*, Cambridge, 1970.

Toland, John, *Infamy: Pearl Harbor And Its Aftermath*, Doubleday, 1982.

Torres, Ramon, *The Right to Travel*, Unpublished Master's Thesis, Northwestern University, 2012.

Tourist Information, Welcome to Puerto Rico, www.topuertorico.org/tinfo .shtml (last accessed May 26, 2014).

Townsley, Jeramy, "Walzer, Citizenship, Globalization and Global Public Goods," Unpublished paper, December 2004.

Transportation Security Administration, "Alternate Acceptable Forms of Identification," www.tsa.gov/travel/security-screening/identification.

Transportation Security Administration, DHS-TSA-PIA-018(g), Secure Flight Program Update, January 5, 2015.

Transportation Security Administration, "Forgot Your ID," visited November 25, 2015.

Transportation Security Administration, "Frequently Asked Questions," visited February 9, 2016, www.tsa.gov/travel/frequently-asked-questions#realid.

Traven, B., *The Death Ship*, Cape, 1940.

Tremmel, Pat Vaughnl, "Long Way Up to Highest Court of the Land." March 2011 (not discussing the distinction). www.northwestern.edu/newscenter/stories/2011/03/sotomayor-trienens-judicial-scholar.html.

Tribe, Laurence, *American Constitutional Law*, Foundation Press, 2000.

Tribe, Laurence, "Saenz Sans Prophecy: Does the Privileges or Immunities Revival Portend for the Future or Reveal the Structure of the Present?," *Harvard Law Review* 113 (1999), pp. 110–198.

Tricot, Bernard, *Les Sentiers de la paix (The Paths of Peace)*, Plon, 1972.

"TSA One Step Closer to Mandating ID for Domestic Flights," by poetloverrebelspy, July 8, 2008, Less than a Shoestring. https://nobudgettravel.wordpress.com/2008/07/08/tsa-one-step-closer-to-mandating-id-for-domestic-flights/.

Tushnet, Mark, *A Court Divided: The Rehnquist Court and the Future of Constitutional Law*, Norton, 2005.

Twight, Charlotte, *Dependent on D.C., The Rise of Federal Control over the Lives of Ordinary Americans*, Palgrave/St. Martins, 2002.

Twight, Charlotte, "Watching You, Systematic Federal Surveillance of Ordinary Americans," *Independent Review*, Cato Institute, 42 (Fall 1999), pp. 165–200.

"Unenumerated Rights," Legal Dictionary, 2015 http://legal-dictionary.thefreedictionary.com/Unenumerated+Rights.

Update to the U.N. Human Rights Committee concerning Violations of the Right to Freedom of Movement (ICCPR Article 12) by the government of the U.S.A., papersplease.org, February 10, 2014.

Urekew, Robert, "Justice Delayed: IBM's Collaboration with Nazi Germany," *Harvard International Review*, 23:4 (Winter 2002), pp. 84–85 (Reviewing Edwin Black, *IBM and The Holocaust: The Strategic Alliance between Nazi Germany and America's Most Powerful Corporation*, 2012).

Urofsky, Melvin, "The Brandeis-Frankfurter Conversations," *The Supreme Court Review*, 1985, pp. 299–399.

Urofsky, Melvin, *Louis D. Brandeis: A Life*, Pantheon, 2009.

Van der Brink, Bert, "Liberalism without Agreement: Political Autonomy and Agonistic Citizenship," in John Christman and Joel Anderson, eds., *Autonomy and the Challenge to Liberalism*, Cambridge University Press, 2005, pp. 121–122.

Walzer, Michael, "Citizenship," in Terrence Ball, ed., *Political Innovation and Conceptual Change*, Cambridge University Press, 1989 (1995), pp. 211–219.

Walzer, Michael, "Education, Democratic Citizenship and Multiculturalism," in Eugenia Weiner, ed., *Handbook of Interethnic Coexistence*, Continuum Publishing, 1998, pp. 153–161.

Walzer, Michael, *Obligations: Essay on Disobedience, War and Citizenship*, Harvard University Press, 1970.

Walzer, Michael, *Spheres of Justice: A Defense of Pluralism and Equality*, Basic Books, 1983.

Walzer, Michael, "What Does It Mean to Be an American?," *Social Research*, 71:3 (Fall 2004), pp. 654–663.

Warren, Samuel D. and Louis D. Brandeis, "The Right to Privacy," *Harvard Law Review*, 4:5 (1890), pp. 193–220.

Wessert, Will, "Gun-friendly Texas Eases into Allowing Open-Carry Pistols," *The Boston Globe*, December 26, 2015. www.bostonglobe .com/news/nation/2015/12/26/texas-police-say-they-take-new-open-carry-law-stride/OEy6MI0VQTrGkR3MrNuy4L/story.html.

"What are Fundamental Rights," 2015, www.wisegeek.org/what-are-fun damental-rights.htm#didyouknowout.

Whitehead, Tom, "Home Secretary Abandons Compulsory ID Cards," *Telegraph*, July 1, 2009.

"You Belong to the State," *Santa Ana Register*, July 14, 1994.

Yadron, Danny, "Senators in Immigration Talks Mull Federal IDs for All Workers," *The Wall Street Journal*, February 20, 2013. www.wsj.com/ articles/SB10001424127887323864304578316434045924350.

Zamora, Lazaro, *Immigration 101: Path to Citizenship*, Bipartisan Policy Center, June 3, 2014.

Zebrowski, Nathaniel, "Dr. Sobel on Personhood and Rights," *Northwestern Chronicle*, December 7, 2007.

Zeliger, Julian, *The Fierce Urgency of Now*, Penguin Publishing Group, 2014.

Zezima, Katie, "McCain Questions Cruz's Eligibility to Run for President," *Washington Post*, January 6, 2015. www.washingtonpost .com/news/post-politics/wp/2016/01/06/mccain-questions-cruzs-elig ibility-to-run-for-president/.

REFERENCES FOR BRIEFS

BRIEFS AND OPINIONS

"Brief for Petitioner," Indiana Democratic Party et al. *Crawford v. Marion County.* 2007. www.americanbar.org/content/dam/aba/publishing/pre view/publiced_preview_briefs_pdfs_07_08_07_25_Petitioner.auth checkdam.pdf.

"Brief of Amici Curiae Cyber Privacy Project," *Privacy Journal,* Privacy Activism, Liberty Coalition, U.S. Bill of Rights Foundation, Robbin Stewart and Joell Palmer in Support of Petitioners, December 2007. *Crawford v. Indiana.* 2007. www.americanbar.org/content/dam/aba/pub lishing/preview/publiced_preview_briefs_pdfs_07_08_07_21_PetitionerA mCu3PrivacyOrgs2LibOrgs.authcheckdam.pdf.

"Brief of Amici Curiae Electronic Privacy Information Center (EPIC) and Legal Scholars and Technical Experts," to the U.S. Supreme Court on *Hiibel v. Nevada,* No. 3-5554, December 13, 2003. http://epic.org/priv acy/hiibel/epic_amicus.pdr.

"Brief of Amici Curiae for the Lawyers' Committee for Civil Rights under Law," *Crawford v. Marion County,* 2007. www.americanbar.org/con tent/dam/aba/publishing/preview/publiced_preview_briefs_pdf s_07_08_07_21_PetitionerAmCu7CivilCommunityOrgs.authcheck dam.pdf.

"Brief of Amici Curiae to the U.S. Supreme Court," PrivacyActivism, Cyber Privacy Project, and FreeToTravel.org In Support of the Petitioner. *Hiibel* v. *The Sixth Judicial District Court of the State of Nevada,* et al., December 15, 2003, http://www.cyberprivacyproject.org/ storage/8113/u10227/Northwestern_Depo_Backup/hiibel_amicus.pdf.

"Brief of Amicus Curiae to the U.S. Supreme Court," by the Program in Psychiatry and the Law at Harvard Medical School. *Citizens for Health, et al. v. Leavitt,* June 14, 2006, http://pipatl.org/data/library/17158%20pdf%20Zalkin.pdf

Posner, Richard. *Frank v. Walker* (Nos. 14-2058 and 14-2059), "On Suggestion of Rehearing En Banc." October 10, 2014.

REFERENCES FOR COURT CASES

AFL v. American Sash and Door, 335 U.S. 538 (1949).

Allen v. State Bd. of Education, 393 U.S. 544 (1969).

Allgeyer v. Louisiana, 165 U.S. 589 (1897).

Aptheker v. Secretary of State, 378 U.S. 500 (1964).

Austin v. New Hampshire, 420 U.S. 656 (1975).

Bauer v. Acheson, 106 F. Supp. 445 (D.C) (1952).

Beach v. Oklahoma, NO. CJ-2011-1469 (2016).

Beckman v. Saratoga & Schenectady Railroad, 3 Paige 45 (1831).

Beer v. United States, 425 U.S. 130 (1976).

Bell v. Leavitt, WL 551853 N.D. IL, 2007.

Berkemer v. McCarty, 468 U.S. 420 (1984).

Bey v. DHS-TSA, 1:15-cf-03188-ENV-VMS, May 28, 2015.

Bey v. TSA, 3:13-cv-01927-PG, December 18, 2013.

Board of Regents of State Colleges v. Roth, 408 U.S. 564 (1972).

Boyd v. United States, 116 U.S. 616 (1886).

Briscoe v. Kusper, Jr. 435 F.2d 1046 (7th cir. 1970).

Buck v. Kuykendall, 267 U.S. 307 (1925).

Burdick v. Takushi, 504 U.S. 428 (1992).

Butchers' Union Co. v. Crescent City Co, 111 U.S. 746 (1884).

Citizens for Health, v. Thompson, 03-2267 (3rd Cir. 2004).

City of Houston v. F.A.A., 679 F.2d 1184 (5th Cir. 1982).

Collins v. City of Harker Heights, 503 U.S. 115 (1992).

Colorado Republican Fed Campaign Comm. v. FEC, 518 U.S. 604 (1996).

Coppage v. Kansas, 236 U.S. 1 (1915).

Corbett v. TSA, 767 F.3d 1171 (11th Cir. 2014).

Corfield v. Coryell, 6 Fed. Cas. 546. No. 3,230 C.C.E.D.Pa (1823).

Cramer v. Skinner, 931 F.2d, 1020 (5th Cir. 1991).

Crandall v. Nevada, 73 U.S. 35 (1867).

Crawford v. Marion County Election Bd, 472 F.3d 949 (7th Cir. 2007).

Crawford v. Marion County Election Bd, 484 F.3d 436 (7th Cir. 2007).

Crawford v. Marion County Election Board, 128 U.S. 1610 (2008).

CSL NAACP v. McCrory, 1:13-CV-658 (2015).

Delaware v. Prouse, 440 U.S. 648 (1979).

Demore v. Kim, 538 U.S. 510 (2003).

District of Columbia v. Heller, 554 U.S. 570 (2008).

Doe v. Bolton, 410 U.S. 179 (1973).

Dred Scott v. Sandford, 60 U.S. 393 (1857).

Dunn v. Blumstein, 405 U.S. 330 (1972).

Edema v. Jordan, 415 U.S. 651 (1974).

Edwards v. California, 314 U.S. 160 (1941).

Elrod v. Burns, 427 U.S. 347 (1976).

Ex parte Mitsuye Endo, 323 U.S. 283 (1944).

Ex parte Siebold, 100 U.S. 371 (1879).

Ex parte Yarbrough, 110 U.S. 651 (1884).

Florida v. Royer, 460 U.S. 491 (1983).

Foley v. Connelie, 435 U.S. 291 (1978).

Frank v. State of Md., 359 U.S. 360 (1959).

Frank v. Walker, 768 F.3d 744 (2014).

FTC v. Am. Tobacco Co., 264 U.S. 298 (1924).

Gibbons v. Ogden, 22 U.S. 1 (1824).

Gilmore v. Gonzalez, 435 F.3d 1125 (9th Cir. 2006).

Gomez v. Turner, 672 F.2d 134 (D.C. Cir. 1982).

Gomez v. United States, 490 U.S. 858 (1989).

Graham v. Richardson, 403 U.S. 365 (1971).

Green v. TSA, 2:05-cv-01210-MCE-Pan, June 16, 2005.

Griffin v. Burns, 570 F.2d 1065 (1st Cir. 1978).

Griswold v. Connecticut, 381 U.S. 479 (1964).

Guinn & Beal v. United States, 238 U.S. 347 (1915).

Hague v. CIO, 307 U.S. 496 (1939).

Haig v. Agee, 453 U.S. 280 (1981).

Hamdi v. Rumsfeld, 542 U.S. 507 (2004).

Harper v. Virginia State Bd. of Educ., 383 U.S. 663 (1966).

Harris v. McRae, 448 U.S. 297 (1980).

Hicklin v. Orbeck, 437 U.S. 518 (1978).

Hiibel v. Sixth Judicial Dist. of Humboldt County, 542 U.S. 177 (2004).

Hirabayashi v. United States, 320 U.S. 81 (1943).

Hoxie v. New York, N.H. & H.R. Co., 82 Conn. 352 (1909).

Hynes v. Mayor and City of Oradell, 425 U.S. 610 (1976).

Ibrahim v. Department of Homeland Security, No. C 06–00545 WHA, 2012 WL 6652362, *7 (N.D. Cal., 2012).

I.C.C. v. Brinson, 154 U.S. 447 (1894).

Illinois v. Wardlow, 538 U.S. 119 (2000).

In re Coy, 127 U.S. 731 (1888).

In re Quarles and Butler and In re McEntire and Goble, 158 U.S. 532 (1895).

In re Sam Kee, 31 F. 680 (C.C.N.D. Cal. 1887).

INS v. Lopez-Mendoza, 468 U.S. 1032 (1984).

Jensen v. Quaring, 472 U.S. 478 (1985).

John Doe No. 1 v. Ga. Dep't of Pub. Safety, 147 F. Supp. 2d 1369 (N.D. Ga. 2001).

Johnson v. De Grandy, 512 U.S. 997 (1994).

Jones v. Helms, 452 U.S. 412 (1981).

Jones v. United States, 132 S. Ct. 945 (2012).

Kent v. Dulles, 357 U.S. 116 (1958).

Kerry v. Din, 135 S. Ct. 2128 (2015).

Kolender v. Lawson, 461 U.S. 352 (1983).

Korematsu v. United States, 323 U.S. 214 (1944).

Latif v. Holder, No. 3:10-cv-750, 2013 WL 4592515, at 8 (D. Or. 2013).

Lawrence v. Texas, 539 IS 559 (2003).

Lawson v. Kolender, 658 F.2d 1362 (9th Cir. 1981).

League of Women Voters of Wisconsin v. Walker, 834 N.W.2d 393 (Wis. Ct. App. 2013).

Lochner v. New York, 198 US 45 (1905).

Logan v. U.S., 144 U.S. 263 (1892).

Lopez v. Monterrey County, 525 U.S. 299 (1999).

Lubin v. Panish, 415 U.S. 709 (1974).

Luis v. United States (No. 14-419, 2016).

McCutcheon v. FEC, 134 U.S. 1434 (2014).

Meyer v. Nebraska, 262 U.S. 390 (1923).

Miller v. Reed, 176 F.3d 1202 (9th Cir. 1999).

Miranda v. Arizona, 384 U.S. 436 (1966).

Mocek v. City of Albuquerque, WL 312881 (DNM, July 14, 2013).

Mohamed v. Holder, 995 F.Supp.2d 520 (E.D. Va. 2014).

Mohamed v. Holder, 1-11-CV50 (AJT/MSM), July 16, 2015.

Monarch Travel Service, Inc. v. Association Cultural Clubs, Inc., 466 F.2d 552 (9th Cir. 1972).

NAACP v. Alabama, 377 U.S. 288 (1964).

National Federation of Independent Business v. Sebelius, 132 U.S. 2566 (2012).

Newton v. INS, 736 F.2d 336 (6th Cir.1984).

Ng Fung Ho v. White, 259 U.S. 276 (1922).

North Carolina NAACP v. McCrory, 1:13-CV-658 (2015).

Olmstead v. United States, 277 U.S. 438 (1928).

Palko v. Connecticut, 302 U.S. 319 (1937).
Papachristou v. City of Jacksonville, 405 U.S. 156 (1972).
Paul v. Virginia, 75 U.S. 168 (1869).
Pierce v. Society of Sisters, 268 U.S. 510 (1925).
Planned Parenthood v. Casey, 505 U.S. 822 (1982).
Plyler v. Doe, 457 U.S. 202 (1982).
Presser v. Illinois, 116 U.S. 252 (1886).
Quaring v. Peterson S. Ct. 781 F.2d 1121 (8th Cir. 1984).
Reynolds v. Sims, 377 U.S. 533 (1964).
Roe v. Wade, 410 U.S. 113 (1973).
Saenz v. Roe, 526 U.S. 489 (1999).
San Antonio Independent School District v. Rodriguez, 411 U.S. 1 (1973).
Santa Clara County v. Southern Pacific Railroad Company, 118 U.S. 398 (1886).
Service Machine & Shipbuilding Corp. v. Edwards, 671 F.2d 70 (5th Cir. 1980).
Shachtman v. Dulles, 225 F.2d 938 (D.C. Cir. 1955).
Shapiro v. Thompson, 394 U.S. 618 (1969).
Shelby County v. Holder, 570 U.S. 1 (2013).
Slaughterhouse Cases, 83 U.S. 36 (1873).
Snyder v. Massachusetts, 291 U.S. 97 (1934).
South Carolina v. Holder, Case No. 12-203, October 2012.
State of New Mexico v. Phillip Mocek, D.C. NO. 1:11-CV-01009-JB-KBM (2013).
Sugarman v. Douglas, 413 U.S. 634 (1973).
Swafford v. Templeton, 185 U.S. 487 (1902).
Tashjian v. Republican Party of Connecticut, 479 U.S. 208 (1986).
Terry v. Ohio, 392 U.S. 1 (1968).
Thornburg v. Gingles, 478 U.S. 30 (1986).
Town of Southold v. Town of East Hampton, 477 F.3d 38, 54 (2nd Cir. 2007).
Tropicana v. United States, 789 F.Supp. 1154 (CIT 1992).
Truax v. Raich, 239 U.S. 33 (1915).
United States v. Albarado, 495 F.2d 799 (2d Cir. 1974).
United States v. Bathgate, 246 U.S. 200 (1918).
United States v. Carolene Products Company, 304 U.S. 144 (1938).
United States v. Classic, 313 U.S. 299 (1941).
United States v. Davis, 482 F.2d 893 (9th Cir. 1973).
United States v. Goldman, 25 F. Cas 1350 (USCC La, 1878).
United States v. Graham, 846 F. Supp. 2d 384 (D. Md. 2012).
United States v. Guest, 383 U.S. 745 (1967).

United States v. Illinois, No. 07–3261, C.D. Ill. (2009).

United States v. Jones, 565 U.S. 1 (2012).

United States v. Kroll, 481 F.2d 884 (8th Cir. 1973).

United States v. Maryland, 79 U.S. 430 (1871).

United States v. Miller, 307 U.S. 174 (1939).

United States v. Mosley, 238 U.S. 383 (1915).

United States v. Verdago-Urquidez, 494 U.S. 259 (1990).

United States v. Wheeler, 254 U.S. 281 (1920).

United States v. White, 401 U.S. 745 (1971).

United States v. Wong Kim Ark, 169 U.S. 649 (1898).

Veasey v. Abbott, 14-41127, July 20, 2016.

Veasey v. Perry, 135 U.S. 9 (2014).

Village of Belle Terre v. Boraas, 416 U.S. 1 (1974).

Wallace v. Palm Beach, 624 F.Supp. 864 (S.D. Fla. 1985).

Ward v. Maryland, 79 U.S. 418 (1871).

Washington v. Glucksberg, 521 U.S. 702 (1997).

Wesberry v. Sanders, 376 U.S. 1 (1964).

Wiley v. Sinkler, 179 U.S. 58 (1900).

Williams v. Fears, 179 U.S. 270 (1900).

Williams v. Salerno, 792 F. 2d 323 (2d Cir. 1986).

Williams v. Sclafani, 444 F.Supp. 906 (SD NY, 1977).

Wong Wing v. United States, 163 U.S. 228 (1896).

Wright v. Mahan, 478 F. Supp. 468 (E.D. Va 1979).

Yick Wo v. Hopkins, 118 U.S. 356 (1886).

Zemel v. Rusk, 381 U.S. 1 (1965).

Zobel v. Williams, 457 U.S. 55 (1982).

INDEX